EXPERT SYSTEMS: THE USER INTERFACE

HUMAN/COMPUTER INTERACTION

A Series of Monographs, Edited Volumes, and Texts

SERIES EDITOR

BEN SHNEIDERMAN

EXPERT SYSTEMS: THE USER INTERFACE

edited by

James A. Hendler
University of Maryland

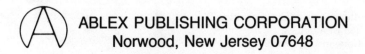

ABLEX PUBLISHING CORPORATION
Norwood, New Jersey 07648

Library of Congress Cataloging-in-Publication Data

Expert systems.

 (Human/computer interaction)
 Bibliography: p.
 Includes index.
 1. Expert systems (Computer science) I. Hendler,
James A. II. Series: Human/computer interaction
(Norwood, N.J.)
QA76.76.E95E985   1987   006.3'3   87-18675
ISBN 0-89391-429-0

Ablex Publishing Corporation
355 Chestnut St.
Norwood, NJ 07648

Contents

Series Editor's Preface

Ben Shneiderman

The Controversy

Enthusiasts see expert systems as a replacement for scarce human experts, the embodiment of a human expert's wisdom, a repository for the collective knowledge of many experts, or a tool to enable novices to behave like experts. Critics complain that the promises are more attractive than the reality and that the term "expert systems" is seductive and possibly misleading.

Some prefer the term "knowledge-based" systems to convey the idea that knowledge is being stored on the computer, not just data or algorithms. A still less flamboyant term—"rule-based" systems describes the programming language style of using multiple, nonsequential IF-THEN groupings. Many hours of debate have been wasted in discussing whether an expert system can be written without a rule-based language.

In spite of the confusion over terminology, it is clear that something new has emerged. The promise of advanced systems that support less-structured decision-making situations has engaged the energy of thousands of researchers, product developers, and commerical designers. Hardware manufacturers have come forward with high-speed machines to support rule-based programming and large screen displays to provide visibility for the complex world of action in many of the applications.

But while there has been tremendous progress in programming methods and hardware, there seems to be little emphasis on the user interface. Designers of early expert systems postulated that a natural language front end would handle all the problems and that a human-like dialogue would be most effective. Of course, these naïve visions generated serious problems with the implementation and the usability of practical systems. Natural language front ends that look good during demonstrations are not sufficiently robust to handle the diversity of input in realistic applications. Human-like dialogue in which the computer prompts the user for answers to a long series of questions are too rigid, tedious, and machine-centered.

Real users of expert systems are not data entry clerks. They have a large body of knowledge about the problem, the computer, and the real world. In many cases they are willing to learn some compact notation to speed problem entry, but they also want more flebility in the sequence of actions. They also want to understand what is happening and be in control. Therefore they are often unsatisfied with the generated explanations of why each rule was invoked, but prefer to be in charge along the way, directing the machine and developing an effective cognitive model of the task domain that reduces their dependency on the expert system.

Turning Toward a Scientific Approach

These unsupported conjectures may not apply to many situations and users, but are meant as an alternate view of the users. Rather than waste further hours of debate, it seems possible to develop a more scientific approach and study explicitly the user interface for expert systems. Instead of vague arguments about the user friendliness of competing approaches, we can turn to controlled psychologically oriented experiments or carefully planned observational and thinking aloud studies of user behavior. Separate measurements are made of the learning time, speed of performance on benchmark tasks, rates and distribution of errors, and retention over time for a variety of user communities. In addition, subjective satisfaction scales and informal comments can provide insight to the problems users experience.

The benefits of these approaches in advanced basic research and in commercial environments have been amply demonstrated in other applications. Usability laboratories and thorough user interface testing have become part of the landscape for successful software companies.

Expert Systems Programmer Interfaces

Programmers, knowledge engineers, and maintainers or expert systems also need effective user interfaces. When there are 1,000 rules of 20 lines each and 80 are invoked to produce a result, tracing and debugging become fighteningly difficult. Successful tools must support rapid and comprehensible browsing of rules and facts, graphic display of

relationships, convenient dynamic execution, meaningful documenta-
tion facilities, and elaborate version control. Still more powerful features are needed when multiple graphics displays or direct manipulation programming is involved.

Creating a Community

With explicit attention to the user interface the advantages of rule-
based programming will be more easily and successfully applied in
many situations. To foster more attention to the user and programmer
interface, we began to organize a workshop. We wanted to bring together the small number of people who had already identified the problems and were working on solutions. In early 1986, about 20 people
were contacted to present their work during 2-day in June 1986. The
organizing committee included James Hendler, Dana Nau, James Reggia, and Roland Simon.

With support from the University of Maryland Institute for Advanced Computer Studies (UMIACS) (Larry Davis, acting director) and
the Department of Computer Science (Victor Basili, chair) we were able
to invite the people we wanted and play host to a stimulating workshop. Johanna Weinstein did a superb job with the administrative issues, resulting in a smooth running workshop.

The Workshop

The thoughtful presentations, lively discussions, and joy at discovering
colleagues with shared interests made for a successful workshop. Many
of the chapters in this volume were prepared especially for the workshop. James Hendler organized the reviewing and editing process and
diligently pursued the researchers who were working on key problems
but could not attend the workshop. The reviewers made numerous
suggestions that strengthened the individual efforts and the cohesiveness of the collection. We hope that the appearance of this book
will stimulate further research in this area.

The Future

Our workshop was just a beginning. We were excited with the enthusi-
astic response of participants and the numerous intriguing directions
for research. I believe that greater attention to the user interface will be

extremely beneficial to the success of expert systems. The work will be challenging, but the payoff substantial. I was very satisfied to see that researchers have come to recognize the central role of user interface design.

The user interface is not the paint put on at the end of the project, but the steel frame on which to hang the details. Designers who are concerned about good user interfaces are finding the ideas to build quality into their systems. I believe that we are getting closer to the goal of building interactive systems that are comprehensible, predictable, safe, and attractive. I think users of well-designed systems experience a higher level of competence, mastery, clarity, potency, and satisfaction.

Preface

James Hendler

As Ben has mentioned in his Preface, this book was originally to be a presentation of the set of papers given at a workshop held at the University of Maryland entitled "Expert systems: The user interface." I was asked to edit because of my interest in the area and my involvement in the workshop. As time progressed, however, it became clear that interest in the book was so high that just presenting a set of workshop papers wouldn't be enough. New papers were sought to try to present a balanced coverage of the field of interface design for expert systems. We felt it important to represent as many of the different people working in the expert systems field as possible. Our goal was to present papers from academics and those working in industry; from diagnosis, classification, and domain modeling; and from the perspective of knowledge engineer, expert, and end user. Thus, I tried my best to provide a broad coverage of the field with no particular viewpoint emphasized.

I wasn't aware how successful this attempt was until I tried to organize the gathered chapters into subsections for this volume. There were so many different overlaps that almost any grouping of the papers provided some sort of classification. The order these papers now appear corresponds in some rough way to a "spectrum" of the field, with "practice" at one end and "theory" at the other. Unfortunately for this ordering, (although fortunately for the reader), this was an artificial distinction at best. Papers on theory cite specific systems and papers on developed systems aim to explain the theory behind their operation.

Each of the authors contributing to this volume was asked not only to contribute a chapter, but also to read and review at least two other papers. The production schedule was frantic and authors were asked to produce these reviews, read their own reviews, and update their papers in a timely manner. Finding time in busy schedules to perform these tasks was a monumental effort for each of the authors, and their labors are most appreciated. Several outside reviewers were also used. In particular, Kate Erhlich of Symbolics Inc., Lorin Wilde of Lisp Machines Inc., and Joy Bush of the University of Maryland took the time to read several articles each and produce useful reviews for me and the authors. Their efforts, too, are greatly appreciated.

The workshop at which several of these papers were first presented was jointly sponsored by the University of Maryland Institute for Advanced Computer Studies (UMIACS) and the University of Maryland Computer Science Department. I am grateful to the help of those organizing the conference technically: James Reggia, Dana Nau, Ben Shneiderman, and Roland Simon, and administratively: Larry Davis (acting director of UMIACS), Victor Basili (chairman of the Computer Science Department). A special thanks to Johanna Weinstein who did much of the administrative work.

Finally, a great many people expressed interest in contributing articles to this book. It was a difficult task to make these decisions, and I must apologize again to all those doing outstanding work whose articles do not appear here. Thanks for your graciousness and understanding.

Jim Hendler
University of Maryland

## ONE

Introduction: Designing Interfaces for Expert Systems

James Hendler

Department of Computer Science
University of Maryland

Clayton Lewis

Department of Computer Science
University of Colorado

Over the past decade the field of expert systems has grown from a few small projects to a major field of both academic and industrial endeavor. The systems have gone from academic laboratories, through industrial development, and are now reaching a substantial user population. In other areas of computer science such explosive growth has often led to systems which are difficult to learn and painful to use. Will expert systems suffer this same fate? In this chapter we compare expert systems with more traditional computer systems and discuss the special needs of this new field. We do this by presenting several short questions, and the corresponding long answers.

Question 1:

Does Fantastic New AI Technology Avoid Traditional System Usability Issues?

When a new technology makes the transition from laboratory to industry, there is a tendency to treat it as if it has a magical nature. Since it solves many previously unsolvable problems one begins to believe it solves all of them. *Expert systems* are no exception to this. The seeming natural language interfaces of many early systems, the windowing and animation facilities of some of the newer systems, the built-in help facilities of present-day Lisp Machines and the like appear to be the necessary tools to cause user interaction problems to all but disappear. Would that it were so.

Unfortunately, interface design is more complicated than just putting up the windows on the screen. The designer must consider many aspects of computer usage ranging from cognitive models of the users' thought processes to the ergonomic issues of body motions and comfort. The designer must concentrate on many aspects of usability, including a focus on users and their tasks, getting empirical evidence about effectiveness, and stressing iteration between designers, implementers, and users (Gould & Lewis, 1985).

Furthermore, far from alleviating the design burden, expert systems bring up new design issues which must be addressed. Developing an expert system usually contains three separate, but highly interacting, components: knowledge capture, programming and debugging the system, and, finally, placing the system before an active user community. Thus, the interface designer must take new factors into consideration in the design of tools for making these stages more efficient and for the development of systems which can be used by the various personnel involved in this process. The designer must now consider:

1. *The issues involved in providing tools for the different personnel involved in each of these stages.* The designer is forced to examine who is involved at each stage. What are their particular needs? How are these needs best addressed in the design of the system?
2. *The special needs of expert system users.* The user community for expert systems is often different from those using editors, operating systems, and other traditional systems. What are the special needs of these professional users who, despite being computer novices, are often experts in their own field of endeavor?
3. *The efficacy of these interfaces.* The design process requires getting empirical evidence about the effectiveness of the tools. The designer must therefore consider how to evaluate the interfaces designed for expert systems. How do we demonstrate that these systems are beneficial to the users? How do we present a rule base such that the eventual user is able to test it.

In short, instead of avoiding the design issues for standard interfaces, expert systems appear to need all these considerations, plus more. This leads us to our next question:

Question 2:

Are Expert Systems Different From More Traditional Technologies in Their Interface Needs?

Along with the new design issues listed above, expert systems create a different set of demands on the interface. An expert system, unlike a traditional computer program, is not just a *tool* that implements a process, but rather it is a *representation* of that process. Further, many of these processes correspond to judgments that can have critical real world consequences. The user interface must often present not only conclusions, but an explication of the processes by which those conclusions are reached.

Compare the behavior of an expert system to that of a more traditional software system, say a compiler. The compiler user cares about ease of input, clarity, and timeliness of error reports, etc. but is willing to trust the compiler designer's decisions as to optimizations in the code, translations, etc. It is a rare user who demands that the interface show the internal workings of the compiler or produce a represention of the algorithms used.

This is not the case, however, for the typical expert system. These systems are often not merely used as a tool for performing a task, but rather as a support tool for performing some decision-making process. Thus, the interface designer must be able to provide support for a knowledge engineer who is trying to enter and debug the representation of the process, and also support, through the same or a different interface, the user who wishes to know how some decision is reached. Issues involving explanation of the reasoning process and display of this reasoning become paramount in the acceptance of the system by users and thus may become paramount to the designer. This implies that the expert systems interface designer has a difficult task on his/her hands. Not only must the designer concentrate on the issues that lead to acceptance in traditional interfaces (which are often overlooked in the design of expert systems), but he/she must also concentrate on these new design areas of import in the system's acceptance.

Question 3:

What Are the Traditional Design Areas Which Are Often Overlooked in the Design of Expert Systems?

As mentioned above, one of the key features an expert system designer must worry about is the acceptance of the system by the intended users. Most of the thrust in many AI systems today is to get the knowledge in and make it work. The interfaces may be designed in advance, as opposed to allowing them to follow from the data, but often the end user of the system is not considered. The system, a perfectly usable one with a well-designed interface, is sent out to a customer, where it sits on the shelf and is never used.

There are many reasons this may occur. One reason may be simply the natural skepticism about *artificial intelligence* that is still seen in many fields and endeavors. These users need much convincing that the underlying technology is sound and that the knowledge contained is correct. Further, many of these users also insist that the knowledge be changeable by themselves. They are not content with someone else's judgments being promoted as "the answer." They want to make sure they will agree. Typical users in this group would be doctors, lawyers, physicists, managers, and others who are traditionally viewed as *experts* in their own field.

These users make many demands on the designer of an expert system interface. The system must be able to explain its behavior and must be able to be updated, using some interaction technique which is natural to these experts. Further, these experts will demand to see data that will convince them of the efficacy of the system. The issue of exactly what needs evaluation and how such evaluation is to be performed is beyond the scope of "interface design," and yet, the interface designer must be sensitive to such issues—the product developer, or the users themselves, will make demands on the interface during this evaluation process.

Further, there is another, probably larger, group of users for whom expert systems are being designed which is not as subject to this "AI fear." These users, often not the experts themselves, but "consumers of expertise," usually *will* trust the results of the system. Yet they too, in many current situations, are refusing to use the new technologies.

In these cases, we believe, it is often the interface, and thus, the interface designer, which is to blame. If the interface doesn't take into account the global needs of the user, that is those beyond the use of the system itself, the program will not be used. Unfortunately, it is these considerations which are often ignored during the design process.

One of the key factors ignored by many designers is the users' environment. The expert system must be designed to match the office or workplace of the system's users. The designer must take into account the users' access to the system, their time to use it, and the compatibility of the expert system with other interfaces the users have been exposed to. Too often, these factors are not taken into account.

Take, for example, a user with some form of PC on his/her desk. If an expert system is imported which must run on a Lisp Machine located in a separate room using a mouse and windows, the user may experience several usability problems. This user may not typically have access to the room in which such a machine is kept. Further, if the system requires many short interactions, the user may not have the time for the extra steps involved in constantly running back and forth between rooms. They may be resistant to the amount of learning required to become proficient at handling the new interface. Why, the user laments, does it not look more like Lotus 1-2-3. There is nothing wrong with the expert system per se; rather, the user's needs have not been taken into account.

Along similar lines is the integration of the expert system with the users' existing *data* environment. If the users are spending much time entering data into an existing data base system, are keeping information on cards for a large COBOL processor, or are even typing large amounts of data on paper for filing in the office cabinets, they are not willing to re-enter much of this data for the expert system. If it is crucial that such information be captured, the expert system interface designer must take the environment into account. This may be as simple as making sure that the expert can make remote calls on the existing data base, or as complex as helping to introduce a new report system which the expert system can use, but which will replace much of the filing presently going on.

Taking into account the users' environment is by no means an easy task. While some guidelines do exist, describing key factors for various types of users and usages (see, e.g., Shneiderman, 1986), many of these systems can only be designed with a knowledge of the users and their environment for some application. The technique that has been used successfully in designing other systems has been that of getting the end users involved early in the design process.

Traditional wisdom has been that the design of an expert system requires iterative interaction with the knowledge engineer. Interviews are held, production rules are written and tested, and the results are shown to the expert. The expert critiques the results, new rules are added and tested, and this process continues until both expert and knowledge engineer are satisfied. We advocate that a similar process must occur between the interface designer and the end user. The interface designer should study the physical environment, the data systems, and the "office culture" of the targeted users. As the interface is designed and prototyped feedback should be solicited. In this way, the final product can be designed to integrate gracefully into the users' workplace.

Another important factor to be considered is the *information re-quirements* of the user. This is particularly true as the uses of expert systems are expanding and the definition of what an expert system can do continues to grow. Expert systems have often been viewed as just that—systems containing the expertise. A user could approach such a system, ask a question (or, as is more common, enter a set of data by filling in forms or answering questions) and get *the answer*. In practice, however, such systems are difficult to write and even more difficult to have accepted into a workplace. Becoming more common are expert systems which are used to help make this expertise more available— the human, often the expert him/herself, is left in the loop.

These new systems are used in many ways. One way is the "second opinion" system, in which the expert system is viewed as a consultation with a colleague. Another way is the "what if" system, where the expert system contains the knowledge about a domain and the human can test various scenarios. Another way is the training system, in which the expert is viewed as helping humans to learn a task, rather than for performing the task itself.

The interface designer must determine the goals of the system and the user and make sure the interface provides support for these new types of interactions. The traditional data-entry technique for the "definitive expert" type of system may not work in these others. Where the traditional expert control the interaction asking questions to ascertain the data it needed, the "what if" system, for example, must let the user be in control. The interfaces for these types of expert systems must be reactive rather than prerogative.

Question 4:

Do You Have An Example of Designing An Expert System Taking These Factors into Account?

Well, not really. We will, however, describe a system whose design either considers these factors **or** shows what happens to you when you don't. The system, called THEO, is a rule-based system for forecasting solar flares, developed jointly by teams from the University of Colorado (Dan Britt, George Engelbeck, Gary Bradshaw, Clayton Lewis, and Dave Shaw) and the Space Environment Laboratory of the National Oceanic and Atmospheric Administration (Pat McIntosh, Jim Winkelman, and Dick Grubb.)

Tool versus representation. When THEO was first conceived the emphasis was on demonstrating the technical feasibility of producing high-quality forecasts without the use of a human expert. The tool conception was that the system would be something to use to generate answers to a range of specific questions. Once technical feasibility of the tool was demonstrated, however, it became clear that just giving the right answers was not sufficient to make THEO useful in some situations. Rather, users need to know the reasoning behind the answers.

There are two reasons for this, corresponding to two applications of the THEO system. In a training application, novice forecasters using THEO need to know not just the correct forecast but the reasoning that led to it. In a "second opinion" application, in which THEO is used by a forecaster to check on his or her own analysis, it is also critical that the system show the basis for its forecast so that user can determine whether to modify his or her judgment.

It might seem that THEO could back up its answers simply by displaying a trace of the rules by which it derives its forecast. Unfortunately this is not so. THEO's rules are adequate to relate symptoms, e.g., observable things on the sun, to the likelihood of flares. But these rules do not contain their own justification. The problem is particularly clear in a training application. Telling a novice that the probability of a flare is high because a sunspot group is of a certain size and is growing in a particular way is not adequate. Rather, the novice needs to know what these symptoms reveal about processes in the sun, and how these processes may produce flares. While the THEO system can store and use several hundred unmotivated connections between symptoms and forecasts, and while these several hundred connections are adequate to produce good forecasts, it would not be possible for a human to learn and apply them with no organizing rationale.

In the knowledge acquisition process for THEO this gap between rules adequate to make good forecasts, and rules that represented the logic behind forecasts, was apparent to us. We were aware of Swartout's (1983) work on this very point. But we still produced a tool system, rather than a representation system, and will face considerable further work to refit it.

New demands on the user interface. THEO has a traditional glass teletype interaction style, in which the system drives the user by displaying a series of questions with multiple-choice and fill-in-the-blanks questions. While this can be improved, we have seen no evidence that this style of interaction is a key issue in user acceptance of THEO. The content of the interaction, however, does differ from what is usual in at least one respect. The interaction allows for help requests about each question. The responses to these provide information not about how to do something, as in traditional systems, but how to decide what to do. The mechanics of interacting with THEO are simple enough that the user needs information about the task and not about the system.

THEO does not address the need for multiple interfaces in expert systems, to support not only end users but experts and other maintainers. Updating is done by writing new rules directly, with no higher-level support. With hindsight we can see that the logic of THEO is sufficiently clear and stereotyped that higher-level maintenance tools could be built. Another need that has emerged in THEO but has not been met, is for reliability information about answers. THEO's forecasts are expressed as probabilities, and so inherently contain an indication of uncertainty, but uncertainty can arise in different ways that THEO does not distinguish. Consider the following hypothetical outputs:

(a)   This situation is one in which flare probability can be confidently assessed to be .5.
(b)   This situation is hard to figure but all in all there's .5 probability of a flare.
(c)   This situation has a flare probability of .5. but the rules used to determine that have not been well tested.
(d)   Expert M's rules indicate a flare probability of .5 here but other experts would disagree with this interpretation.

All of these would appear in the current THEO as a simple forecast of flare probability .5.

Fitting into the user environment. THEO has had only occasional real use, despite expressions of interest by forecasters. It was initially available on a machine different from the one forecasters use, in another room, and no outreach operation was mounted to introduce potential users to the system. Interested users would have had to obtain an account and password on this new machine before investigating THEO. Steps have been taken to lower these barriers; no new technology is sufficiently glittering to overcome obstacles like these (or at least expert systems technology is not).

A further problem has been the time available to forecasters to work with THEO. Learning a new system takes time, and busy people don't have that kind of time unless specific action is taken to make time available.

Fitting into the data environment. THEO started life as an interactive system, like the classic MYCIN, which obtained its knowledge of the problem at hand by asking questions of a human operator. It soon became apparent that the great majority of the information that THEO needs is available in on-line data bases, and so the required user interaction has been progressively replaced by automatic (and invisible) access to these data bases. There is now a version of THEO which carries on no user interaction at all, not because all of the desirable information is available on-line, but because the gaps are small enough that at least a rough forecast can be made with no added information. It appears likely that in a "second opinion" application the degradation in the forecast due to these information gaps will be outweighed by the convenience of being able to get a forecast from THEO with no inter-action.

The need for iterative design. The above discussion has illustrated more than one way in which THEO has evolved over its lifetime, and is continuing to evolve. Being unfamiliar, expert systems are even more likely than more traditional software to require adjustments in design and even in goals as they develop. THEO provides a dramatic illustra-tion of the importance of this evolution: for one application its user interface has disappeared entirely!

Question 5:

What Else Must Be Considered When Designing An Expert System?

As we mentioned earlier, the designer of an interface for an expert systems is faced with many of the same decisions as the designer of an interface for a traditional system. Some issues relating to traditional design, however, must be rethought in terms of the new technology being used and the purposes to which expert systems are being put. In the remainder of this chapter we briefly describe some of these, with pointers to longer articles appearing in this book discussing these topics.

Several models have been proposed for describing the levels of inter-face design (cf. Card, Moran, & Newell, 1983; Foley & Van Dam, 1982; Shneiderman & Mayer, 1979). These theories suggest that a high-level "conceptual model" of the interface is of major importance to the users' ability to learn an interface and to their comfort and efficiency in using it. When users approach a new system they are trying to build a model of what the system does and how they are to get it to do it. If the interface either encourages formation of a correct model, or at least doesn't discourage formation of such, the users' ability to learn and use a system is enhanced.

In expert systems it appears to be the case that the mental model is even more important. It is crucial to a user, particularly an expert in a field, that the system be doing the reasoning "correctly." If users can-not understand the coverage of the system, the inference processes, and the match to their own reasoning processes their ability to use the system is diminished and acceptance is longer in coming. Experimental evidence suggests that the ability to build a correct mental model of an expert system is a dominant factor in the quality of the user/expert system interaction as discussed in Chapter 13 (Lehner & Kralj). Further, as expert systems start to stress domain modeling (as in "what if," "second opinion," and training expert systems) the mental modeling issues become a significant part of the interface design (Chap 12, Stelzner & Williams).

Of key importance in the ability of a user to be able to model the processes of the expert system is the system's ability to "explain" both the reasoning process it uses and how that process is represented in the system. Explanation is also critical to the acceptance of systems by the user. In fact, the ability of a system to describe its reasoning may be more important to the users than the overall correctness of the interface. Early medical expert systems based on Bayes Theorems, for example, often arrived at a correct conclusion more often than later systems designed using other techniques. The users, however, were unable to predict what questions the system would ask, were unable to follow the reasoning involved, and had no access to the "knowledge base" of the system. These systems were not accepted by the medical community and, in fact, became difficult for even the designers of the system to use.

The ability of an expert system to explain its behavior is not something that can be "tacked on" at the end of its design. Explanation must be built into the system throughout. Thus, the interface designer must be involved in the design of the system itself, making sure that the eventual interface will have access to the knowledge necessary for explaining the system's behavior. Further, this explanation is not critical solely to the end user, the designer must also make it available for the knowledge engineer's use in testing and debugging the system. Issues concerning explanation are the central theme of Chapter 10 (Chandrasekaran, Tanner, & Josephson).

Below the level of the conceptual model comes what is usually called the "semantic" level. At this level the designer is concerned with the meanings conveyed by the user's command input and by the computer's output display (Foley & Van Dam 1982). At this level the interface designer is concerned with the capabilities of the system and with what "commands" (in any type of form: command language, menu, graphics, etc.) the system can perform.

In the case of the interface design for an expert system, this level is complicated by the number of different types of users who may be involved. If the system is to be defined by an expert, captured by a knowledge engineer, and then employed by a separate end user, the interface designer must be familiar with the commands each may be able to apply and to the demands which each might have for the system's usage. The designer must decide between separate interfaces for knowledge capture and end use or a single interface that can be employed throughout the systems' various stages.

If, as is typically the case, a knowledge engineer is to build the system, then the interface designer must cater to that engineer's needs as well as to the requirements of the end users of the system. Designing the semantic level of this type of interface, often a prime concern of the designer of the *expert systems shell*, requires attending to a very different set of issues.

One of the demands on the knowledge engineer may be to have command over the control level of the system. Thus, he/she may need to be able to examine and change not only the rule base, but the inference strategies employed. The knowledge engineer might wish, for example, to change the conflict resolution strategy employed by the system. Traditionally, the burden for such activities is put on the knowledge engineer, not the interface designer. The knowledge engineer is expected to be facile in both the interaction language used by the system and the underlying language it is implemented in. Thus, he/she may need to be knowledgeable about both the shell the system is using for inferencing and the implementation language (LISP in many cases) of the shell. As may be imagined, this puts tremendous demands on this programmer. These problems are exacerbated by the lack of a software engineering discipline used for creating and maintaining these expert systems. The design of such a methodology is one mechanism for easing the burden on the knowledge engineer. A proposal for such a design is found in Chapter 11 (Jacob & Froscher).

Another approach to this problem is to switch the onus to the designers of expert systems tools, and to the interface design of those systems. Thus, instead of forcing the knowledge engineer to become proficient in several languages, the expert systems language designer provides mechanisms for explicitly changing the behavior of the system. An example of such a program is the ORBS system described in Chapter 7 (Fickas). In this system the knowledge engineer is presented with an environment for developing and debugging of expert systems.

Another way to avoid the problem of developing separate interfaces for the varying users is by letting experts enter the knowledge on their own. This removes the knowledge engineer from the loop entirely. In fact, in many such systems the expert is also intended as the primary user of the system. The interface designer is thus trying to build one consistent interface, rather than several interrelated ones. The merging of knowledge engineer and expert also has the added advantage of increasing user acceptance of the system. This is discussed in Chapter 3 (Tuhrim, Reggia, & Floor).

One problem with such an approach is that the traditional expert systems knowledge base, composed of production rules and working memory elements, is difficult for these experts to use. The interface designer is forced to devise new methods of representing the knowledge to provide a better match of the expectations and capabilities of the expert. One such approach is described in Chapter 5 (Nau & Gray) where a frame-based representation is substituted for a production rule base; another is described in Chapter 6 (Baroff, Simon, Gilman, & Shneiderman), where special purpose tools for expert systems designers are proposed.

Another difficulty in letting experts enter such knowledge is that some domains require procedural, rather than declarative, information. For example, in the ONCOCIN medical expert system, a doctor needs to be able to enter information specifying the procedures used in the treatment of cancer patients. In such cases the interface designer must create new languages to deal with the semantic issues involved in capturing such procedural knowledge. The ONCOCIN system, for example, uses graphics to specify these procedures as described in Chapter 2 (Musen, Fagan, & Shortliffe).

Yet another approach being explored with an eye toward an interface for knowledge capture is that of the DARN system discussed in Chapter 4 (Mittal, Bobrow, & DeKleer). DARN's purpose is to serve as a tool for aiding inexperienced users in a complex diagnosis and repair task. It works by capturing the knowledge of a group of experts and letting the experts use a sort of "peer review" process for revising data and helping to solve each other's problems.

Question 6:

All These Extra Things to Consider! Isn't Anything Made Easier for the Designer of an Expert System's Interface?

Given the importance of the interface to the acceptance of the expert system, it is no surprise that the burden on the interface designer is increased. Not only must all the issues above (and the approaches suggested in the chapters mentioned) be considered, but all the traditional interface questions as far as command languages, menus, mice, and the many other ways of providing communication between human and computer. Do the expert systems provide any real advantage?

One technology proposed for helping interface designers to cope with the ever-increasing demands on their systems is that of User Interface Management Systems (Hayes, Lerner, & Szekely, 1983; Tanner &

Buxton, 1985). This method advocates creating tools which allow the designer to define the interface in a declarative manner, usually via some special language features. This form of interaction allows the designer of the interface to experiment with different forms more easily.

Of even greater use to an interface designer is a UIMS in which the interface design language closely matches the underlying language of the system. In such a system, if tools are written for the programmers of the underlying language, the interface designer can now take advantage of these tools. This may include syntax-directed editors, browsers, debugging tools, and the like. The interface designer's own productivity is given a boost by this form of interaction.

In an expert system the underlying language for implementation is the expert system language (or shell) itself. The "knowledge bases" used in these systems are generally stored as production rules, or in some other manner allowing the representation of inferential knowledge. Such rules, however, appear to correspond nicely to the types of rules one might wish to use in the design of interfaces. Thus, expert system languages appear to be good vehicles for the development of UIMS systems in general, and of expert systems interface management systems in particular. Two variations on this theme are presented in Chapter 9 (Faneuf and Kirk) and Chapter 8 (Hayes).

References

Card, S. K., Moran, T. P., & Newell, A. (1983). *The psychology of human-computer interactions.* Hillsdale, NJ: Erlbaum.

Foley, J. D., & Van Dam, A. (1982). *Fundamentals of interactive computer graphics.* Reading, MA: Addison–Wesley.

Gould, C., & Lewis, C. (1985). Designing for usability: Key principles and what designers think. *Communications of the ACM, 28*(3), 300–311.

Hayes, P. J., Lerner, R. A., & Szekely, P. A. (1985). Design Alternatives for User Interface Management Systems, *Proceedings CHI-85,* 169–175.

Shneiderman, B. (1986). *Designing the user interface: Strategies for effective human-computer interaction.* Reading, MA: Addison–Wesley.

Shneiderman, B., & Mayer, R. (1979). Syntactic/semantic interactions in programmer behavior: A model and experimental results. *International Journal of Computer & Information Sciences, 8*(3), 219–239.

Swartout, W. R. (1983). XPLAIN: A system for creating and explaining expert consulting programs. *Artificial Intelligence, 21,* 285–325.

Tanner, P. P. & Buxton, W. (1985) Some Issues in Future User Interface Management System (UIMS) Development. In G. Pfaff, (ed), *User Interface Management Systems,* 67–79, Springer Verlag: Berlin.

TWO

Graphical Specification of Procedural Knowledge for an Expert System

Mark A. Musen,
Lawrence M. Fagan,
Edward H. Shortliffe

Medical Computer Science Group,
Knowledge Systems Laboratory,
Stanford University School of Medicine

Abstract

Tools that allow experts to enter knowledge about given domains directly into computers will greatly facilitate the creation of new expert systems. OPAL is a knowledge entry program that has been developed to allow oncologists to specify new cancer treatment plans to be executed by an expert system called ONCOCIN. This chapter describes the portion of OPAL that is used by physicians to specify the procedural knowledge for treating cancer patients. This knowledge is customarily represented as a flow chart, or schema, in oncology treatment documents. The OPAL schema entry system represents a visual programming environment that permits complex therapy plans to be drawn graphically as a flow chart. The visual program can then be translated into an internal format for use by the ONCOCIN consultation program. Visual programming languages can be particularly useful in acquiring domain knowledge from experts and can expedite development of certain classes of expert systems.

Introduction

The development of expert systems has become an important focus of work in artificial intelligence. Knowledge acquisition, the process of

15

interviewing experts and encoding their expertise in machine-under-standable format, has become widely recognized as a principal bot-tleneck in the construction of expert systems (Buchanan et al., 1983). Knowledge acquisition is difficult because the computer scientists who build expert systems (referred to as *knowledge engineers*) often lack the background needed to pose optimal questions, while experts in the application area often have difficulty appreciating how their knowl-edge is to be captured in the computer. It has long been suggested that if domain experts could somehow encode their knowledge directly with-out relying on programmers as intermediaries, the development of ex-pert systems might be greatly expedited (Davis, 1979).

Because it is unrealistic to expect collaborators to learn traditional programming languages and knowledge representation techniques, the use of computer-based "knowledge editors" has been suggested as a means to reduce dependence on computer scientists during knowledge base construction. Previously reported knowledge editors for use by domain experts have either proven too general in purpose for develop-ment of truly robust expert systems (Bennett, 1985; Boose, 1984) or have encountered significant problems in parsing natural language (Davis, 1979). None has emphasized the use of graphical interfaces for initial knowledge entry.

We describe a new knowledge editor, OPAL, that incorporates an icon-based graphical programming language (Raeder, 1985) to capture the procedural aspects of cancer treatment from clinical experts. OPAL allows physicians to create and modify knowledge bases for an expert system called ONCOCIN (Shortliffe et al., 1981) without dependence on a knowledge engineer to serve as intermediary (Figure 1).

Cancer Therapy and the ONCOCIN System

Optimal therapy for most cancers is not known. In academic medical centers, patients are often enrolled in formal experiments or "clinical trials" that compare the effects of alternative treatment plans for given types of cancer. The written descriptions of these experiments are called *protocols*. Individual patients are typically assigned at random to one of a protocol's alternative treatment plans. Cancer protocols contain extremely detailed specifications for how patients with given tumors should be managed by their physicians. When large numbers of patients complete treatment on a protocol, analysis of their outcomes permits determination of which treatment plan might be preferred.

Cancer protocols may be comprised of chemotherapies—groups of one or more drugs given over time—and radiation treatments (radi-

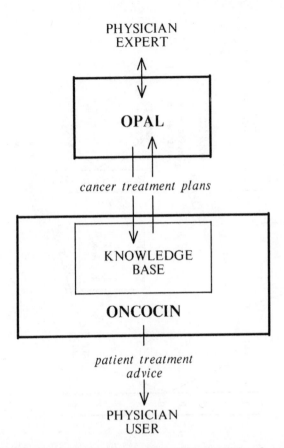

PHYSICIAN
EXPERT

OPAL

cancer treatment plans

KNOWLEDGE
BASE

ONCOCIN

patient treatment
advice

PHYSICIAN
USER

Figure 1.   Relationship of OPAL and ONCOCIN. OPAL is a knowledge editor that permits oncologists to enter and review cancer treatment plans stored in the ONCOCIN knowledge base. ONCOCIN is an expert system that provides advice concerning the management of cancer patients receiving treatment according to the plans entered via OPAL.

otherapy). Protocols may combine various chemotherapies (each with its own sequence of drugs) with radiotherapy. Each repeated administration of the drugs in a chemotherapy is called a *cycle* of treatment; chemotherapy cycles are often repeated a prescribed number of times and then followed by different treatment. Sometimes a sequence of operations is repeated until a change occurs in the patient's condition. As patients can receive simultaneous chemotherapy and radiation, protocols may also dictate concurrent actions.

Oncologists draw flow charts, or *schemas*, to provide high-level descriptions of these often complex protocols. The schema for a protocol developed by the Northern California Oncology Group to treat a form of lung cancer is shown in Figure 2.

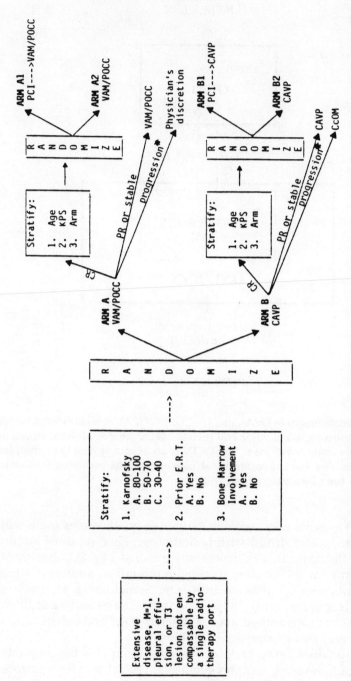

Figure 2. Sample protocol schema. This diagram is taken directly from Northern California Oncology Group protocol 20–83–1 for small-cell lung cancer. VAM, POCC, CAVP, and CcOM are chemotherapies. CR and PR represent *complete response* and *partial response*, respectively.

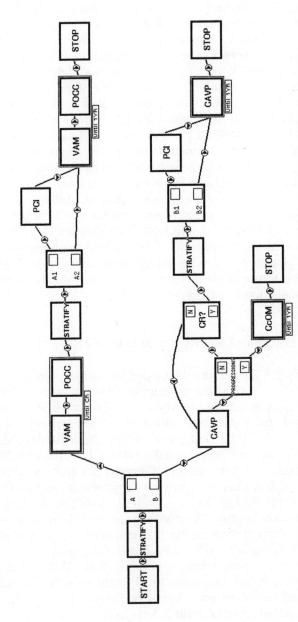

Figure 3. Schema for protocol entered with OPAL. This is a modified version of the schema for Northern California Oncology Group protocol 20–83–1 entered with OPAL. Note the relationship of this graphical description to the flow diagram from the protocol document reproduced in Figure 2.

ONCOCIN is able to recommend treatment for cancer patients because it has a large knowledge base of oncology protocols. This knowledge base contains two separate classes of knowledge, one "procedural," one "inferential." *Procedural knowledge* consists of the sequences of operations to take over time as represented in the protocol schemas. This procedural knowledge is discussed in detail in the next section. ONCOCIN's *inferential knowledge*, on the other hand, is more static in nature and reflects how treatments dictated by the procedural knowledge should be modified, based on the current situation. The inferential knowledge in ONCOCIN is represented largely as production rules. The rules are used to conclude the values of special variables called *parameters*, which establish such concepts as the clinical condition of the patient, interpretations for various laboratory tests, and required adjustments in drug dosages (Shortliffe et al., 1981).

OPAL has been designed as a high-level graphic editor for both procedural and inferential knowledge in ONCOCIN (Musen et al., 1986a). This chapter focuses on the portion of OPAL that captures the *procedural* knowledge of protocol schemas by means of a visual programming language. An example of an actual protocol specification created using this language appears in Figure 3.

Procedural Knowledge in ONCOCIN

The version of ONCOCIN we have developed for use on personal workstations (Musen et al., 1985) uses augmented finite state transition tables to represent the procedural specifications of the various protocols in the knowledge base. A state in a transition table is represented as a unique name followed by a list of possible transitions to other states. Each transition has an associated *condition*. If the condition evaluates to *true* then the transition is executed; otherwise the next transition in the list is considered. A transition may be "augmented" in that it may indicate actions for ONCOCIN to take, such as the administration of a chemotherapy or radiotherapy. To arrive at a recommendation for treatment, ONCOCIN follows transitions in the state table, taking note of the actions specified by each transition executed. Traversal of the state table stops when the system encounters a transition that dictates an action which will not be completed until some time in the future. Having established the necessary actions for the current consultation, *inferential knowledge* is then brought to bear in determining the specific recommendation. For example, once the procedural component of the knowledge base determines that a certain chemotherapy should be given, inferential knowledge is used to conclude the particular drugs to administer and the required dosages.

Each transition table and the name of its associated *state variable*— the particular parameter that gives the table's "current" state—are stored together in a data structure known as a *generator* (Figure 4). The precise assignment of the state variable is different from patient to patient, depending on the individual stage of treatment. At the start of a consultation, the ONCOCIN reasoning program retrieves the patient-specific value of the state variable from a time-oriented data base (Kahn et al., 1985), having identified the particular generator in the knowledge base defining the appropriate protocol. A generator interpreter then executes transitions in the state transition table of the generator, updating the state variable each time. At the conclusion of the consultation, the new value of the state variable is stored back in the patient data base so that it will be available the next time ONCOCIN must reason about the same patient.

The knowledge in the generators corresponds to the procedures expressed in protocol schema diagrams. Because the schemas can be complex, the generators often represent the equivalent of rather complicated computer programs. However, generators in ONCOCIN are never created by programmers in the usual sense; physicians use a graphical language provided by OPAL to describe the schemas for new protocols. OPAL then converts the visual representations into generators for the ONCOCIN knowledge base.

The Schema Entry Environment

OPAL has been developed for use on Xerox 1100 series LISP work stations. The initial display is devoted to a large rectangular region where the user will create the visual program that represents a particular protocol schema. Beneath this area is a menu of "reference" icons which correspond to some of the basic syntactical elements of the visual language (Figure 5). These elements include control operators such as START (begin execution), STOP (end execution), and DECIDE (binary branch), as well as the basic treatment modalities CHEMOTHERAPY and RADIOTHERAPY. An operator labeled WAIT can be used to designate explicit pauses.

When the user selects one of the reference icons with the mouse pointing device, a copy of the icon appears in the main graph region. The new icon may be positioned anywhere in the graph by moving the mouse. If the user adds a CHEMOTHERAPY or RADIOTHERAPY icon to the

NAME: GENERATOR

STATE VARIABLE: PROTOCOL.STATE

STATES:

START/1
CONDITION: *true*
NEXT STATE: **CHEMO/2**
ACTIONS: *none*
TRANSITION TYPE: NON-RETURN

CHEMO/2
CONDITION: *true*
NEXT STATE: **CHEMO/3**
ACTIONS: VAM Chemotherapy
TRANSITION TYPE: RETURN

CHEMO/3
CONDITION: *true*
NEXT STATE: **DECIDE/4**
ACTIONS: POCC Chemotherapy
TRANSITION TYPE: RETURN

DECIDE/4
CONDITION: *If* CR *is false*
NEXT STATE: **CHEMO/3**
ACTIONS: *none*
TRANSITION TYPE: NON-RETURN

CONDITION: *If* CR *is true*
NEXT STATE: STOP/5
ACTIONS: *none*
TRANSITION TYPE: NON-RETURN

STOP/5
CONDITION: *true*
NEXT STATE: *none*
ACTIONS: STOP
TRANSITION TYPE: RETURN

Figure 4. Stylized ONCOCIN generator. A generator contains the name of a *state variable* (here PROTOCOL.STATE) and a *transition table*. Each state in the table has a unique name, followed by a list of possible transitions. If the *condition* associated with a transition evaluates as *true*, the transition is executed, applying any associated actions. When a transition of type RETURN is encountered, execution of the generator is suspended; when the same patient returns for a subsequent consultation, execution of the generator resumes from where it left off. The generator shown here specifies that patients receive a single cycle of VAM chemotherapy followed by repeated cycles of POCC chemotherapy until the value of the parameter CR (complete response) is concluded to be *true*.

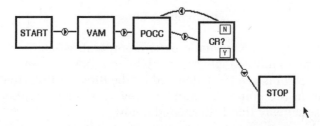

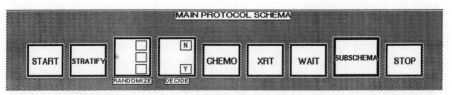

Figure 5.   The OPAL schema entry environment. Below the region where the user edits the schema is a menu of "reference" icons, used to add new nodes to the graph. These icons include basic control elements, such as START, STOP, and DECIDE, as well as specific domain processes, such as chemotherapy cycles (CHEMO) and radiation treatments (XRT, for X-Ray Therapy). The schema that has been constructed above calls for a single cycle of VAM chemotherapy to be administered, followed by cycles of POCC chemotherapy until the parameter CR (complete response) becomes *true*. The visual program corresponds to the generator shown in Figure 4.

graph, the particular form of the treatment is selected from a menu that pops up once the icon is moved into place. The name chosen from the menu then appears as a label for the icon. Similarly, if the user creates a DECIDE node in the graph, a menu of ONCOCIN parameters is displayed. The user is asked to specify the name of the parameter whose Boolean value during the ONCOCIN consultation will determine the flow of control at the branch point.

The user creates a visual program for the protocol schema by adding icons to the graph, positioning the icons appropriately, and drawing links between them. When icons previously added to the graph are selected with the mouse, a menu appears to allow the icon to be moved elsewhere, erased from the graph, or linked to another icon. The mouse is then used to carry out the desired operation. If a link between icons is selected with the mouse, the user can erase the link from the diagram or change the link's destination. OPAL thus provides a "what you see is what you get" environment for drawing out protocol schemas. The use of intuitive icons and a direct manipulation interface (Shneiderman, 1983) has allowed physicians to learn to use OPAL quickly with a minimum of training.

The Schema Language

A syntactically correct visual program represents a deterministic finite state diagram with a single START node and one or more STOP nodes. Flow of control is generally denoted by the directed links that connect the icons in the graph. Iteration, however, is often represented in a more abstract way that is discussed below.

Conditionality

As in typical flow chart languages, the links between icons are un-labeled. Conditionality is expressed by the use of DECIDE nodes in the graph. For example, as part of the protocol diagrammed in Figure 5, a chemotherapy called POCC is administered one cycle at a time until ONCOCIN can conclude that the parameter CR (complete response to treatment) is *true*. Rules that determine the values of the parameters tested by DECIDE nodes may be defined by OPAL, but not at the level of the schema entry component. (Rules are part of the *inferential knowl-edge* and not represented in the schema.) Thus the schema language can use ONCOCIN parameters to alter the flow of control but cannot reset the values of these parameters directly.

A special form of conditionality is represented by the RANDOMIZE icon. Such a node allows oncologists to indicate conveniently when protocol patients are to be randomly assigned to alternative treatments. Although one could theoretically represent the same flow of control by using one or more DECIDE nodes, we have chosen to tailor the visual language more specifically for the application domain. This considera-tion is important because OPAL is designed to be used by doctors, not programmers.

Iteration

In our experience, physicians who are not familiar with programming seem to have difficulty thinking of iterative sequences (as in Figure 5) in terms of explicit branch points and state transitions. The oncologists with whom we collaborate much prefer flow charts where the concept of iteration is either ignored or at best represented as an annotation to the graph. In the protocol schema shown in Figure 2, for example, the chemotherapies POCC, VAM, CAVP, and CcOM are not drawn ex-plicitly as elements that recur over time, despite the *verbal* specifica-tions for their repeated administration elsewhere in the protocol document.

The OPAL schema language buffers the user from the details of the flow of control needed for iteration. To specify a repeating sequence of operations, the user enters the basic sequence of nodes and draws a box around the relevant icons with the mouse. A menu then asks the user whether the enclosed sequence is to be repeated (1) a fixed number of times, (2) until a condition, (3) a number of times *then* until a condition, or (4) a number of times *or* until a condition, whichever occurs first. Further menus solicit the number of iterations or precise condition to test. OPAL then replaces the original sequence of icons with a single icon whose image is a graph of the procedure to be repeated. The new REPEAT icon is annotated with a phrase describing the test that determines when the iterative loop should terminate. The process of specifying repeating elements graphically is shown in Figure 6.

An icon representing a repeating sequence of operations can be manipulated like any other node in the graph. The user can thus include a REPEAT icon among those nodes designated as part of some higher order repeating sequence. The superposition of icons in the graph adds a third dimension to the visual representation, defining a hierarchy of nested operations. Iteration can be nested to any level (Figure 7).

Concurrency

A physician can designate two or more sequences as "concurrent" by using the mouse to draw a box around the corresponding groups of nodes, similar to the way in which repeating sequences are specified. The concurrent sequences may be of any complexity and may themselves specify concurrent sequences (Figure 8).

The semantics are such that the individual operations drawn within the CONCURRENT icon independently proceed in parallel; when all of the simultaneous sequences have terminated, control passes to the node in the superior graph that follows the CONCURRENT icon. Concurrency is implemented by creating a hierarchical set of generators in the knowledge base. At the time the visual program is translated, a "subgenerator" is created for each one of the separate concurrent sequences. At run time, when the main generator interpreter enters the state corresponding to a CONCURRENT node, the interpreter calls itself recursively on each of the subgenerators, causing the subgenerators to execute appropriate transitions. Then, if any of the subgenerator sequences remain in progress, the main generator interpreter simply returns without advancing. If, however, all of the subgenerators are in their terminal states, the main generator proceeds to its own next state, first resetting the subgenerator state variables.

It is not possible to encode coordination among concurrent processes directly using the generator hierarchy, unlike other representation schemes for procedural knowledge (Zisman, 1978). However, by explicitly using the WAIT operator to specify a pause until some param-

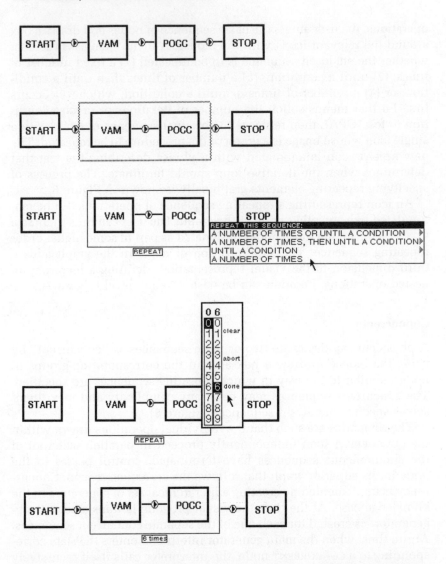

Figure 6.   Specifying a repeating sequence in OPAL. A. Basic icons are entered. B. The iterative sequence is specified by using the mouse pointing device to draw a box around the involved nodes. C. The type of iteration is selected using a menu. Sequences may repeat a fixed number of times, until a condition becomes true, or a combination of both. D. The values of the terminating conditions are entered. Here, the number of iterations is selected from an input device called a *register*. E. The system annotates the REPEAT icon with the specific terminating condition.

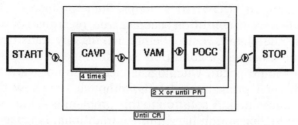

Figure 7. Nested iterative sequences. Iterative sequences may be nested to any level. Each "loop" has its own terminating condition with which the corresponding REPEAT icon is annotated.

eter set by another process becomes *true*, the user can synchronize concurrent sequences in mid-course. Concurrent processes can be simultaneously aborted using the "exception handling" mechanism described in the next section.

Abstraction

The readability and modifiability of programs written in textual languages largely depend on the languages' ability to represent control structures and data at an adequate level of abstraction. Because OPAL is designed for nonprogrammers, removing unnecessary procedural detail is a particularly important goal.

OPAL allows *control abstraction* with its ability to denote iteration without having to specify the precise transitions back to a loop's starting point. Yet a further degree of abstraction is often necessary because the iterative sequences in oncology protocols are often more compli-

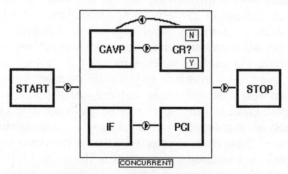

Figure 8. Concurrent sequences. In this example, cycles of CAVP chemotherapy are administered until the parameter *CR* becomes *true*. Simultaneously, two radiation treatments (IF followed by PCI) are given.

cated than standard "DO WHILE" loops. Some protocols call for exiting a loop *whenever* a condition becomes true, regardless of whether an iteration has completed. Hence, before making any transitions within the loop, one must test a condition to determine whether premature termination should occur. Oncologists clearly do not want to be concerned with such procedural details, although somehow the details have to be represented. A solution to this problem is achieved by what is equivalent to "exception handling" in traditional languages such as PL/I or Ada. The OPAL user can create an iterative sequence and specify that the termination condition is to be checked *implicitly* before making any transitions within the sequence; if at any time the condition becomes *true*, control passes out of the loop. A nested iterative sequence inherits any exceptions that might apply to the enclosing loops and may, of course, have a local terminating condition of its own.

Procedural abstraction is achieved by using auxiliary graphs called *subschemas*. These "graphical subroutines" make the representation of complex procedures easier, particularly when a visual program might otherwise be too big to fit in one graph. Similar constructs have been used in other graphical programming languages (Jacob, 1985; Wasserman, 1985).

Specifically, if the user selects the reference SUBSCHEMA icon with the mouse, a copy of that icon can be positioned in the current graph. The user then assigns a name to the icon either from a predefined menu or by typing it in. Whenever a SUBSCHEMA node in the graph is selected, one of the choices in the resultant menu allows the user to specify the details of the subschema procedure. The current graph is then replaced with a new graph (initially blank) corresponding to the particular subschema. Once the procedure for the subschema has been diagrammed, the user simply returns to the original graph.

A graph may have multiple instances of the same subschema, each referring to the identical procedural specification. Subschemas may call other subschemas to any level of nesting. However, the user is prevented from allowing subschemas to call themselves recursively, either directly or via another subschema.

Similarly, the OPAL interface imposes its own form of procedural abstraction on the protocol being entered. Although administering chemotherapies and radiotherapies can be quite complex, these intricate treatments are represented in the schema language as simple icons. Whenever one of these icons is selected with the mouse, it is possible to enter a special environment for describing the *inferential knowledge* needed to apply the particular therapy. This separate portion of OPAL is discussed in detail elsewhere (Musen et al., 1986a) and uses graphical "forms" to allow specification of knowledge using a "fill in the

Alterations for Blood Counts

Drug Combination: _____POCC_____   Subcycle: _____A_____

Drug: ╱ _____PROCARBAZINE_____

| Copy to Clipboard | Copy from Clipboard | Change Table Format? | Delete Table? |

WBC (x 1000)	Platelets (x 1000)			
	>= 150	100 - 150	75 - 100	< 75
>= 3.5	100% of STD	75% of STD	Delay	Delay
3.0 - 3.5	75% of STD	Delay	Delay	Delay
2.5 - 3.0	Delay	Delay	Delay	Delay
< 2.5	Delay	Delay	Delay	Delay

| Specify Abort Info | Specify Delay Info |

Figure 9.   Inferential knowledge entry. Inferential knowledge is specified by filling in the blanks of standardized graphical "forms." OPAL then converts the knowledge to the internal representations used by the ONCOCIN reasoning program. The table shown here specifies the actions to take for the drug procarbazine in the *A* subcycle of POCC chemotherapy. The highlighted choice indicates that when a patient's white blood cell count is greater than or equal to 3,500 and the platelet count is between 100,000 and 150,000, 75% of the standard dose of the drug should be administered.

blanks" approach (Figure 9). Once the details of the chemotherapy or radiotherapy have been entered, OPAL reverts back to the schema environment where the iconic representation is redisplayed. The system thus encourages a "top–down" approach to knowledge entry.

As mentioned previously, the OPAL interface also allows entire iterative sequences to be manipulated as individual icons during schema editing. Similar "structural abstraction" can be found in other systems such as the structure editor in Interlisp.

Syntax Validation

Many of the syntax errors that occur in textual languages are simply not possible in OPAL because of the direct manipulation interface

(Shneiderman, 1983). Because the user specifies elements in the visual program by pointing at them with the mouse, it is impossible to point to a nonexistent object. As all the operations one can perform in building the visual program are dictated by menu selections, it is impossible to specify an unrecognized command. The effects of all operations are displayed visually as they are performed, providing the user with immediate feedback at each step.

Other kinds of syntax errors are actively prevented by the user interface. For example, if a graph node already has a transition to another node, it is impossible to join the former node to some other icon until the existing transition is erased. The interface prevents the user from specifying transitions that (1) enter the START node, (2) exit from a STOP node, or (3) go from a node to itself. Attempts to designate more than a single iterative sequence within a REPEAT node are also identified immediately and reported to the user. Checks for other kinds of syntax errors do not take place until translation of the visual program into a generator is attempted. Any incomplete specifications, missing transitions, or apparent nonterminating loops are then reported to the user.

Translation

When the physician indicates that he or she is done entering the schema, the visual program is checked for correct syntax. Assuming no errors are found, a recursive algorithm traces through all the icons and produces an ONCOCIN generator to be incorporated directly into the knowledge base. The process of constructing the state transition table is totally transparent to the user.

The completed generator also contains certain system data to allow precise regeneration of the graphical representation directly from the state transition table, removing the need to store the iconic version as well. This approach does have the disadvantage that it is not possible to save a partly entered schema for later editing if the visual program is syntactically incorrect. Users must rectify any errors before saving their work.

Because the resultant generator is a direct translation of the visual program, neither physicians nor ONCOCIN knowledge engineers need ever be concerned with the details of the transition table actually encoded in the knowledge base. If a knowledge engineer wishes to review or modify an ONCOCIN generator, the visual program is simply examined using OPAL. Although originally designed for physicians, OPAL has also become an important tool for computer scientists working on ONCOCIN.

Discussion

The emergence of high-performance personal work stations with bit-mapped displays is having a major impact on work in artificial intelligence. The ability to develop software in multitasking environments where both programs and data can be displayed graphically and where commands can be issued by pointing rather than by typing has almost changed what it means to program in LISP (Sheil, 1983). More important, the interactive graphics capabilities of these new LISP work stations have sparked development of powerful tools for perusing and editing large knowledge bases (Richer & Clancey, 1985; Tsuji & Shortliffe, 1986). However, despite the interest given to the use of visual display techniques by knowledge engineers, few workers in AI have emphasized the potential for graphics in the traditionally arduous problem of acquiring domain knowledge from nonprogrammers.

Building the prototype version of ONCOCIN, before the development of OPAL, required nearly two years and some 800 hours of an expert oncologist's time to encode the knowledge of 23 similar protocols for lymph node cancer. Adding three more protocols for breast cancer took several additional months. The length of time needed to develop clinically acceptable knowledge bases could be traced to ambiguities in the protocol documents and difficulty in capturing the judgmental knowledge with which practicing physicians tend to supplement the written protocol guidelines (Musen et al., 1986b). By providing a language with which oncologists themselves can express precise concepts about their domain, OPAL now permits new protocols to be specified for ONCOCIN in a matter of days or even hours. (Formal testing and validation of the knowledge may subsequently require several additional days of effort.)

For most developing expert systems, knowledge acquisition remains a tedious, highly iterative process whereby domain experts are interviewed by knowledge engineers, prototype systems are built, and performance of the completed prototypes is then evaluated by the domain experts. Repetitive prototyping may be useful in domains where the knowledge itself is poorly formalized. Often, however, the cycles of testing and rebuilding are necessary simply because of the communication difficulties that arise when programmers are not knowledgeable about a domain and when experts do not understand programming (Buchanan et al., 1983). A similar bottleneck has been identified in the development of applications programs for management information processing. Both a recognized shortage of programmers and difficulty on the part of managers in explaining what they want to outsiders have been cited as leading to an increasing backlog of needed applications software. MacDonald (1982) suggests that an impending crisis in data processing can only be avoided with the development of graphical tools that will permit end users to program their own applications.

For years, direct manipulation interfaces have allowed printed circuits, newspaper layouts, and various mechanical devices to be designed and fabricated automatically by domain experts working alone. In a similar fashion, visual programming environments such as OPAL can permit "computer-aided design" of knowledge bases for expert systems without the direct need for traditional programmers. Just as CAD/CAM systems are tailored for specific, repetitive design problems, computer-aided knowledge entry will have greatest applicability in areas where the knowledge is already formalized, highly stereotypic, and constrained. There are many such domains in which the ability to generate new expert systems for particular tasks would be valuable. Clinical trials in medicine and general process control applications are but two examples.

The schema entry language in OPAL has been designed to mimic the notations used by oncologists in drawing protocol flow charts. It is our belief that a visual representation approximating the way our experts actually depict their knowledge in protocol documents is important for user acceptability. Physicians using OPAL seem more at ease with the system when they think of their work as "drawing a flow chart" rather than as "programming a knowledge base." Providing control abstraction by means of a visually familiar paradigm is an important part of getting domain experts to feel comfortable with a system such as OPAL.

Although the schema entry system ultimately has the same expressive power as a Turing machine, it is not designed as a general-purpose flow chart language. ONCOCIN's somewhat artificial separation between *procedural* and *inferential* knowledge constrains the way knowledge base parameters may be manipulated in a visual program. The schema language can test the values of parameters to alter flow of control; however, because the values of the parameters are concluded by rules in the inferential part of the knowledge base, the language provides no *explicit* way to rebind these parameters. The only "variable assignment" permitted involves the incrementing and resetting of loop counters. Yet the control abstraction used for iteration makes it impossible to examine or reassign these counters directly. Although one could postulate extensions to the schema language to permit a more direct interface between the procedural and inferential components of the knowledge base, expanding the syntax would have clear tradeoffs. The schema language currently provides adequate facility for encoding new protocols for ONCOCIN. To add more complexity to the procedural language might only make it more cumbersome for use by doctors and thus be counterproductive. The present division of knowledge between procedural and inferential components seems intuitive to physicians and has the advantage of helping to organize their thinking about the protocol knowledge entered through OPAL.

Whereas the icons manipulated in the OPAL schema environment represent the structural elements of oncology protocols, the system could be readily reconfigured to capture procedural knowledge in other domains. The syntax of the visual language is extremely general. Both the appearance and behavior of the icons can be defined using data structures in OPAL that are easily modified by knowledge engineers. However, the meaning of any visual program is established by the way the ONCOCIN reasoning program ultimately interprets the resultant generator, a function of special *control knowledge* built into the system. Extending OPAL for other domains requires more than just attention to elements of the visual syntax; the *semantics* applied to the entered knowledge by the underlying expert system must also be considered. Generalizing OPAL for entry of clinical trials in areas of medicine beyond oncology should be possible with the existing ONCOCIN implementation. Modifications to ONCOCIN's control knowledge could permit OPAL to create expert systems in yet other domains that have large procedural components.

The use of visual flow chart languages has already shown promise in allowing rapid prototyping of user interfaces for applications programs (Jacob, 1985; Wasserman, 1985). Our work extends visual programming as a method by which "computer-naïve" domain experts can enter procedural knowledge for a working expert system. By providing an intuitive graphical syntax that hides unnecessary details, we have created an environment that allows doctors to encode new protocol schemas directly without dependence on knowledge engineers. In an era of increasing expectations for the application of artificial intelligence, knowledge editors such as OPAL may finally break the knowledge acquisition bottleneck for certain classes of expert systems.

Acknowledgements

This work has been supported by grants LM-04420, LM-07033, and RR-01631 from the National Institutes of Health. Computer facilities were provided by the SUMEX-AIM resource under NIH grant RR-00785 and through gifts from Xerox Corporation and Corning Medical. Dr. Musen and Dr. Shortliffe have also received support from the Henry J. Kaiser

Family Foundation. Dave Combs, Michael Kahn, Christopher Lane, Rick Lenon, Hank Rappaport, Janice Rohn, and Samson Tu provided important evaluations of the developing system. Robert Noble designed the system software for icon manipulation.

References

Bennett, J. S. (1985). ROGET: A knowledge-based system for acquiring the conceptual structure of a diagnostic expert system. *Journal of Automated Reasoning, 1*(1), 49–74.

Boose, J. H. (1984). Personal construct theory and the transfer of human expertise. *Proceedings of the Fourth National Conference on Artificial Intelligence*, pp. 27–33, American Association for Artificial Intelligence, Austin, TX, August.

Buchanan, B. G., Barstow, D., Bechtal, R., Bennett, J., Clancey, W., Kulikowski, C., Mitchell, T., & Waterman, D. A. (1983). Constructing an expert system. In F. Hayes–Roth, D. A. Waterman, & D. B. Lenat (Eds.), *Building Expert Systems*, chap. 5, pp. 127–167. Reading, MA: Addison–Wesley.

Davis, R. (1979). Interactive transfer of expertise: Acquisition of new inference rules. *Artificial Intelligence, 12*(2), 121–157.

Jacob, R. J. K. (1985). A state transition diagram language for visual programming. *Computer, 18* (8), 51–59.

Kahn, M. G., Ferguson, J. C., Shortliffe, E. H., & Fagan, L. M. (1985). Representation and use of temporal information in ONCOCIN. *Proceedings of the Ninth Annual Symposium on Computer Applications in Medical Care*, pp. 172–176, Baltimore. November.

MacDonald, A. (1982). Visual programming. *Datamation, 28*(11), 132–140.

Musen, M. A., Combs, D. M., Walton, J. D., Shortliffe, E. H., & Fagan, L. M. (1986a). OPAL: Toward the computer-aided design of oncology advice systems. *Proceedings of the Tenth Annual Symposium on Computer Applications in Medical Care*, pp. 43–52 Washington, DC, October.

Musen, M. A., Langlotz, C. P., Fagan, L. M., & Shortliffe, E. H. (1985). Rationale for knowledge base redesign in a medical advice system. *Proceedings of AAMSI Congress 85*, 197–201, American Association for Medical Systems and Informatics, San Francisco, May.

Musen, M. A., Rohn, J. A., Fagan, L. M., & Shortliffe, E. H. (1986b). Knowledge engineering for a clinical trial advice system: Uncovering errors in protocol specification. *Proceedings of AAMSI Congress 86*, pp. 24–27, American Association for Medical Systems and Informatics, Anaheim, CA, May.

Raeder, G. (1985). A survey of current graphical programming techniques. *Computer, 18*(8), 11–25.

Richer, M. H., & Clancey, W. J. (1985). GUIDON-WATCH: A graphic interface for viewing a knowledge-based system. *IEEE Computer Graphics & Applications, 5*(11), 51–64.

Sheil, B. (1983). Power tools for programmers. *Datamation, 29*(2), 131–144.

Shneiderman, B. (1983). Direct Manipulation: A step beyond programming languages. *Computer, 16*(8), 57–69.

Shortliffe, E. H., Scott, A. C., Bischoff, M. B., van Melle, W., & Jacobs, C. D. (1981). ONCOCIN: An expert system for oncology protocol management. *Proceedings of the Seventh International Joint Conference on Artificial Intelligence,* pp. 876–881, Vancouver, BC, August.

Tsuji, S., & Shortliffe, E. H. (1986). Graphical access to medical expert systems: I. Design of a knowledge engineer's interface. *Methods of Information in Medicine, 25*(2), 62–70.

Wasserman, A. I. (1985). Extending state transition diagrams for the specification of human-computer interaction. *IEEE Transactions on Software Engineering, SE–11*(8), 699–713.

Zisman, M. D. (1978). Use of production systems for modeling asynchronous, concurrent processes. *Pattern Directed Inference Systems,* 53–68. New York: Academic Press.

THREE

Expert System Development: Letting the Domain Specialist Directly Author Knowledge Bases

Stanley Tuhrim, M.D.,
James A. Reggia, M.D., Ph.D.,
Marianne Floor, M.D., M.P.H.

University of Maryland

Abstract

More widespread use of expert system technology is currently limited by a knowledge acquisition bottleneck. Transferring the domain specialist's expertise to an expert system's knowledge base has proven difficult and time consuming, in part because the traditional approach requires the interposition of a computer scientist/knowledge engineer between the human expert and computer. An alternative approach supports a high-level knowledge representation language so that an application specialist can implement an expert system directly. This chapter describes procedures for doing this and the evaluation of the practical use of the high-level language by application specialists. The advantages and disadvantages of this approach are then discussed.

Acknowledgement

This work was supported in part by NIH Grant NS-163332. Dr. Tuhrim is the recipient of an NINCDS Teacher Investigator Development Award (1K07NS00913). Dr. Reggia is the recipient of an NSF Presidential Young Investigator Award (DCR-8451430) with matching support from Software A&E, AT&T Information Systems, and Allied.

Introduction

Expert systems can be viewed as consisting of a domain-specific knowledge base and a domain-independent inference mechanism. For example, in medicine the knowledge base is a collection of encoded knowledge needed to solve or analyze problems in some medical area. The inference mechanism is a program which, given a patient description, uses the information in the knowledge base to generate useful information about the patient (e.g., diagnosis, prognosis).

Although they have existed for more than 25 years, expert systems have had a very limited impact on real world decision making. In part, this is the result of the inefficiency and expense of developing them. The major limiting factor in more widespread use of expert system technology may be the knowledge acquisition problem: it has proven in general to be very difficult to transfer a human expert's knowledge into an evolving expert system's knowledge base. This reflects, in part, an inability to achieve a direct interaction between the domain expert and knowledge-based system during the process of system development. Typically, a computer scientist or "knowledge engineer" acts as an intermediary, translating the domain specialist's knowledge into appropriate data structures that can be processed by computer (Figure 1a). This requires a domain specialist (e.g., a medical doctor) to explain application concepts to a computer scientist, and to describe explicitly a decision-making process of which he or she may not normally be conscious. Consequently, the translation of knowledge into a form suitable for computer processing has proven costly and inefficient, thereby impeding the production and dissemination of functional systems (Reggia & Tuhrim, 1985). With the traditional approach to system development, it has been estimated that "Even for the best understood problems, experienced researchers using the best-understood technologies still require at least five man-years to develop a system that begins to be robust" (Davis, 1982).

In the past, the role of the knowledge engineer in the knowledge acquisition process has been viewed as critical. The general opinion has been that domain experts usually lack the skills necessary to organize and structure their knowledge, select an appropriate inference method, and write the necessary computer programs (Weiss & Kulikowski, 1984). Recent efforts have been made to develop tools facilitating direct construction of expert systems by the noncomputer scientist. A variety of approaches have been taken, leading to "intelligent" editors (e.g., TIERESIAS, Davis, 1978), and expert systems whose expertise is in the area of knowledge acquisition (e.g., AGE, Nii

(a)

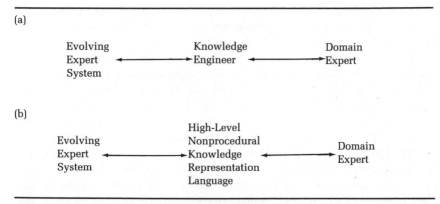

(b)

Figure 1. (a) How Most Knowledge-based Systems are Constructed; (b) The Alternative Approach Advocated in this chapter

& Aiello, 1979). However, to date this approach has not received widespread use nor critical evaluation in practice.

In this chapter, we advocate an alternative approach to the development of knowledge-based systems. Specifically, we suggest that the direct use by a domain specialist of a suitable high-level, nonprocedural knowledge representation language during expert system development would hasten the amelioration of the existing knowledge acquisition bottleneck (Figure 1b). Not only would such an approach avoid the need for an application specialist to explain domain-specific aspects of a problem to a computer scientist, but it would also contribute to system portability and facilitate a clean separation of artificial intelligence (AI) issues and application-specific concepts during system construction. In addition, providing a "hands-on" experience to domain experts may increase their willingness to accept these systems and put them to use, in contradistinction to the widespread resistance which currently exists.

The idea of devising a high-level, nonprocedural language that would permit a computer-inexperienced application specialist to implement expert systems directly raises a number of questions and undoubtedly a healthy skepticism in the reader. How should such a language be designed? What primitive features should it have? Could a computer-inexperienced individual really be expected to use it to construct an expert system independently? How could a language sufficiently simple for such use also be sufficiently powerful?

To investigate the feasibility of such an approach, we developed an expert system generator (or "shell") called KMS (the Knowledge Management System) based on a high-level representation language intended for direct use by noncomputer scientists (Reggia, 1981). The language KMS supports can be described as nonprocedural and object-oriented. The primitive generic "entities" available in the system are problem attributes or features, the values these attributes can have and various actions that an expert system can perform. We recently completed a 5-year study of the use of this language to construct expert systems (Tuhrim & Reggia, 1986). In the following, we first summarize KMS and the high-level knowledge representation language it embodies. We then describe its use by a group of medical students to implement small expert systems, as well as its use by other computer-inexperienced individuals. As a result of this experience, we conclude that very high-level knowledge representation languages can be used directly by application specialists to construct expert systems.

Creating Knowledge-Based Systems with KMS

The Knowledge Management System (KMS) is a domain-independent expert system generator intended to enable application specialists without computer expertise to author knowledge bases in their area of expertise without a computer scientist acting as an intermediary (Reggia, 1981). KMS provides all of the necessary software for a knowledge-based expert system in prepackaged form (inference mechanisms plus user interface). The application specialist is only required to provide a knowledge base written in the KMS language.

The end product derived from the use of KMS by a knowledge base author is an interactive system that can carry on a "conversation" with a user of the type illustrated in Figure 2 (user typing has been underlined for clarity). KMS-generated expert systems can do three things: display their knowledge, apply it to solve problems, and justify the solution derived. The knowledge-base author gives KMS a knowledge base written in the KMS language, and KMS in turn uses that knowledge base to support interactive sessions with users such as the one demonstrated here. The knowledge-base author can structure the interactive sessions by specifying a detailed "actions" section or leave the specific form of the session to KMS by simply specifying the answers to be obtained. This example illustrates the format of questions asked by KMS, how the user answers them, generation of useful information (e.g., American Cancer Society recommendations), and answer justification. While we are currently using KMS in the setting of medical decision making and thus present medically oriented examples, KMS is applicable to virtually any domain involving semistructured

THIS DECISION SUPPORT SYSTEM WILL HELP ASSESS AN INDIVIDUAL FOR CANCER RISK AND RECOMMEND APPROPRIATE SCREENING TESTS. IT IS ONLY FOR ASYMPTOM- ATIC PEOPLE AND ITS SUGGESTIONS ARE SUBJECT TO THE PHYSICIAN'S JUDGEMENT IN EVERY CASE. THE RECOMMENDATIONS, WHICH ONLY APPLY TO SCREENING FOR EARLY CANCER AND NOT TO SCREENING FOR THE DETECTION OF OTHER DISEASES, ARE BASED ON THE LATEST ACS (AMERICAN CANCER SOCIETY) RECOMMENDATIONS DESCRIBED IN

> THE CANCER RELATED HEALTH CHECKUP
> AMERICAN CANCER SOCIETY, FEB. 8, 1980

NOTE: THIS IS AN EXPERIMENTAL SYSTEM THAT HAS NOT BEEN APPROVED FOR USE IN PRACTICE

TYPE 'CONTINUE.' TO BEGIN

<u>continue.</u>

LET'S BEGIN BY DETERMINING IF THE INDIVIDUAL IN QUESTION IS AT INCREASED RISK FOR ANY OF THE COMMON TYPES OF CANCER. PLEASE ANSWER THE FOLLOWING ABOUT HIM OR HER.

SEX:
  (1) MALE
  (2) FEMALE
= ?
<u>2</u>

AGE = ? (ENTER A NUMERIC VALUE)
<u>35</u>
  .
  .
  .

OK—AT THIS POINT WE CAN SAY THAT THIS PERSON IS AT INCREASED RISK FOR THE FOLLOWING TYPES OF CANCER:

    ENDOMETRIAL CANCER
    COLON OR RECTAL CANCER

NOW LET'S DETERMINE WHAT THE AMERICAN CANCER SOCIETY RECOMMENDS AS SCREENING TESTS FOR THIS INDIVIDUAL . . .

NEGATIVE PAP SMEAR ANNUALLY FOR TWO YEARS:
  (1) YES
  (2) NO
= ?
<u>1</u>

PREVIOUS NEGATIVE MAMMOGRAM:
  (1) YES
  (2) NO
= ?
<u>2</u>

Figure 2.   Examples of KMS-user Session

Figure 2. (continued)

OK—THE AMERICAN CANCER SOCIETY RECOMMENDS ('RECS') THAT THIS INDIVIDUAL
BE SCREENED FOR CANCER AS FOLLOWS:

    PAP TEST EVERY THREE YEARS
    PELVIC EXAMINATION EVERY THREE YEARS
    BREAST EXAM BY PHYSICIAN EVERY THREE YEARS
    BREAST SELF—EXAMINATION MONTHLY
    BASELINE MAMMOGRAPHY
    EXAMINATION OF OVARIES EVERY THREE YEARS
    —THYROID —LYMPHATIC —SKIN AND —ORAL EXAM EVERY THREE YEARS

NOTE THAT ROUTINE CHEST XRAY AND SPUTUM CYTOLOGY FOR EARLY DETECTION OF
LUNG CANCER ARE SPECIFICALLY EXCLUDED FROM THESE RECOMMENDATIONS.

READY FOR COMMAND:

justify recs = baseline mammography.
    SEX = FEMALE
    & AGE GE 35
    & AGE LE 50
    & PREVIOUS NEGATIVE MAMMOGRAM = NO
    (BY RULE SCREEN20)

READY FOR COMMAND:
   .
   .
   .

---

decision making (e.g., legal analysis, corporate planning, governmental decisions).

KMS provides multiple inference methods and knowledge representation formats, and correspondingly is broken into subsystems where each subsystem is based on a different approach to knowledge processing. Originally, KMS required the knowledge-base author to select a single approach from among those available when constructing an expert system (subsequent KMS-like software does not make this restriction). Having different knowledge-processing methods in KMS reflects the belief that there is no "best" method for developing knowledge-based systems. On the contrary, there exist several good methods (statistical pattern classification, rule-based deduction, association-based abduction, etc.). The appropriate ones for any situation depend on several factors such as the structure of the problem involved and the availability of appropriate problem-solving knowledge.

Conceptually, the knowledge base for an expert system created using KMS can be viewed as consisting of four components:

1. *data schema:* a list of relevant attributes and their possible values for some specific problem;
2. *associations:* the network of associations that relate the values of one attribute to those of another;
3. *actions:* instructions to KMS about how the knowledge base is to be used; and,
4. *free text:* supplementary free text (string data) such as definitions, references, etc.

KMS is composed of a collection of subsystems, each of which implements (1) a knowledge-base parser and interpreter, (2) an inference system for supporting goal-directed behavior, and (3) a user interface implementing commands (e.g., DISPLAY and NEXT) and question-and-answer interactions. Significant attention has been given to keeping KMS as modular as possible. We have tried to keep KMS simple from the viewpoint of the knowledge-base author by emphasizing standardized features throughout.

We illustrate the knowledge acquisition process with a simple example. Briefly, using KMS to develop an expert system involves the following steps: (1) Conceptually organizing the underlying knowledge in terms of the relevant attributes of a problem and the associations between them; (2) Selecting the most appropriate knowledge-processing method in KMS to use; (3) Writing the knowledge base using the high-level, nonprocedural knowledge representation language supported by KMS; and (4) Testing and certifying the resultant expert system.

Example: The American Cancer Society (ACS) published a 50-page booklet describing which routine screening tests for cancer should be performed by physicians on apparently healthy adults (ACS, 1980).

To create an expert system that generates the ACS recommendations illustrated in Figure 2 one would begin by organizing the underlying knowledge into a "problem-oriented attribute hierarchy." Such a hierarchy consists of nodes which are problem attributes and links representing the relation "depends on." It provides a general conceptual framework, understandable by computer-inexperienced application specialists, for representing information about the specific problem for which an expert system is to be built. It also forms the basis for the resultant expert system's goal-directed behavior. In this case, the ultimate goal is the determination of the ACS RECOMMENDATIONS. This attribute is therefore placed at the top of the attribute hierarchy as depicted in Figure 3. CANCERS AT INCREASED RISK represents another attribute whose values must be inferred and upon which the value of ACS RECOMMENDATIONS depends. The remaining 12 at-

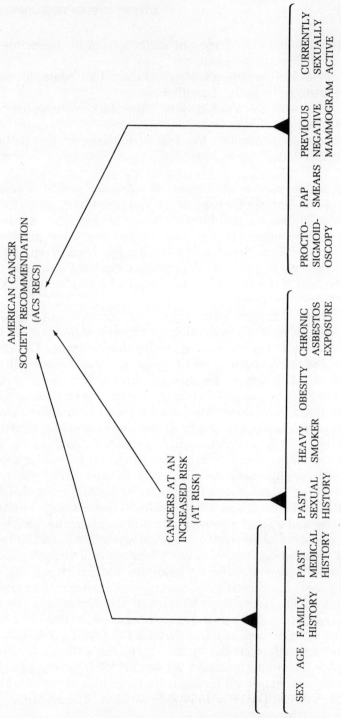

Figure 3.   Attribute Hierarchy for the ACS Knowledge Base

tributes at the bottom of this hierarchy are input attributes whose values must be obtained from the user. This attribute hierarchy will guide the inference process during problem solving. For example, if the ACS expert system is given the goal of obtaining a value for ACS RECOMMENDATIONS, it will automatically set up subgoals for itself of first obtaining values for attributes below that node in the attribute hierarchy.

A set of possible values is conceptually associated with each attribute in Figure 3 but is not shown explicitly. For example, the attribute SEX has possible values MALE and FEMALE. The second step that the knowledge-base author would take in building the expert system is to select an approach to managing the system's knowledge (i.e., select a representation and inference method from among those available in KMS). In this case, since the ACS recommendations are effectively a set of rules about when an individual is at risk for cancer and what specific tests should be done, it would be appropriate to represent the knowledge involved as a collection of rules or productions and use deduction as the inference method.

The third step in development would be to encode the actual knowledge base using the nonprocedural knowledge representation language supported by KMS. The schema in this case consists of declarations such as

SEX(SGL): MALE, FEMALE.

indicating that the attribute SEX can take on the value of MALE or FEMALE but not both, because only a single (SGL) value is permitted at any one time. In general, attributes are tagged as SGL indicating "single valued," MLT indicating multiple valued (e.g., PAST MEDICAL HISTORY is tagged MLT as an individual may have had zero or more medical problems in the past), or INT (REAL) indicating integers (reals) only.

The associations in this example are specified as a collection of nonprocedural rules or productions, such as

```
RISK1
IF SEX = FEMALE, & AGE GE 20,
   & PMH = INFERTILITY / FAILURE OF OVULATION /
           ABNORMAL UTERINE BLEEDING
           /ESTROGEN THERAPY,
      / OBESITY
THEN AT RISK = ENDOMETRIAL CA.
```

This rule, named RISK1, states that *if* a woman is 20 years old or older *and* has either a past medical history (PMH) of infertility, failure of ovulation, abnormal uterine bleeding, or estrogen therapy, or she is obese, then it follows that she is at increased risk for endometrial cancer. In this knowledge base, 5 rules (RISK1 through RISK5) assess whether or not an individual is at special risk for common types of cancer. Twenty-eight rules (SCREEN1 through SCREEN28) generate the ACS recommendations for screening based on an individual's age, sex, special risk, etc. Note that these rules are a nonprocedural description of the knowledge needed to generate the ACS screening recommendations; they are in general not evaluated in the order given.

The "actions" included in a knowledge base are control information representing a description of how the knowledge base is to be used in a consultation session. In our example, the actions the ACS expert system should perform might be indicated as

```
MESSAGE
    "THIS DECISION . . ." . . .
PAUSE.
MESSAGE
    "LET'S BEGIN BY . . ." . . .
OBTAIN CANCERS AT AN INCREASED RISK.
MESSAGE
    "OK—AT THIS POINT . . ."
DISPLAY VALUE (CANCERS AT AN INCREASED RISK).
MESSAGE ". . ."
OBTAIN RECS.
MESSAGE ". . ."
DISPLAY VALUES(RECS).
    . . .
```

by the knowledge-base author. This indicates that the expert system generated by KMS should first print out an introductory message to the user, and then PAUSE until the user types 'CONTINUE.' At that time, the system should generate another brief message, and then should OBTAIN the value of the attribute CANCERS AT AN INCREASED RISK and DISPLAY this value. Finally, the expert system should OBTAIN and DISPLAY the ACS screening recommendations (RECS is a synonym for this declared in the schema). Once the expert system has executed the above commands it will default to asking the user what to do next. The reader should compare this control information with the "conversation" in Figure 2.

The final component of a knowledge base is free text. At the beginning of a knowledge base, one can specify a CERTIFICATION for the knowledge base, such as who was the author, who has reviewed it, and what sort of testing it has undergone. One can also specify tutorial INSTRUCTION and REFERENCES. In addition, one can add free text throughout the knowledge base, and educational messages. All of this free text material is much more than "comments" in that it can be selectively displayed as desired by the knowledge base author or eventual users by using the DISPLAY command (e.g., DISPLAY DEFI-NITION(OBESITY) or DISPLAY CERTIFICATION).

After writing the knowledge base its author submits it to KMS. The KMS parser examines the knowledge base for syntactical and a limited number of semantic errors. Diagnostic error messages may be generated. The errors must be corrected by the knowledge-base author before KMS will "accept" the knowledge base. Once this is accomplished the expert system can be used to support conversations such as that illustrated in Figure 2. Much of the apparent "intelligence" in the conversation is due to the goal-directed behavior produced by the OBTAIN command. This command creates a goal of obtaining the value of the attribute specified as part of the command. The expert system achieves this goal by looking at information in the knowledge base. For example, the OBTAIN CANCERS AT AN INCREASED RISK command sets up the goal of assigning a value to the attribute CANCERS AT AN IN-CREASED RISK. All rules which could assign a value to this attribute are retrieved and evaluated one at a time. Rule evaluation involves first seeing if a rule's antecedents are true (Does SEX = FEMALE ?, etc.), and if they are then assigning the appropriate values to the consequent attributes. Note that to evaluate antecedent statements requires KMS to check first to see whether the values of the antecedent statement attributes are known. If not, KMS must determine a value for them either by evaluating other rules or by asking the user for their values if no suitable rules exist. This is the basis of the questions generated in the conversation previously illustrated. In general, one can view the goal-directed behavior of KMS as an implementation of an exhaustive, depth-first evaluation of a goal tree. This behavior is effectively the same regardless of whether the underlying knowledge is specified as rules, calculations, probabilities, or descriptions.

The above example demonstrates how one can author a knowledge base consisting of rules or productions. There are several other ways in which one can represent knowledge in a knowledge base.

Calculations can be represented in mathematical formulae that employ operations on appropriate attributes. For example, a RISK SCORE for complications from arteriography (Faught, Trader, & Hanna, 1979) can be described as

```
RISK SCORE (INT)
  [CALCULATION:
        8 * NUMBER OF TRANSIENT ISCHEMIC ATTACKS
     +  6 * NUMBER OF ARTERIES TO BE CATHETERIZED
     + 14 * PRESENCE (DIABETES MELLITUS)
     + 11 * PRESENCE (SEX = FEMALE) ].
```

Here, PRESENCE is a function with a value of 1 if something is present and a value of 0 otherwise. Besides creating linear discriminant equations like this, the knowledge base author has access to a full range of mathematical functions (log, cos, abs, exponentiation, etc.).

Statistical pattern classification can be done using Bayes' Theorem with the independence assumption. An example of the schema and the associations components of a very simple Bayesian knowledge base is (based on Snyder, Ramirez–Lassepas, & Lippert, 1977):

```
RESPIRATORY STATUS(SGL): SPONTANEOUS ACTIVITY, ON
      RESPIRATOR AND NOT TRIGGERING.
RESPONSE TO STIMULI(SGL):
      PURPOSEFUL RESPONSE TO PAIN,
      NONPURPOSEFUL RESPONSE TO PAIN.
PUPILLARY LIGHT REFLEX(SGL): PRESENT, ABSENT.
OCULOCEPHALIC REFLEX(SGL): PRESENT, ABSENT.

NEUROLOGICAL OUTCOME(SGL):
      FUNCTIONAL ⟨0.62⟩
         0.67 0.33;
         0.57 0.43;
         0.89 0.11;
         0.69 0.31,
      IMPAIRED ⟨0.38⟩
         0.15 0.85;
         0.15 0.85;
         0.42 0.58;
         0.33 0.67 %%
```

For the attribute whose value is to be inferred (NEUROLOGICAL OUTCOME), each possible value (e.g., FUNCTIONAL) is followed by a prior probability in angular brackets and all of the necessary conditional probabilities needed for Bayesian classification. These conditional probabilities are listed in the same order as the values of the input attributes to which they correspond. For example, in the article from which this knowledge base was derived 67% of those patients who eventually recovered from coma following a cardiac arrest (i.e., NEUROLOGICAL OUTCOME = FUNCTIONAL) were initially breathing

spontaneously (i.e., RESPIRATORY STATUS = SPONTANEOUS AC-
TIVITY) while 33% were not. (In general, attributes are *not* restricted to
having two possible values as is the case in this simple example.) The
inference mechanism uses these numbers to calculate the probabilities
of the outcomes and then ranks them.

Descriptions can be used by a knowledge-base author to supply the
information needed for tasks involving diagnostic reasoning. For example, one can describe the different syndromes associated with peroneal
muscular atrophy (Dyck & Lambert, 1968), such as Refsum's Syndrome
as:

```
REFSUM'S SYNDROME
  [DESCRIPTION:
    AGE OF ONSET = CHILDHOOD OR ADOLESCENCE;
    INHERITANCE = RECESSIVE;
    SEVERITY OF MOTOR DEFICIT = MODERATE⟨L⟩, SEVERE⟨H⟩;
    SENSORY DEFICIT ⟨A⟩
      [SEVERITY = MODERATE⟨L⟩, SEVERE⟨H⟩];
    HYPERTROPHIC NERVES⟨H⟩;
    OTHER NEUROLOGICAL FINDINGS = DEAFNESS⟨M⟩,
      RETINITIS PIGMENTOSA⟨M⟩,
      CEREBELLAR ATAXIA⟨L⟩;
    CSF PROTEIN = ELEVATED⟨H⟩;
    MOTOR CONDUCTION VELOCITIES = VERY SLOW⟨A⟩;
    SENSORY ACTION POTENTIAL = ABNORMAL⟨A⟩].
```

Here the features of this disorder are described in a series of statements
and "symbolic probabilities" are indicated in angular brackets (A =
always, H = high likelihood, M = medium likelihood, L = low likelihood, and N = never). All of the attributes and values used in statements in this DESCRIPTION were defined previously in the schema of
the knowledge base.

Knowledge represented in this descriptive manner is utilized by a
hypothesize-and-test inference mechanism modeled on human diagnostic reasoning (Reggia, Nau, & Wang, 1983). Given one or more initial
problem features, the expert system generates a set of potential hypotheses or "causes" which can explain the problem features. The system
employs a "parsimonious covering" model (Reggia et al., 1985).

Evaluation in Practice

Having summarized the basic features of KMS and the knowledge representation language it supports, we now review our experiences with

the use of this system over the last several years. To test the hypothesis that the high-level language in KMS could be used by computer-inexperienced domain experts to build expert systems, we evaluated its use by medical students over a 4-year period. In the following, we first describe this evaluation, and then turn to other experiences with this approach to developing both medical and nonmedical expert systems.

Evaluation of Use by Medical Students

From 1981 to 1984 we offered an annual 15-hour elective course on medical decision making at the University of Maryland School of Medicine. We monitored the experience of 70 medical students who took the course. At the beginning of the course students completed a questionnaire describing their previous computer experience. On the basis of this questionnaire, the students' previous experience, ranging from none to an undergraduate degree in computer science or engineering, was graded on a 4-point scale (Table 1).

During the course formal models of decision making, including Bayesian classification, decision analysis, rule-based deduction and association-based abduction (a method of drawing plausible inferences commonly used in an intuitive way by physician; given that a causes b if we find b we conclude probably a) were discussed. Students learned to use the language supported by KMS to build two small expert systems. The purpose of these exercises was to reinforce the basic decision-making concepts introduced in class. One system developed by students used Bayesian classification to diagnose thyroid disorders on the basis of probabilities published in an article in the medical literature (Nordyke, Kulikowski, & Kulikowski, 1971). Students also developed a small rule-based system which staged the disease of lung cancer patients and estimated prognosis on the basis of published data (Rosenow & Carr, 1979). In addition, they were given an examination covering basic decision-making concepts. At the conclusion of the course, students were asked to rate, anonymously, the difficulty in learning

TABLE 1.   Experience Scores of 70 Students Using the Knowledge Managements System (KMS)

Category	Description	Number
1	No previous programming experience	27
2	One previous computer course involving actual programming, individual programming experience	28
3	Two or three previous computer programming courses	8
4	Several computer programming courses or substantial work as a programmer	7

KMS and its utility as an adjunct to lecture material in learning about decision-making concepts. They also recorded the length of time spent on each project. Performance scores, a composite of test and project grades, were calculated for each student. The correlation between performance and experience scores was evaluated by Spearman's r.

The mean performance score was 87 (range 79 to 97). The mean experience score was 1.9 (range 1 to 4, see Table 1). There was no association between performance and experience scores ($r = 0.02$). Thirty-two of 47 students responding anonymously rated the expert system generator easy to use; 15 felt it was of moderate difficulty; no one thought it difficult. The mean amount of time spent implementing the Bayesian system was 4.7 hours (range 1 to 13). For the rule-based system it was 8.4 hours (range 2 to 20). By way of comparison the mean time reported to learn to use the text editor (a simple line editor) to the degree necessary to write the knowledge bases was 1.9 hours. All students completed the course.

These data support the belief that it is possible for computer-inexperienced students to learn to use a high-level knowledge representation language to develop expert systems quickly and easily. The amount of previous computer experience was unrelated to the quality of performance, although greater previous experience appeared to allow students to build the systems faster. Subjective evaluations by the students involved indicated that the use of the expert system generator enhanced their classroom learning experience.

This study demonstrates that computer-inexperienced physicians can, in a reasonable period of time, learn to build directly at least small expert systems by using a high-level knowledge representation language. However, it should be emphasized that in the study described above we have demonstrated only the feasibility of developing decision aids in the manner stated. The expert systems developed were not "field ready" and would require modification or enhancement and testing in practice before becoming practical tools. Hence, this study does not address the length of time actually required to develop a finished and tested system.

Other Experiences Using the KMS Language

The high-level knowledge representation language supported by KMS has been used to develop a variety of real world as well as "toy" systems in both medical and nonmedical areas. For example, in medicine it has been used to develop a robust, rule-based expert system to assist physicians with the difficult task of assessing and managing patients with possible transient ischemic attacks (TIAs) (Reggia et al.,

1984). This system uses approximately 400 rules to classify a patient's illness, localize the neurological deficit, screen for 46 causative or mimicking disorders, recommend additional diagnostic tests, and suggest management alternatives. We evaluated this system on 103 patients with possible TIAs by comparing its judgements with those of physicians. The system's localization and classification of patients generally agreed with those made by the specialists, whose knowledge and opinions had formed the basis for the system's rules. This demonstrated that the TIA system can reproduce the decision criteria of the experts using it. The patients used in the study were usually cared for by general neurologists or internists and not by the specialists who helped develop the expert system. So, not surprisingly, the expert system's management recommendations often differed significantly from what was actually done with the patient.

KMS has also been used in computer sciences courses at the University of Maryland to give students experience with building expert systems as class projects. Students were easily able to build demonstration systems which performed the same task but used different inference mechanisms. This helped them develop an understanding of the advantages and disadvantages of different approaches.

Similarly, KMS has served as the basis for comparative analysis of the methods used in expert systems (Ramsey et al., 1986). In each case multiple expert systems for the same task were built, one using statistical pattern classification, one using rule-based deduction, and/or one using association-based abduction. Example applications include determining the type of water pollutant at a chemical spill site, predicting prognosis following subarachnoid hemorrhage, and diagnosing the source of low productivity during software development projects. The ease of construction and general accuracy and efficiency of the systems have been compared and the strengths and weaknesses of each approach have been described elsewhere (Ramsey et al. 1986).

A commercial system[1] modeled after KMS has been used to develop expert systems for a wide variety of industrial, commercial, military, and government applications. While this involved applications developed by "knowledge engineers" in some cases, in many applications domain specialists with very limited previous exposure to computer science and artificial intelligence used the knowledge representation language directly during system development. These experiences suggest that the direct use of high-level languages by computer-inexperienced individuals to construct expert systems may be viable in many nonmedical domains.

---

[1] KES, from Software A&E, Inc., Arlington, VA.

Conclusion

To our knowledge the high-level knowledge representation language supported by KMS is the only such language which has been systematically evaluated in practice. This evaluation through its use by medical students has served to demonstrate the feasibility of this approach and illustrates many of its advantages. Some limitations of this approach have also been brought to light, pointing the way for further research. Some of the advantages and disadvantages of direct use of high-level knowledge representation languages by domain specialists are discussed below.

A number of limitations of this approach came to light. Some training of application experts is required and consultation with computer scientists or more experienced knowledge-base authors may be necessary. The KMS language cannot conveniently represent all of the concepts necessary for adequately describing the knowledge necessary for many application domains. In particular, spatial and temporal relationships are difficult to represent. The obvious efficiencies of prepackaged inference mechanisms are counterbalanced by forcing the knowledge-base author to use existing inference mechanisms which may not be ideally suited for the type of information available or powerful or efficient enough for the decision-making task required (this is, of course, a limitation of current AI technology in general). Finally, it must be emphasized that this is not primarily a research-oriented approach but rather a utilitarian one, aimed at providing a tool for application to specific domains.

On the other hand, our experiences as outlined in this chapter have convinced us of the following advantages of this approach. First, systems supporting high-level, domain-independent knowledge representation languages greatly improve the efficiency of the expert system development process. All of the software that is needed to create a complete expert system (inference method, user interface, etc.) is already available in prepackaged form and does not have to be reprogrammed for each system. Knowledge-base parsers facilitate the detection of errors and thus expedite the process of acquiring the needed knowledge. This newfound productivity makes it possible to create a potent library of computer-processable knowledge to support human-machine problem-solving activities.

Second, high-level languages permit direct interaction between the computer and the application specialist during the creation and testing of knowledge bases. Our experience with the use of KMS by previously computer-inexperienced physicians and medical students has clearly demonstrated the feasibility of this interaction. This contrasts sharply to the currently predominent approach to developing expert systems in which a computer scientist effectively serves as an intermediary between the computer and the application specialist (Feigenbaum, 1977). A more direct interaction improves efficiency by eliminating the difficulties involved when a computer scientist and application specialist try to communicate their expertise to one another. It also contributes to the acceptability of the resultant expert systems to application specialists because of their personal involvement with and control over knowledge-base creation.

Third, the number of people who will be able to build expert systems can be increased dramatically since all that is required is access to a computing environment which supports a system like KMS. This may facilitate the development of a "critical mass" of knowledge bases making expert system use more widespread.

Fourth, high-level languages such as those in KMS make expression of the relevant concepts needed for a knowledge base much easier than other existing languages (e.g., FORTRAN). This is not surprising since other languages were never specifically intended for expressing human knowledge of the type required for semistructured problem solving. In contrast, KMS provides a variety of abstract formalisms (rules, descriptions, etc.) for encoding knowledge in a format that is reasonably understandable to application specialists and relatively easy for them to learn.

Fifth, high-level languages raise the possibility of a qualitative improvement in the portability of knowledge-based expert systems. Even when successful in the past, knowledge-based expert systems have been very resistant to transfer to different sites. High-level languages could change the question from one of portability of expert systems to one of portability of knowledge bases. In other words, since KMS supports machine-independent representation and command languages, any computer facility with an implemented version of KMS would potentially be able to use suitable knowledge bases authored at other sites.

Finally, a high-level language forces the separation of application-specific aspects of problem solving (expressed in knowledge bases) from the theoretical concepts of human-machine problem solving (expressed in the programs of KMS). This permits the latter, general problem-solving methods to be studied separately, at times with new ideas being readily tested on a variety of problems simply by applying them to existing knowledge bases.

We are attempting to eliminate some of the above-mentioned shortcomings in developing our next generation of knowledge representation languages. This is being done in the context of developing a system for neurological localization, the process of identifying a region in the nervous system whose dysfunction is producing a patient's symptoms (Reggia et al., in press). This process requires an understanding of the spatial relationships among the nuclei and tracts of the nervous system as well as their functional capacities. We are attempting to combine probabilities and hypothesize-and-test mechanisms to perform more complex reasoning capabilities, provide a natural language interface for patient descriptions, more sophisticated answer justification based on causal reasoning and a pictorial depiction of lesions in the nervous system. We hope this system will serve as a prototype for an improved system more conducive to widespread use by computer-inexperienced application specialists.

References

ACS. (1980). *The Cancer Related Health Checkup*, American Cancer Society, February.

Davis R. (1982). Expert systems: Where are we? and where do we go from here? *AI Magazine, 3*, pp. 3–22.

Davis R. (1978). Knowledge acquisition in rule-based systems—Knowledge about representations as a basis for system construction and maintenance. In D. A. Waterman & F. Hayes–Roth (Eds.), *Pattern directed inference systems*. New York: Academic Press, pp. 99–134.

Dyck, P., & Lambert, E. (1968). Lower motor and primary sensory neuron diseases with peroneal muscular atrophy. *Archives of Neurology, 18,* 603–625.

Faught, E., Trader, S., & Hanna, G. (1979). Cerebral complications of angiography for transient ischemia and stroke: Prediction of risk. *Neurology, 29,* 4–15.

Feigenbaum, E. (1977). The art of artificial intelligence—Themes and case studies of knowledge engineering. *Proceedings Fifth IJCAI,* pp. 1014–1029.

Nii, H. P., & Aiello, N. (1979). AGE (Attempt to Generalize): A knowledge-based program for building knowledge-based programs. *Proceedings Sixth International Joint Conference Artificial Intelligence,* pp. 645–655.

Nordyke, R. A., Kulikowski, C. A., Kulikowski, C. W. (1971). A comparison of methods for the automated diagnosis of thyroid dysfunction. *Computer Biomedical Research, 4,* 374–389.

Ramsey, C., Reggia, J., Nau, D., & Ferrentino, A. (1986). A comparative analysis of methods for expert systems, *International Journal of Man-Machine Studies, 24,* 475–479.

Reggia, J. (1981). *Knowledge-based decision support system: Development through KMS, TR–1121.* University of Maryland, College Park.

Reggia, J., Nau, S., & Wang, P. (1983). Diagnostic expert systems based on a set covering model. *International Journal of Man-machine Studies, 19*, 437–460.

Reggia, J., Nau, D., Wang, P., & Peng, Y. (1985). A formal model of diagnostic inference. *Information Sciences, 37*, 227–285.

Reggia, J., Tabb, D. R., Price, T. R., et al. (1984). Computer-aided assessment of transient ischemic attacks. *Archives of Neurology, 41*, 1248–1254.

Reggia, J. A., & Tuhrim, S. (1985). An overview of methods for computer-assisted medical decision making. In J. A. Reggia & S. Tuhrim (Eds.), *Computer-assisted medical decision making* (Vol. 1). New York: Springer.

Reggia, J., Tuhrim, S., Ahuja, S., et al. (1986). Plausible reasoning during neurological problem-solving. *Proceedings Fifth World Conference on Medical Informatics*, pp. 17–21.

Rosenow, E. C., Carr, D. T. (1979). Bronchogenic carcinoma. *Ca—Cancer J Clinicians, 29*, 233–245.

Snyder, B., Ramirez–Lassepas, M., & Lippert, D. (1977). Neurologic status and prognosis after cardiopulmonary arrest. *Neurology, 27*, 807–811.

Tuhrim, S., & Reggia, J. (1986). Feasibility of physician-developed expert systems. *Medical Decision Making, 6*, 23–26.

Weiss, S. M., Kulikowski, C. A. (1984). *A practical guide to designing expert systems*. Totowa, NJ: Rowman & Allanheld, p. 12.

FOUR

DARN: Toward a Community Memory for Diagnosis and Repair Tasks

Sanjay Mittal,
Daniel G. Bobrow,
Johan de Kleer

Intelligent Systems Laboratory
Xerox Palo Alto Research Center
Palo Alto, CA

Abstract

DARN is a plan-based knowledge system designed to aid an inexperienced technician in a diagnosis and repair task. Our approach to building this knowledge system is contrasted with theory-based systems such as Sophie, or a classification-based system such as MDX, using a characterization of the tasks, and the leverage for the different approaches. DARN provides a compact and convenient representation for capturing knowledge available in the community of experts for this task. Graphic interfaces are used to guide rookie technicians in the repair task. DARN also provides an "expert's interface" that allows members of the community to extend and modify the knowledge base without intervention of "knowledge engineers."

I. Introduction

DARN is a knowledge-based system to aid in a diagnosis and repair task. In this task, the problem is to localize the cause of a malfunction sufficiently to allow an action that will repair the faulty artifact. Traditional approaches to the development of knowledge-based troubleshooting systems have been based on deep models of the artifact or on a classification of ways in which the artifact can malfunction. In this chapter we identify a third approach, called plan-based, which may be more suitable for some systems. The plan-based approach derives its power from plans for debugging developed by a set of experts, *and allowing them to formalize, extend, and propagate their community knowledge base.* We have focused on the development of a representation to express this diagnostic and repair experience. We support the use of this representation with an interface to enable experts to create and modify the knowledge bases without the mediation of a knowledge engineer.

A spectrum of approaches are possible for the debugging task depending on characteristics of the artifact being debugged. To understand when a plan-based approach is useful, we look at sources of leverage in the computer programs based on existing approaches, and the assumptions made by these approaches about the nature of the artifact being debugged.

Theory-based systems derive their leverage from use of a number of domain-independent reasoning mechanisms operating on large amounts of domain-specific knowledge. For these systems, one must build models of their structure and function. It is then possible to reason from differences between their modeled and actual behavior to locate the cause of the malfunction. SOPHIE (Brown, Burton, & de Kleer, 1982) and DART (Genesereth, 1982) are programs that typify this approach. These programs derive their power from general-purpose reasoning methods that include dependency-directed backtracking (de Kleer et al., 1979; Sussman & Stallman, 1975) and envisioning (de Kleer, 1984). These programs can reason about behavior based on descriptions of the artifact. In order for this approach to succeed, one must assume, of course, that the artifact can be completely described. This is true for circuits analyzed by SOPHIE but is often not true for electro-mechanical systems or hardware-software systems.

Classification-based systems derive their leverage by classifying malfunctions in equivalence classes based on effective actions to ameliorate the malfunction. Medicine is a typical domain in which this approach is used; although they may wish to know more, it is often sufficient for doctors to find differential diagnosis on which suitable therapeutic measures can be devised. MDX (Chandrasekaran & Mittal, 1982), a computer program for medical diagnosis, organized knowledge about liver disorders as a hierarchy of diagnostic states. Szolovits and Pauker (1978) have argued that even rule-based diagnostic systems such as MYCIN are really performing such classification. These systems derive their power from appropriately structured diagnostic hierarchies and employ a more special purpose problem-solving technique called heuristic classification (Chandrasekaran, 1984; Clancey, 1985).

A major cost in the development of classification-based diagnostic programs is the creation and maintenance of suitable hierarchies. One reason for this is that such hierarchies have often not been made explicit by practitioners, though the practitioner's behaviors may be described that way. Even in medicine, where there are many extant ways to classify any given set of diseases, it is clear that none of the existing classifications are a suitable basis for organizing diagnostic knowledge in this way. A medical diagnosis hierarchy has to be crafted from pieces of anatomical, physiological, biochemical, and other views (see Mittal, 1980, for an extended discussion of this issue). It would seem, therefore, that a classification approach would be pragmatically useful only for systems which have a long lifespan of interest over which they stay relatively stable. Some other suitable examples would seem to be nuclear power plants, the space shuttle, automobiles, and Boeing 707 airplanes.

Plan-based systems for diagnosis and repair are based on capturing the plans of experienced technicians for debugging an artifact. They capitalize on the incremental nature of the knowledge acquisition process and the combination of modeling and testing knowledge that the technicians have. It seems most useful for complex systems containing a number of different kinds of subsystems, for example, electrical, mechanical, and software, that have alternative implementations. Examples are computers, printers, copiers, modern automobiles, and maybe even semiconductor fabrication processes. Complications often arise from the short lifespan of these systems, which is often caused by obsolescence. These systems can be further characterized by unavailability of complete underlying models, and complex interaction between the different subsystems. The rapid advancement in technology is causing a maintenance nightmare in many areas. The short lifespan of an artifact prevents the development of a sustained body of experience in troubleshooting these systems, often a precondition for the development of classification of malfunctions.

We believe that the development of knowledge-based tools for assisting in the maintenance of this latter class of artifacts requires a shift in paradigm away from reasoning and deep knowledge structures. A more suitable paradigm is suggested by the metaphors of a knowledge medium (Stefik, 1986) or a community memory. The basic idea is that one should provide a framework in which the experts can themselves articulate their relevant knowledge precisely enough that it can then be used by the computer not only to aid in solving problems in the domain but also made subject to peer review and revision. Such a community memory may, over time, integrate the knowledge from many experts.

In this paper we describe one experiment towards better understanding how to build such community memories. The problem domain for our study was the diagnosis and repair of a class of personal computer at Xerox. As part of this experiment we also developed a knowledge-based system called DARN (Diagnosis and Repair Network). This chapter is organized as follows: We start by reporting some observations about the problem domain and the current practice of repairing these computers. In the next section, we present a relatively simple representation which can be used to encode a large fraction of the experiential plans and knowledge of the computer technicians. Next, we discuss some of the user interface issues in enabling a community of users to themselves create and modify a knowledge base. We also describe some of the user interface tools that were implemented as part of the DARN system. The concluding section summarizes our experience in trying to use DARN, including a follow-up experiment in trying to adapt the DARN framework for the repair of copiers.

II. Observations About the Repair of Personal Computers

Most personal computers, regardless of size or price, are very complex electro-mechanical systems. While our observations here are based on the Xerox 8000 (Star or Dandelion) series machines, many of them are also relevant for other popular series such as the IBM PC or Apple II. A typical Dandelion is configured with a bit-mapped display, a pointing mouse device, a floppy drive, a high-capacity fixed disk, an ethernet connection, and a CPU. We talked to a number of people involved in servicing these machines—technicians in research labs, field service technicians, diagnostic manual writers, and people providing service advice over the phone. The problem of diagnosing and repairing the fixed disk emerged as one of the more challenging and time-consuming problems. We have focused primarily on the disk subsystem in the work reported here.

A fixed disk has electronic (control circuitry), mechanical (disk drive, platters), and electrical (power supply, cooling fan cables) components which can interact in a complex way, especially when there are problems. The problem of how to diagnose and repair problems relating to a malfunctioning disk system in a personal computer has a number of interesting aspects. First, it is not just a diagnosis problem; one is required to find actions which restore the disk to a state where it can continue to be used. This requirement raises interesting issues because of the interplay of hardware and software models. The diagnostic procedures are often programs whose outputs do not precisely indicate a single hardware fault. Moreover, many of the diagnosed problems are *soft* in nature e.g., garbled data fields on a disk, which have been caused by hardware malfunctions. However, these soft faults often cannot be diagnosed until the malfunctioning hardware has been fixed. This interplay presents an interesting challenge in representing the interaction between hardware and software during diagnosis and repair.

Second, there are situations in which there are multiple faults in the machine, and where repairs can fail because newly replaced parts are faulty. In general this is a hard problem. However, there seem to be interesting heuristics for dealing with the more common cases. Finally, the disk repair problem is complicated by the tension between competing constraints: one wants to minimize the amount of hardware replaced on the machine, minimize the amount of time the machine is unavailable to the user, and minimize loss of data on the current disk. The problem of loss of data is often critical when fixing disks.

Current Practice

We started out by taking some very detailed protocols from a couple of the expert technicians of their diagnosis and repair strategies when faced with a problem with a fixed head disk. It was clear that the experts knew a lot about the computer system—they were not approaching it as just a black box. They had a fairly complete model of the architecture (which subsystem was connected to which one and how) and knew how the various subsystems functioned, at least at some level. They also had some partial theories about how the various diagnostic programs worked.

At the same time it was striking to observe how much their ability to troubleshoot the machines was limited by the availability of the diagnostic tools. For example, the diagnostic programs have limited coverage, perform tests in inflexible sequences, and often make unarticulated assumptions about the state of the computer system. Similarly, complex electro-mechanical systems, such as a disk, can malfunction in numerous ways, only a small fraction of which can be directly observed. The real issue, we believe, is not really one of devising better diagnostic procedures, which is always possible, but of using the existing ones to get the job done. In this and many other similar situations the primary objective is making the machine functional again under some of the constraints discussed earlier. We found that our experts

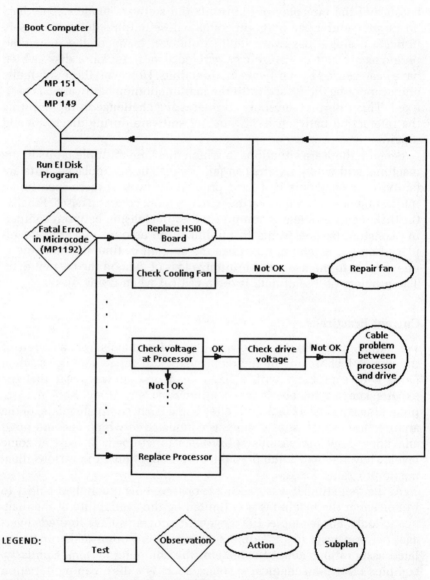

Boot Computer

MP 151 or MP 149

Run EI Disk Program

Fatal Error in Micirocode (MP1192)

Replace HSIO Board

Check Cooling Fan — Not OK → **Repair fan**

Check voltage at Processor — OK → **Check drive voltage** — Not OK → **Cable problem between processor and drive**

Not OK

Replace Processor

LEGEND: Test   Observation   Action   Subplan

Figure 1. Plan Fragment from Protocols A fragment of a plan to repair one of the fixed-disk malfunctions. The plan is based on the initial protocols from the expert technicians before a computer system was implemented.

were articulating their knowledge in the form of diagnosis and repair plans. *These plans were organized around the typical problems that were encountered by the technicians and encoded their experience of how to go about isolating and fixing the problem.* Figure 1 shows a plan fragment from our initial protocols. This figure encodes the plan for fixing one of the problems that shows up when a user boots the machine. The plan might be read as:

> After booting the machine for a cold start, if the maintenance panel (MP) shows 151 or 149, then run EI Disk diagnostic program. If the computer stops with MP code 1192, then execute the following plan. First, try replacing the HSIO (High-Speed I/O board) and rerunning the EI Disk program. If the computer runs fine, then the problem is fixed. Else, check the cooling fan. If the fan is faulty, then fix the fan and rerun the EI Disk program. . . .

We will defer a discussion of these plans to the next section, but a few general comments are in order here. There were many such plans, with each plan being designed to cover a family of problems. As we will see, the plans were not completely independent and often shared subplans. Interestingly, there were variations even among the two experts that we probed in some depth. The plans seemed to compile the experience of and constraints under which the experts were working. It is easy to speculate that the plan variations reflected different experiences and attempts to cope with an imperfect diagnostic situation.

Finally, we had to confront the issue of who would be the users of a computer-based system such as DARN. The experts whose knowledge was encoded in the system would possibly benefit from a precise articulation of their expertise in a form that could aid them in later situations. In the longer term, the experts could share their expertise with other experts, possibly combining their knowledge to form a whole that was larger then the sum of its parts. However, the one clear class of users that could immediately benefit were the so-called "rookie" technicians, i.e., people just being trained to service a new machine.

Currently, inexperienced technicians are provided with manuals of repair that encode Fault Identification Procedures (FIPs). These FIPs suffer from some major problems. First, they are often prepared before any serious experience has accumulated about a machine. Thus, they are incomplete at best and grossly incorrect at worst. Second, while they are occasionally updated, they are usually obsolete before they become available. Furthermore, much of the experience of the expert technicians rarely (or too late) makes its way into the field service manuals. Finally, even though our experts seemed to have a relatively simple way of expressing their repair plans, these plans, nevertheless, could not be suitably expressed in or used from the medium of printed books. This last point should become clear as we move to a discussion of the plan representation.

III. Representation of Repair Plans

In this section we describe a language for representing repair plans. Our primary criterion in devising a representation was to ensure that there be a conceptual match between the representation in the machine and the apparent representations used by the technicians. This criterion is itself motivated by the requirement that the domain experts themselves create the knowledge base, modify parts of it, understand the representation well enough to know the implications of their representational choices, and have confidence in the advice provided by a system that uses the knowledge base. Some recent projects such as PIES (Pan & Tenenbaum, 1986), are also exploring similar set of issues.

Plan Elements

The representation in DARN is based on the following observations. Most of the repair plans such as the one discussed in the previous section (see Figure 1) have a fairly similar form. Typically, a plan includes starting with some initial *test* on the machine which indicates a malfunction, running some diagnostic tests to pinpoint the problem, applying a *fix* for the problem, verifying that the problem is indeed fixed, otherwise iterating this process.

A plan can thus be viewed as a graph where the nodes can be classified into a fixed number of abstract classes. As a first approximation, we have found that three abstract types—Tests, Observations, and Actions—are sufficient to represent the different elements of the plans. Examples of these from the plan described in the previous section are: *tests* (booting the machine, running EIDisk, checking cooling fan); *observations* (MP151, fatal error microcode, processor voltage OK); and *actions* (replace HSIO board, replace cable).

Rules of Composition

The primitive plan elements (graph nodes) are not composed in arbitrary fashion. Instead, there are some well-defined rules that dictate how nodes of a certain class can be linked to nodes of other classes to form legal plans. The basic rules are:

A *test* can be connected to *observations* only, representing the results of running a test.

An *observation* can be connected to either *actions* and/or further *tests*. The former case represents actions to be taken in fixing the problem manifested by the observation. The latter case enables further exploration to pinpoint the problem.

An *action* is implicitly connected to a *test* which is used to verify that the action indeed fixed the problem. More complex rules about representing actions are described later.

These rules not only define the plan structure but in effect describe the semantics of the structure as a plan for diagnosing and repairing the target machine. In other words, an element of the plan that is marked as a test node, represents a test to be performed because it is followed by the observations that can be made from running the test. Similarly, an observation node derives its meaning from two structural properties. One, that it follows a test and thus represents a possible result of running the test. Two, it is followed by further actions or tests which represent what should be done with this observed state of the machine in further identifying or fixing the malfunction. *We hypothesize that such a structural transparency is crucial in enabling the experts to manipulate the knowledge base comfortably.*

Extensions to the Plan Representation

The basic TAO (Test–Action–Observation) framework described above is rather abstract because it is only sufficient in a computational sense. It does not capture many nuances and specializations that the experts use in describing the repair plans. Here we discuss some of the extensions. Most of the extensions can be viewed as specializations of the three abstract classes. Each of the specialized plan element may also specialize the structural rules associated with that class. Figure 2 shows some of the specializations as a class lattice.

Tests

A top-level test in DARN describes the context in which the user discovered a malfunction. For example, at the top level the system uses the following query as a test to discover the context:

```
Which situation are we in:
1) Testing a new disk
```

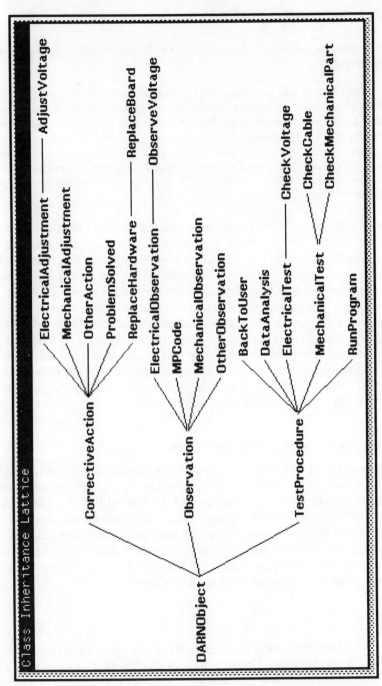

Figure 2. Primitives for Describing Plans A class lattice showing the ontological primitives for describing repair plans.

2) A problem found while booting the machine for a cold start
3) A problem found while running user software

Performing a test leads to *observations*, often indications of problems to be fixed. Often some action may be taken to try to "fix" the problem. If the action (or any of its subactions) changes the machine, a test indicating a problem must be run again to verify whether the change affected the problematic observation. For example, suppose we have the test:

```
Check voltage at Processor
None   —ReplacePowerSupply
Not24V—CheckPowerCable
OK     —CheckVoltageAtDrive
```

If no voltage is found at the processor, then after replacing the power supply, we must check that the new power supply is providing the correct voltage at the processor.

Verifying correct behavior is more crucial when running a diagnostic program, and choosing one of a number of potential repairs for the problem. For example:

```
Select the result of running the ElDisk diagnostic
program:
1) Fatal Error in Microcode
2) Maintenance Panel says 1611—No interface signals
3) . . .
4) No errors
```

If (1) Fatal Error in the Microcode is the symptom reported by ElDisk, the technicians can replace one of several printed circuit boards that could cause this error. After replacement of one, the diagnostic program is run again to test whether replacing that board fixed the problem. If not, the technician will try other possible replacements.

The generic notion of a test is further elaborated by the kinds of tests available in a particular domain. For example, in the disk domain, some of the elaborations of *test* are: *Electrical Test, Mechanical Test, Diagnostic Program, Query User*. Each of these may be further specialized. Similar elaborations exist for *observations* and *actions*. The importance of these domain-dependent elaborations lies in providing the system restrictions on the general rules of interconnections between nodes. For example, the observations of a *diagnostic program*, in our domain, are restricted to *maintenance panel codes* (*MP Codes*) and something which signals successful completion of the test. These restrictions are exploited in customizing the user interface as discussed in the next section. Eventually, these elaborations provide a means for attaching deeper models. For example, knowing that the MP Codes are generated in an ascending sequence allows the actual MP Code observed to be used to rule out problems associated with other codes lower in the sequence.

Observations

There are two classes of observations: ones which indicate successful completion of the associated test and ones which indicate some problem. The former need not be connected to any further nodes, thereby modifying the default interpretation of the associated test. For example, if a test is used for further elucidation of the problem (discussed later in this section), then a successful completion of the test *without any following action* implies that a different action must be taken for fixing the original problem.

Actions

The kinds of nodes that can follow after an observation may be another *Test*, or actions such as *SimpleRepair, FixList* or *CompoundAction*. These nodes are ordered on the basis of the desirability. Desirability is an implicit combination of likelihood of the action specified fixing the problem, the cost of trying the repair, etc. Some *SimpleRepairs* are:

Replacement of a part, e.g., Read Write Board
Adjustment within the system, e.g., 5=Volt Level
Software changes to data on disk, e.g., Rewrite Broken
Headers

Fault Isolation

For some tests, the symptom found may not uniquely determine a repair for the problem found. At this point, one possibility is to try to isolate the problem. The simplest option is to just ask the user to narrow the choices (using a *QueryUser* test). Our experts often suggested this course in the intermediate stages of building the knowledge network. In this case, the original *Test* must be used to verify if any action taken fixed the problem. Sometimes a fault may be isolated by performing a secondary test; in this case both the primary and secondary test must be used to verify any fix. Finally, isolation can be done with a *SubTest*; in this new type of *Test*, verification of the *SubTest* is deemed sufficient to verify a fix for the primary *Test*.

Trying Alternatives

In some situations, no tests may be available to isolate the fault. In this case, experts (and the DARN system) suggest an ordered sequence of actions. If any of the actions on this *FixList* lead to a change in the machine, the last test indicating a fault symptom is tried to verify if the change had the desired effect. For example, in running the ElDisk diagnostic, when one gets a fatal error in the microcode, one tries in turn: Replacing the HSIO Board; Checking the Cooling Fan; Replacing the Control Board; . . . ; Replacing the Disk. After trying each action, the ElDisk diagnostic is run again.

The ordering of actions in a *FixList* is dependent on much information not explicit in the model. It depends on the frequency of occurrence of a particular action in fixing a particular symptom, the cost to the technicians of trying the repair, and the ease of performing an action after having taken other actions. We discuss later how such information might be explicitly embedded in the model as annotations for particular purposes.

Remembering the Context of Fixes

Sometimes the same sequence of potential fixes is applicable in response to different symptoms found by other tests run by the technicians. In each case, the verification condition is determined by the test which manifested the symptom to be fixed. This requires that the DARN interpreter remember the "caller" of the *FixList* in order to use the correct test for verification.

Expert technicians often use previously defined *FixLists* as models for later lists. For example, they would say things like "First replace the ControlBoard, then replace the VFOBoard, and then do the rest of the actions taken for Fatal Error in the Microcode." Implicit in this statement is the fact that any actions already taken should not be repeated. *DoRest* nodes in DARN directly model this expression of the technicians. This of course requires that the DARN interpreter keep a history of actions that have already been done.

A special class of actions were created to express concisely another combination of activities. For some parts of the system, one could guarantee that if a symptom were found, then the associated repair would fix that symptom. For example, if the voltage level in the power supply was outside some specified tolerance, then adjusting it would ensure that it was then within tolerance. Similarly, replacing a broken cooling fan by an obviously working one would not require checking the cooling fan again. These actions are generically called *VerifiedAction*.

Fault Identification

How does DARN recognize when it has identified a problem? When it runs a test a second time after taking some action A, and the symptom has changed, there are two possibilities. First, if the symptom changes from an error indication to OK, then clearly the action A fixed the problem. If the action was the replacement of a part, then the replaced part was faulty and can be labeled as such. The action could also have been an adjustment, and the system can record that there was a need for such an adjustment on this particular machine.

The situation is more complicated if the symptom changes from one error indication, E_1, to another, E_2, when replacing a part P_o. It could be that the original part, P_o, had no fault and that the replacement part Pr_1 has a fault. We have been told that this is not completely unlikely. To test this hypothesis, a second replacement part Pr_2 is inserted in the machine. If the error indication returns to E_1 then the original part, P_o, is determined to be fault-free, and P_{r1} is marked as being faulty. If the error indication stays at E_2, then P_o is marked as being faulty, P_{r1} as being all right, and there is a second fault in the machine.

In some circumstances the technicians know that a symptom cannot be caused by a newly replaced board, and there is no need for the above *majority verification procedure*. There are two different cases. The rare case is when a second hardware fault is recognized, but the symptom precludes it from being the replaced part. In this case, the replaced part P_o is marked as faulty, and the repair process is continued. Much more frequently, the second error seen is a *software fault*, which may have been caused by the hardware fault (now fixed)—for example, data have been garbled on the disk by the formerly malfunctioning hardware. In this case, P_o is marked as faulty, and a second procedure is used to try to restore the disk data. A similar diagnostic and repair network also represents the procedures to be followed in this case of servicing.

IV. User Interfaces

There are two distinct sets of users for this system, and the interfaces for the two reflect the differences in their needs. One type of user is a *consumer* of the knowledge base—say a less-experienced technician trying to use this knowledge as a guide through a service session. The second is an expert technician trying to examine and augment the knowledge base, i.e., a *producer* of the knowledge. Both kinds of users need the capability to interact with the system for solving cases, but the producers also need to have an overview of the entire knowledge base so that the knowledge base can be easily extended and modified. We have experimented with a variety of interfaces and in this section we describe some of these interfaces, paying particular attention to the different kinds of needs.

A Browser for Repair Plans

A basic need for all users is the ability to browse around in the plan structure. The graph-like structure of the plans makes it easy to build graphical browsers in languages such as Interlisp-D (Sannella, 1983). DARN was implemented in Loops (Bobrow & Stefik, 1982; Stefik & Bobrow, 1985), an object-oriented extension of Interlisp-D. Figure 3 shows a fragment of the plan being browsed inside a display window on the screen of a Dandelion lisp machine. The plan browser explicitly shows the plan elements as distinguished nodes. For example, the *observation* nodes are shown enclosed inside braces ({}), *test* nodes are enclosed inside square brackets ([]), and *actions* are enclosed inside angle brackets (⟨⟩). Some of the newer extensions to the browsers in Interlisp/Loops allow even more iconic display of the nodes.

The plans are usually too big to fit inside a window. Some of the basic scrolling mechanisms provided by Interlisp allow a user to traverse the graph structure easily. Sometimes, a user might want to restrict their attention to some subplan. This can be accomplished by creating a subbrowser rooted at any of the nodes in the original browser. We have also experimented with path browsers. These browsers grow as the user traverses them, keeping the branching factor low.

Plan Creation Interface

The *producers* (including the knowledge engineers) of the knowledge base need a specialized interface that lets them easily create and modify the plan structures. Our working hypothesis was that it is easier for users to create the plans by directly manipulating the graph structure of the plan, rather than by describing the plan in some textual form. The structural transparency of the plan structure was an important consideration in this regard. In other words, given that the graphical representation of the plan adequately mirrored its structure, it should be possible for producers to enter new knowledge or modify existing one by directly modifying the graphical representation. The plan browser described earlier was extended to allow plan creation and modification actions at any of the nodes in the plan. Each node in the browser was made "active," i.e., it could be selected by a pointing device such as the

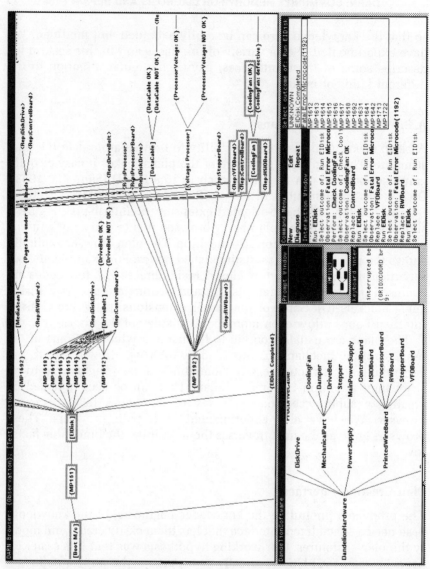

Figure 3. Typical Screen Layout During Interaction with DARN The top
half of the screen shows the plan browser. A node in the browser is either a
Test, an *Observation,* or an *Action.* The browser window can be scrolled or
reshaped. Selection of a node with left-button presents a menu of choices
which allows addition of new information or modification of existing information. The menu on the bottom right of the screen shows an example of the
menu typically presented to a user while the system is being used for servicing
a broken machine. The other window on the bottom right shows a brief history
of the current interaction with the system.

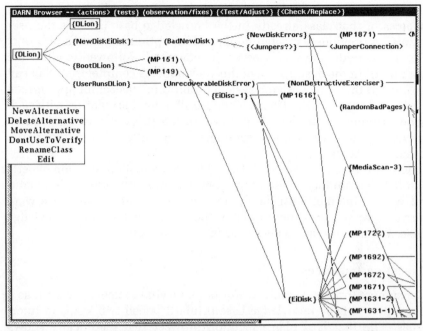

Figure 4. Plan Creation Interface   The plan browser is shown with a menu that comes up when a node is selected for making plan modifications. Complete plans can be created by interactively creating nodes and extending them.

mouse to bring up a menu of choices. Selection with the left button brough up a menu of plan-editing choices and selection with the middle button brought up a menu of plan execution choices (to be discussed later). Figure 4 shows a plan browser with the menu of choices for modifying the plan. Some of the basic options are:

```
NewAlternative
DeleteAlternative
MoveAlternative
Rename
Edit
```

Notice that these commands are generic commands which are interpreted differently by the different kinds of plan elements. Generically, *NewAlternative* allows a plan to be extended from any of its elements. However, the permissible extensions are dependent on the selected node. For example, selecting the *NewAlternative* command for an *observation* displays a browser menu showing all the generic tests and actions known to the system. Once the user selects a class from this menu, the system displays a second menu listing all the known instances of that class already in the knowledge base (in case the user wanted a previously created node) and an option to create a new one. For a new node, the same process is recursively followed to allow the user to fill in the description of this new node. A complete subplan can be created this way, with the system prompting the user for appropriate choices along the way. This is made possible by representing with each kind of node a complete description of the rules of interconnection, including the specializations for domain-dependent elaborations of the basic representation.

Our initial experience with DARN has been that our domain experts (knowledge producers) found the graphical representation to be a natural way to interact with the system with minimal training. We were very impressed with how quickly they could extend the knowledge base. We discuss our experiences in the last section.

Execution Interfaces

Consumers (trainee technicians or others trying to use the system as a consultant) of the knowledge base primarily need two kinds of interfaces. The first is a plan execution browser that graphically shows where the user is in the plan. The second is a history interface that contains a summary of the interaction with the system and can be used as a transcript of the consultation. We briefly describe both kinds of interfaces.

Plan Execution Interface

DARN can guide a user through a diagnosis and repair process by executing the plans in the knowledge base. The test and action elements are used to prompt the user to perform the relevant action. The observations are typically used to prompt the user so they could inform the system of the results of performing some test. The following is a simplified consultation session between a rookie and an expert (or the rookie and DARN if not taken literally). [Bold face indicates remarks by the rookie, and italics indicate advice by an expert technician]:

> **The machine was booted. Stopped with maintenance panel code (MP) showing 151.**
> *Run ElDisk diagnostic program.*

> **The machine stopped with MP 1192 (Fatal Error Microcode).**
> *Replace HSIO board.*
> *Rerun ElDisk.*

The machine stopped with MP 1192.
Check cooling fan.

Cooling fan is OK.
Replace control board and rerun EIDisk.

The machine stopped with MP1192
Check voltage at processor.

Processor voltage is OK.
Check voltage at disk drive.

Drive voltage is Not OK.
Replace the cable connecting the processor and the disk drive.
Rerun EIDisk.

EIDisk ran successfully.

What you just saw was fine as a transcript of the consultation, but is clearly not suitable as the primary interface to help the user during the consultation. It is insufficient because it does not let the user see the plan as it is being executed. It does not show the choices at each stage. It does not visually focus the user on what has happened and what else is possible. It also does not allow a user to ask questions about the purpose of the actions taken. We have extended the basic plan browser to provide a more active execution interface. Essentially, the plan browser can be made active at any test node by selecting the service command at that node. This starts a service consultation session, primarily driven by the system but allowing some override by the user. Figure 5 shows a snapshot of the screen in the middle of a consultation. Notice that in the browser, the nodes that have been traversed at any given time are highlighted, giving a visual summary of where the user is in the plan. The system uses the alternatives in the plan to prompt the user. Thus the user can be prompted to select the correct observation after running a test or taking a action. A user can also see what other actions are possible when they are asked to carry out a particular action from a *FixList*. A user can override the order of fixes by selecting an action that makes more sense in a given situation. As the plan execution proceeds, the browser automatically scrolls, always positioning the relevant part of the plan in the display window.

Case History Interface

A complete history of the service consultation is kept in the browser as discussed above. It is also kept in a textual form in a separate window

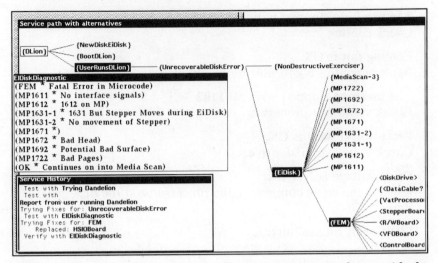

Figure 5.   Plan Execution Interface   The plan browser is shown with the path followed in the current consultation highlighted. The menu in the left middle of the window prompts the user to select the observation from running the *EIDisk* test. The user's selection, *Fatal Error Microcode* (*FEM*), is also highlighted. The window in the bottom left provides a continually updated history of the dialogue.

(shown in the bottom left of Figure 5). This allows the user to scan the chronological sequence of events, as opposed to the logical sequence presented by the plan browser.

Discussion

Experience with DARN

The initial prototype developed by us contained only a fraction of the knowledge needed to repair the fixed disk. The first experiment we conducted was to try to get our expert collaborators to extend the knowledge base. We were surprised by how quickly they were able to learn enough both to extend the knowledge base as well as use the system as a consultant on test problems. In a matter of few days we were able to double the coverage of the system. Our experts were also very excited about using the system as a medium for making their experience available to new technicians. However, for a variety of reasons the project was terminated. One key reason was that the particular fixed disk model that was our initial domain was proving to be too much of a maintenance headache and was phased out in the product line. The replacement disk had fewer replaceable parts and the new repair strategy was simply to replace the complete drive.

Version of DARN for Copier Repair

A second major experiment that we conducted was to try to represent the knowledge for diagnosing and repairing a Xerox copier. Two important classes of copier faults were selected for the experiment: copy quality and paper tray elevator faults. Our collaborator on this project, who is an expert at repairing printers, tried to represent the knowledge in the Fault Isolation Procedures (FIPs). He found that, while he could represent the knowledge using the plan language, there were some significant differences between the disk and printer domains that called for extensions to the DARN framework. For example, copier diagnostics are far more complicated than those of disks. Failures need to isolated at different levels before a suitable repair can be made; or there is often a long series of steps that have to be taken to create the proper context for performing a diagnostic test or corrective action.

Some of these observations suggest a need for a richer representation that allows setup procedures to be described, including guiding a technician who might make a mistake during these procedures. Another extension that was clearly needed was some abstraction capability that would allow a plan element to be expanded into a more detailed subplan when needed. The size and complexity of the copier repair plans also severely taxed the browsing features in DARN. It was clear that more powerful browsers are needed that could for example suppress selective detail, provide a top-down view, or maybe act like fish-eye lens, where the details are blurred around the edges, allowing more information to be displayed in a window.

Other Shortcomings

There are both omissions in current capabilities of the system, and problems with the system by virtue of its structure. As an example of the former, we cannot handle in any easy way intermittent errors, or some types of dependent faults. The latter form of errors comes about because the repair plans contain no model of the function or structure of the system, and no real reasoning capability. Another problem is that the relatively simple interpreter in DARN forces an order in which data are gathered, precluding situations where a technician has already run some tests and fixes and needs assistance.

Implicit Information

In its current form, the plans embody different kinds of implicit information. For example, suppose we have a nested test which checks for the voltage at a disk after finding that the voltage at the processor is all right. If the voltage at the disk is "all right," then the conclusion is drawn that the cable between the two should be replaced. DARN does not have any explicit information about that connection, and this structural information is implicit in the network. Furthermore, if some other node was connected to the node which tested the voltage at the disk in another context, but it did not follow the measurement of the voltage at the processor, then the implicit context of the measurement would be violated, and the conclusion drawn would be invalid.

Annotations

Currently, we provide the users with the capability of annotating plan nodes with information to be used for construction and explanation purposes. Annotation of a node can indicate that it must appear as a subTest of a particular other Test. This kind of structural information can also be included in the descriptions attached to the nodes so that the system can itself check for violations and prevent them. Annotation can also indicate reasons for the ordering of actions. Information compiled into the order includes things like probability of fault causing a particular symptom, or the cost of trying a particular action (e.g., it takes 15 minutes to change this board, and only 5 for most other boards).

Acknowledgements

We are very grateful to our domain experts, Milt Mallory, Ron Brown, and Ted Manley, for their time, patience, and energy. Julian Orr was primarily responsible for trying to adapt the DARN framework for the copier repair problem. We are also pleased to acknowledge the support and helpful criticisms of Mark Stefik. Clive Dym and some anonymous referees provided valuable comments on earlier drafts of this paper.

References

Bobrow, D. G., & Stefik, M. J. (1983). *Loops Manual*. Xerox PARC, December.
Brown, J. S., Burton, R., & de Kleer, J. (1982). Pedagogical, natural language and knowledge engineering techniques in SOPHIE I, II and III. In D. Sleeman

& J. S. Brown (Eds.), *Intelligent tutoring systems*. New York: Academic Press.

Chandrasekaran, B. (1984). Expert systems: Matching techniques to tasks. In W. Reitman (Ed.), *AI applications for business*. Norwood, NJ: Ablex, pp. 116–132.

Chandrasekaran, B., & Mittal, S., (1983). Conceptual representation of medical knowledge for diagnosis by computer: MDX and related systems. In M. C. Yovits (Ed.), *Advances in computers*, Vol. 22.

Chandrasekaran, B., & Mittal, S. (1982). Deep versus compiled knowledge approaches to diagnostic problem-solving. *Proceedings AAAI-82*, Pittsburgh, August.

Clancey, W. J. (1985). Heuristic Classification. *Artificial Intelligence, 27*(3).

de Kleer, J., et al. (1979). Explicit control of reasoning. In P. H. Winston & R. H. Brown (Eds.), *Artificial intelligence: An MIT perspective*. Cambridge, MA: MIT Press.

de Kleer, J., (1984). How circuits work. *Artificial Intelligence, 24*(1–3).

Genesereth, M. (1984). The use of design descriptions in automated diagnosis. *Artificial Intelligence, 24*(1–3).

Mittal, S. (1980). *Design of a distributed medical diagnosis and database system*. Ph.D. dissertation, Department of Computer and Information Science. Ohio State University, Columbus.

Pan, J., & Tenenbaum, J. M. (1986). PIES: An engineer's "Do it yourself" knowledge system for interpretation of parametric test data. *Proceedings AAAI-86*, Philadelphia, August.

Sanella, M. (Ed.) (1983). *Interlisp reference manual*. Xerox Corpo. October.

Stefik, M. J. (1986). The next knowledge medium. *AI Magazine*, Spring.

Stefik, M. J., & Bobrow, D. G. (1986). Object-oriented programming: Themes and Variations. *AI Magazine*, Winter.

Sussman, G. J., & Stallman, R. (1975). Heuristic techniques in computer-aided circuit analysis. *IEEE Transactions Circuits & Systems*, CAS–22.

Szolovits, P., & Pauker, S. G. (1978). Categorical and probabilistic reasoning in medical diagnosis. *Artificial Intelligence, 11*, 115–144.

FIVE

Hierarchical Knowledge Clustering: A Way to Represent and Use Problem-solving Knowledge*

Dana Nau
Michael Gray

University of Maryland

Abstract

In most frame-based reasoning systems, the data manipulated by the system are represented using frames, but the problem-solving knowledge used to manipulate this data is represented using rules. However, this is not always the best approach. Rules are not always a natural way to represent knowledge—and in addition, rule-based systems containing large knowledge bases may require large amounts of computation in order to determine which rules match the current state in a problem to be solved. This chapter describes a way to address these problems using a new technique called hierarchical knowledge clustering.

A prototypical version of hierarchical knowledge clustering was implemented in Prolog, in a system called SIPP. An improved version has been implemented in Lisp, in a system called SIPS (Semi-Intelligent Process Selector), which plans what machining processes to use in manufacturing metal parts. This chapter gives an overview of SIPS, and describes its knowledge representation and problem solving methods.

---

* This work was supported in part by an NSF Presidential Young Investigator Award, IBM Research, General Motors Research Laboratories, Martin Marietta Laboratories, the National Bureau of Standards, and NSF grant NSFD CPR-85-00108 to the University of Maryland Systems Research Center.

1. Introduction

In many frame-based reasoning systems, the information being manipulated is stored in the form of frames, but the problem-solving knowledge that manipulates the frames is stored separately in the form of rules. One problem with this approach is that rules are not always a natural way to represent knowledge; another is that systems containing lots of rules may require excessive amounts of computation to determine which rules match the current state during problem solving.

This chapter describes a way to address these problems using a new approach called *hierarchical knowledge clustering*. In this approach, problem-solving knowledge is organized into a taxonomic hierarchy in which each node represents a set of possible actions, and its children represent different subsets of that set. Restrictions are associated with each node which determine whether or not the set of actions represented by that node are feasible actions to perform, and problem solving is done using an adaptation of Branch and Bound. For some problem domains, this approach can be more natural than rule-based representation, and can alleviate the computational inefficiencies that can arise with rule-based systems.

Hierarchical knowledge clustering was first implemented prototypically in Prolog, in a system called SIPP (Nau & Chang, 1986). Experience with SIPP led to refinements of the idea, resulting in a second implementation—this time in Lisp. The Lisp implementation, called SIPS (Semi-Intelligent Process Selector), is the topic of this chapter.

This chapter gives an overview of SIPS, and describes its knowledge representation and problem-solving methods. The chapter also discusses the implications of this work for AI knowledge representation and problem solving.

2. Problem Domain

SIPS was developed to produce plans of action for the creation of metal parts using metal removal operations such as milling, drilling, reaming, etc. Each of these operations is called a *machining process*, and each machining process is used to create a *feature* on the metal part, such as a hole, a slot, a pocket, etc. Given a specification for what the final part is supposed to look like, the task of deciding which sequence of machining processes to use in creating the part is known as *process planning*.

A number of computer systems exist which provide partial automation of process planning. In most existing systems, process planning is done by retrieving from a data base a process plan for another part similar to the desired part, and modifying this plan by hand to produce a process plan for the desired part. (For more detailed descriptions of such systems, cf. Nau & Chang, 1985; Nau et al., 1984.)

Devising a complete process plan automatically using a part's specifications (e.g., a full technical drawing) is a very difficult problem. There are several systems which attempt to produce a process plan for the exact part desired, but most such systems are experimental and have limited capabilities. Systems which use AI techniques include GARI (Descotte & Latombe, 1981), TOM (Matushima, Okada, & Sata, 1982), and SIPP (a predecessor to SIPS, implemented in Prolog; cf. Nau & Chang, 1986).

The approach used in both SIPP and SIPS is to reason about the intrinsic capabilities of each machining operation in order to produce least-cost process plans. Further extensions of SIPS are expected to address fundamental research issues in reasoning about three-dimensional objects. SIPS is currently being integrated into the AMRF (Automated Manufacturing Research Facility) project at the National Bureau of Standards, where it will be used in producing process plans for an automated machine shop; and plans are under way for integrating it with software being developed at General Motors Research Laboratories.

3. Motivation

In most knowledge-based problem-solving systems that use frames, problem solving is done by manipulating the frames using rules of the form "**if** *conditions* **then** *action*." This approach has proved quite powerful in a number of problem domains, but in some circumstances problems can arise.

One problem with rule-based systems is the problem of efficiency; this problem will be discussed in more detail in Section 6. Another problem is that the way in which the knowledge is represented can sometimes be unnatural. Several ways in which this can occur have been pointed out in the literature (Davis, Buchanan, & Shortliffe, 1977; Reggia, Nau, & Wang, 1983), but the particular one we will consider is this: Since human beings often approach problems hierarchically, a hierarchical representation of problem-solving knowledge can sometimes be easier to understand.

For example, suppose someone is writing a knowledge base about the following milling processes:

rough face milling
finish face milling
rough end milling
finish end milling
rough peripheral milling
finish peripheral milling

The knowledge base presumably consists of a set of rules to determine which of these processes to use in creating some goal feature f. Each process has various restrictions on its capabilities, but since they are all milling processes, some of these restrictions will be common to all of the processes. And since rough face milling and finish face milling are both face-milling operations, they will have even more restrictions in common. If one were to write a single rule for each operation, the result might be the set of rules shown in Figure 1, where $A, B, \ldots, J$ are different sets of restrictions and S is the current state.

One problem with this set of rules is that it does not include any way to decide which rule to invoke when more than one rule is applicable. Suppose, for example, that f may be made either by rough face milling or by rough end milling. If face milling is a less costly process than end milling, then one would want R1 to fire instead of R3, and the rules include no way to assure this. What is needed is to attach priorities to the rules corresponding to the costs of the machining processes. Although there is no conceptual difficulty with doing this (it is in some ways analogous to the certainty factors used in Mycin; cf. Davis, Buchanan, & Shortliffe, 1977), the problem is that these priorities are not really available beforehand, but need to be computed in the knowledge base as functions of other machining processes. (How this needs to be done is illustrated in Section 4 in the discussion of SIPS's and `projected cost` slots

Another problem is that the approach illustrated in Figure 1 is not particularly natural—it requires that for each machining operation, one must describe the characteristics that distinguish this operation from

R1: if S = 'goal(f)' & $A(f)$ & $B(f)$ & $C(f)$ then S := 'rough-face-mill(f)'
R2: if S = 'goal(f)' & $A(f)$ & $B(f)$ & $D(f)$ then S := 'finish-face-mill(f)'
R3: if S = 'goal(f)' & $A(f)$ & $E(f)$ & $F(f)$ then S := 'rough-end-mill(f)'
R4: if S = 'goal(f)' & $A(f)$ & $E(f)$ & $G(f)$ then S := 'finish-end-mill(f)'
R5: if S = 'goal(f)' & $A(f)$ & $H(f)$ & $I(f)$ then S := 'rough-peripheral-mill (f)'
R6: if S = 'goal(f)' & $A(f)$ & $H(f)$ & $J(f)$ then S := 'finish-peripheral-mill(f)'

Figure 1.   Rules Telling which Milling Operations to Use to Create a Feature f.
Each of A, B, . . . , J is a Different Set of Restrictions.

if S = 'goal(f)' & A(f) then S := 'mill(f)'
if S = 'mill(f)' & B(f) then S := 'face-mill(f)'
if S = 'mill(f)' & E(f) then S := 'end-mill(f)'
if S = 'mill(f)' & H(f) then S := 'peripheral-mill(f)'
if S = 'face-mill(f)' & C(f) then S := 'rough-face-mill(f)'
if S = 'face-mill(f) & D(f) then S := 'finish-face-mill(f)'
if S = 'end-mill(f)' & F(f) then S := 'rough-end-mill(f)'
if S = 'end-mill(f)' & G(f) then S := 'finish-end-mill(f)'
if S = 'peripheral-mill(f)' & H(f) then S := 'rough-peripheral-mill(f)'
if S = 'peripheral-mill(f)' & I(f) then S := 'finish-peripheral-mill(f)'

Figure 2.   A Modified Set of Rules for Milling Operations.

every other machining operation in the entire knowledge base. It would be more natural—and probably more efficient—to write rules that describe each of the milling processes only in terms of what distinguishes it from other milling processes, and use these rules only after it has been decided that milling can be used to create f. This approach would yield the set of rules shown in Figure 2.

The rules shown in Figure 2 still do not provide a way to handle the computation of the process costs and the use of these costs in determining rule priorities, but it is interesting to note that each of the rules shown in Figure 2 corresponds to a node of the tree shown in Figure 3. If one were to represent each node in the tree as a frame, one could represent the process costs as values of slots in these frames, and compute the process costs as functions of slots in other frames. One could also represent various other relevant properties of the processes—feed rates, cutting speeds, location of the machine in the factory, etc.

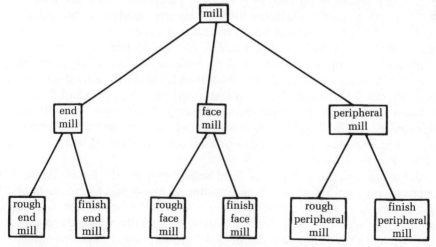

Figure 3.   A Tree Corresponding to the Rules in Figure 2

The biggest problem with representing the processes as frames would be how to represent and invoke the **if** and **then** parts of the rules. One approach would be to use procedural attachment and message passing, using the following protocol: If a "consider-yourself-for-creating(f)" message were sent to a frame (say, the *mill* frame) and if this frame's restrictions (in this case, A(f)) were satisfied, then this frame would send the same message to each of its children (the *face-mill*, *end-mill*, and *peripheral-mill* frames). However, this approach would make it very difficult to keep the message from being sent to the *end-mill* frame if face milling were less costly than end milling.

A solution to this problem would be not to use message passing, but instead to write a global control strategy to supervise the activation of the frames. Such a strategy would maintain a list of all frames eligible to be activated, activating first those of least cost. The combination of this control strategy with the frame representation shown in Figure 3 we refer to as *hierarchical knowledge clustering*.

In addition to being a more natural way to organize information about some problem domains (such as process planning), hierarchical knowledge clustering can also be more efficient computationally than a rule-based approach. This is discussed in more detail in the concluding section of this chapter.

4. Knowledge Representation

As described in the previous section, hierarchical knowledge clustering is applicable to situations where the problem-solving knowledge corresponds to a set of actions which can be organized into a taxonomic hierarchy. The hierarchy is set up so that each node represents a set of possible actions that can be performed, and the node's children represent different subsets of that set. Each node is represented by a frame which has restrictions associated with it. A node is eligible for consideration only if the restrictions associated with its parent are satisfied. If a node is eligible for consideration, it may or may not actually be considered, depending on the choices made by a global control strategy. To make this idea clearer, we discuss the way it is implemented in SIPS.

SIPS has two basic types of frames: archetypes and items. Archetypes correspond roughly to sets, and items correspond to members of sets. Normally, the knowledge about a problem domain consists of archetypes, and the data used in solving a specific problem in that domain (both the input data defining the problem and the intermediate data created while the problem is being solved) consist of items. Items have slots into which values can be stored, and archetypes have slots into which default values can be stored. The frame system has general inheritance mechanisms which allow default values either to be inherited in the usual way, or to be computed as arbitrary functions of values stored in other frames.

One purpose of SIPS's frame system is to represent static knowledge about features (holes, pockets, flat surfaces, slots, etc.). These features are organized into the obvious kind of taxonomy, with archetypes representing abstract features and items representing specific instantiations of those features. For example, the hole archetype is a child of the cylindrical-surface archetype, which is a child of the surface archetype. A specific hole in a specific metal part might be represented bx an item called, say, *hole-21. This is not particularly different from how such knowledge would be represented in any other frame system, so we will not discuss it further.

Another purpose of the frame system is to represent problem-solving knowledge—the kind of knowledge which other systems would represent using rules. Information about the capabilities of machining processes is organized into a taxonomy similar to the taxonomy used for features, with archetypes representing abstract machining processes and items representing specific instantiations of those processes. For example, the twist-drill archetype is a child of the hole-create-process archetype, which is a child of the hole-process archetype; and the specific twist drilling process used to create *hole-21 might be represented by an item called *twist-drill-13.

The rest of this section consists of a simple example (much simpler than the information actually appearing in SIPS's knowledge base) of how SIPS represents problem-solving knowledge. The first statement in the example is this:

```
(defarchetype process () (
    (cost $type posnumberp
        $init (min-child-cost current-frame 'cost)
    (projected-cost $type posnumberp
        $init (min-child-cost current-frame
        'projected-coat)))
```

This statement defines an archetype called process which has two slots called cost and projected-cost. The $type specification (which is used to specify data types for slots) says that any values put into the cost and projected-cost slots must satisfy a LISP predicate called posnumberp.

The cost and projected-cost slots are intended to contain lower bounds on, respectively, the cost of performing a machining process and the cost of any other processes which might be required beforehand. To achieve this intent, the $init specification (which is used to specify initial values for slots) says that the initial value for the cost slot is the minimum of the cost slots of process's children, and the initial value for projected-cost is the minimum of the projected-cost slots of these children. Since the only child of process is hole-process (see below), this means that the initial values are 1 for cost and 0 for projected-cost.

```
(defarchetype hole-process (process) ())
```

This statement says that hole-process is a child of process. No slots are given explicitly for hole-process, but since hole-process is a child of process, it has cost and projected-cost slots whose initial values are the minimum values of these slots in hole-process's children. Since the children of hole-process are twist-drill and rough-bore (see below), this means that the initial values are 1 for cost and 0 for projected-cost.

```
(relevant hole-process hole)
```

This statement says that hole-process is relevant for creating any item which is a hole. In general, when SIPS starts planning the creation of some feature, it starts by looking at all processes which have been declared to be relevant for creating the feature. n this example, neither this statement nor any other statements declare any other process to be relevant for creating a hole, so to create a hole SIPS would start by considering only hole-process. A more detailed description of what SIPS would do at this point appears in Section 5.

```
(defrestriction hole-process (h) (surface)
    (setq surface (getval h 'contained-in))
    (equal (get-archetype surface) 'flat)
    (parallel (getval h 'axis) (getval surface
        'norm)))
```

Every machining process (or class of machining processes) has restrictions on its capabilities—for example, restrictions on the size of the feature it can create, and restrictions on how tight a set of tolerances it can achieve. The above statement describes those restrictions which apply to every hole-process—and since twist-drill and rough-bore are both children of hole-process (see below), this means that the restrictions given in this statement must be satisfied before SIPS will consider twist-drill or rough-bore.

In this statement, h is a parameter which SIPS will bind to the item feature describing the frame to be created, surface is a local variable, and the rest of the statement is a conjunct of conditions to be satisfied. These conditions state that a hole–process can be used to create a hole h only if the surface containing h is a flat surface whose normal vector is parallel to the axis of h.

```
(defarchetype twist–drill (hole–process) (
    (cost $init 1)
    (projected–cost $init 0)))
```

If SIPS has decided that a hole-process can be used to create some feature, then any child of the hole–process frame may be considered. According to the above statement, one of these children is twist–drill. The statement says that twist–drill's cost and projected–cost slots have initial values of 1 and 0, respectively.

```
(defrestriction twist–drill (h) (diam)
    (setq diam (getval h 'diameter))
    () diam 0.0625)
    (( diam 2)
    (( (getval h 'depth) 6)
    () (getval h 'roundness) 0.004))
```

Like hole–process, twist–drill has a set of restrictions which must be satisfied if they are to be successful. In the above statement, h is a parameter which SIPS will bind to the item frame describing the feature to be created, and diam is a local variable. The statement says that twist–drill cannot be used to create h unless the diameter of h is greater than 0.0625 and less than six times the depth of h, and unless h's permissible deviation from perfect roundness exceeds 0.004.

```
(defaction twist–drill (p h) ()
    (success p))
```

If SIPS decides that a particular machining process can be used to create some feature, actions must be taken to accomplish this. When creating a plan for the creation of some feature, SIPS searches backwards from the ultimate goal to be achieved—and so the actions associated with a machining process set up subgoals to be achieved before the machining process can be performed. Since hole–process denotes a class of machining operations rather than any particular machining operation, it does not have any actions associated with it—but twist–drill does have actions, as given in the above statement. In this statement, h and p are parameters which SIPS will bind to item frames describing the hole to be created and the particular twist drilling pro-

cess to be used to create it. The statement says that the twist-drilling
process p succeeds directly, without the necessity of achieving any
subgoals.

```
(defarchetype rough-bore (hole-process) (
    (cost $init 3)
    (projected-cost $init (getval 'hole-process
        'cost))))
```

The only other child of hole-process is rough-bore. As described in the above statement, the initial value for rough-bore's
cost slot is 3, and the initial value for the projected-cost slot is the
value of hole-process's cost slot, which is 1.

```
(defrestriction rough-bore (f) ()
    () (getval f 'roundness) 0.0003))
```

This statement sets up the restrictions for rough boring. It says that
that rough-bore cannot be used to create a hole f unless f's permissible deviation from perfect roundness exceeds 0.0003.

```
(defaction rough-bore (p h) (g diam)
    (setq g (copy-item h))
    (setq diam (getval h 'diameter))
    (putval g 'diameter (- diam (* 0.01 (sqrt diam)))))
    (putval g 'roundness 0.01)
    (subgoal p g))
```

This statement says that if SIPS decides to use a rough boring process p to create the hole h, this can be done provided that another hole
called g is created first. The hole g has a smaller diameter than h, and
g need not be as round as h. In order to produce the description of g,
this statement uses copy-item to make g an exact copy of the item h,
and uses putval to assign values into g's diameter and roundness
slots. The subgoal function tells SIPS to consider the creation of g as a
subgoal to be achieved before rough-bore can be successful.

5. Control Strategy

When using SIPS, one normally represents a metal part as some collection of surface features (holes, flat surfaces, slots, etc.). Each such feature is represented by an item frame. The user invokes SIPS separately
on each feature in order to produce a process plan for creating that
feature.

In considering how to create some feature such as a hole, SIPS does

procedure make(f):
    Active := {(p, f)| p is a process archetype relevant for
                      creating whatever kind of feature is}
    /*for example, hole-process is relevant for creating a hole */
    loop
        if *Active* is empty, then return failure
        select $t = (p_1, f_1, p_2, f_2, \ldots)$ as described in the text
        remove t from *Active*
        if the restrictions for p_1 are satisfied then begin
           expand t as described in the text
           if success has been achieved, then return the successful plan
           /* the plan returned is guaranteed to have the least possible cost */
    end
    repeat
end make

Figure 4.   SIPS's Control Strategy

not consider a process such as twist–drill unless the restrictions
have been satisfied for twist–drill's ancestors. This is accomplished by means of the least-cost-first Branch and Bound procedure
shown in Figure 4.

SIPS uses an *active list* containing all alternative process plans being
actively considered. Each plan consists of some sequence of processes,
along with the features these processes create, culminating in the creation of the desired feature f. For example, if we let $t = (p_1, f_1, p_2, f_2, p_3,$
$f)$, then t represents the following plan:

    first use process p_1 to create the feature f_1,
    then use p_2 to transform f_1 into f_2,
    then use p_3 to transform f_2 into f.

Each of p_1, f_1, p_2, f_2, p_3, and f are represented by frames.

SIPS expands plans backwards from the ultimate goal of creating f,
until a complete and successful plan for creating f is found. Since this
expansion is done backwards, the processes $p_2, p_3, \ldots$ in the plan t
will have already been completely determined, but the process p_1 may
not yet be completely determined.

If p_1 has not been completely determined, it will be represented by
an archetype (such as hole–process or mill) which represents a
class containing several different kinds of processes. If the restrictions
specified in the frame for p_1 are not satisfied, then the expansion of t is
empty; otherwise, the expansion of t consists of the set of plans

    {$(q_1, f_1, p_2, f_2, p_3, f)|q_1$ is a child of p_1}.

If p_1 has been completely determined, it will be represented by an archetype (such as twist–drill or rough–face–mill) which falls at the bottom of the hierarchy and thus only represents one kind of process. In this case, if the restrictions given in the frame for p_1 are satisfied, SIPS will create an item frame describing the particular instance of p_1 that is to be used to create f_1, and will perform the actions specified in the action statement for p_1. Normally, these actions will state one of the following:

1. that this instance of p_1 is a process that can be performed directly (in which case SIPS has found a complete and successful process plan). An example of this was given in the action statement for twist–drill in Section 4.
2. that some other feature f_0 must first be created in order for this instance of p_1 to be performed. (There are several ways to specify this, depending on what is known about how to create the feature— but one example is the subgoal statement discussed in Section 4.) In this case, the expansion of t is

    $\{(p_0, f_0, p_1, f_1, p_2, f_2, p_3, f) | p_0$ is relevant for whatever kind of feature f_0 is$\}$.

SIPS selects plans for expansion one at a time. Which plan is selected is determined by means of lower bounds on the costs of the plans. For example, the lower bound on the plan $t = (p_1, f_1, p_2, f_2, p_3, f)$ is

$$B(t) = (\text{getval } p_1 \text{ projected-cost}) + \sum_{i=1}^{3} (\text{getval } p_i \text{ cost}).$$

Two significant features of the procedure described above are:

1. Several different possible plans are explored in parallel. At each point, SIPS considers the plan that currently looks the best (i.e., the one that has the lowest lower bound). As a result, the first successful plan found by SIPS is guaranteed to be the cheapest possible successful plan.
2. A process p will never appear as part of a plan on the active list unless its restrictions have been satisfied. Thus, unless the restrictions for p are satisfied, the children of p will never be examined.

6. Related Work

Hierarchical knowledge clustering can be viewed as a way to do planning based on abstraction. For example, the hole–process frame discussed earlier is basically a representation of an abstract machining process which has several possible instantiations: twist–drill and rough–bore.

Several types of abstraction have been explored in the literature on planning. One type of abstraction is that used in NOAH (Sacerdoti, 1977), in which an action A is an abstraction of actions A_1 and A_2 if A_1 and A_2 are each steps in the performance of A. This is rather different from the abstraction used in SIPS: in SIPS, A is an abstraction of actions A_1 and A_2 if A_1 and A_2 are alternate instantiations of A.

Another type of abstraction is that used in ABSTRIPS (Nilsson, 1980), in which a complete plan is constructed ignoring some of the preconditions of each action and the plan is then modified to meet the preconditions which were ignored. This type of abstraction is more closely related to that used in SIPS, in the following senses: an instantiation of an action A is an action A_1 which must satisfy the preconditions of A and also some additional preconditions, and both SIPS and ABSTRIPS refine a plan containing A by checking those preconditions of A_1 which differ from the preconditions of A. However, there are several important differences:

1. SIPS completely instantiates the last action in a plan before considering what actions should precede this action, whereas ABSTRIPS generates a complete (but possibly incorrect) plan and then tries to fix it up.
2. In SIPS, an abstract action has several possible alternate instantiations, but in ABSTRIPS, only one instantiation is possible. Thus in ABSTRIPS, the notion of considering alternate instantiations of an action and choosing the one of least estimated cost does not make sense.

Another type of abstraction which is quite close to that used in SIPS is proposed by Tenenberg (1986). This approach is similar to SIPS in the sense that each abstract action may have more than one possible instantiation. It is potentially more general than that used in SIPS, in the sense that the effects of actions are represented hierarchically, as well as their preconditions—but this approach has not yet been implemented on any problem.

Several systems for diagnostic problem solving make use of certain kinds of taxonomic hierarchies. Both MDX (Mittal, Chandrasekaran, & Smith, 1979) and Centaur (Jackson, 1986) use taxonomies of various diagnostic problems, in which knowledge about each class of problems is located at the node in the hierarchy that represents that class. These approaches yield some of the same benefits as SIPS in terms of representational clarity and efficiency of problem solving. However, the details of how they represent and manipulate their knowledge are rather different from what SIPS does.

7. Concluding Remarks

7.1 Current Status

A predecessor to SIPS was implemented using Prolog (Nau & Chang, 1985, 1986). SIPS, which is implemented in Lisp, incorporates a number of refinements and improvements—particularly in the operation of the frame system. SIPS is currently being integrated into the AMRF (Automated Manufacturing Research Facility) project at the National Bureau of Standards, where it will be used in producing process plans for an automated machine shop; and plans are under way for integrating it with software being developed at General Motors Research Laboratories.

SIPS is currently up and running in Franz Lisp. It can either read prepared data from a file, or (if some of this data are omitted) run interactively, asking the user for any needed information. Various user features have been implemented in SIPS. For example, if SIPS produces a plan for producing some feature, the user can later tell SIPS to go back and find other alternative plans for producing this feature.

7.2 Computational Considerations

It is well known that rule-based systems having large rule bases can require substantial computational overhead. Suppose a rule-based system is trying to solve a problem in some problem domain D, and suppose R is the set of rules for D. Each time the system applies a rule, this changes the system's current state S—and in order to decide what rule to apply next, the system must determine which rules in R match S. If the system searched through all the rules in R to find the ones matching S, the computational overhead would be tremendous.

Several approaches have been tried for alleviating this problem. One approach, which is used in KEE (Fikes & Kehler, 1985), is to provide facilities whereby the user can divide a set of rules into smaller subsets

$R_1, R_2, \ldots, R_n$, such that each subset is relevant for a different problem domain.[1] Given a problem to solve, the system starts out by determining which problem domain the problem is in. It then selects the rule set R_i for that domain, and then uses R_i exclusively from that point on, ignoring all the other rules. Since R_i is smaller than R, the problems with efficiency are alleviated.

Although hierarchical knowledge clustering was developed without any knowledge of the approach used in KEE, it can be thought of as an extension of that approach. Hierarchical knowledge clustering provides a way to tell, directly from the current state R, that only some subset R_S of the rules in R is relevant to S.[2] Thus, all rules not in R_S can temporarily be ignored. Since R_S is normally quite small, this provides improved efficiency.

Another approach to reducing the computational overhead of computing rule matches is the rete match algorithm used in OPS5 (Forgy, 1980) and YAPS (Allen, 1982). This algorithm provides a way to store partial rule matches in a network so that the system can determine whether a rule matches the current state without having to re-evaluate all of its preconditions each time the current state changes. This makes the complexity of computing matches dependent not on the size of D, but instead on the size of the set P_S of rules whose preconditions partially match S. If P_S is small, then the rete match procedure is efficient, but if P_S is large, significant computational overhead will occur in the elaboration of partial matches.

Hierarchical knowledge clustering can be thought of as a way to control the elaboration of partial matches, by distributing the preconditions of a rule throughout the levels of a hierarchical structure and elaborating a partial match only if it looks promising. Thus, the approach used in SIPS may potentially be useful in increasing the efficiency of the rete match procedure.

7.3 Interface Considerations

For the process planning problem domain, hierarchical knowledge clustering appears to be more natural to use than a "flat" set of production rules. It yields many of the same advantages as hierarchical representation of static information. For example, in the frame representing

---

[1] By "problem domain," we simply mean some class of problems.

[2] In particular, finding R_S corresponds either to retrieving the children of some archetype or (in the case of the subgoal function) retrieving all archetypes relevant to the creation of a feature. In each case, only a few of SIPS's process frames are relevant—and which frames are relevant is determined easily from the frame system.

rough face milling, one can concentrate on describing the restrictions and capabilities that distinguish it from other kinds of face milling processes, rather than having to distinguish it from every other kind of machining operation. This experience has been borne out in the experience of a manufacturing engineer who is currently implementing a SIPS knowledge base for the task of selecting cutting tools once the machining processes are known (Luce, work in progress).

An even more sophisticated interface for SIPS is currently being developed. Work done by the author and others General Motors Research Laboratories has resulted in an interface between SIPS and a solid modeling system, so that the user can build up an object to be created by giving graphical specifications of its machinable features, and have SIPS select sequences of machining processes capable of creating those features. This work will be described in more detail in a subsequent paper (Nau & Sinha, in preparation).

There are certainly some problem domains for which hierarchical knowledge clustering is not appropriate—but for some problem domains it appears to provide a way to represent knowledge more naturally than with production rules, and a way to reduce some of the computational overhead that can occur with rule-based systems.

References

Allen, E. M. (1982). *Yaps: Yet another production system* (Tech. Rep. TR-1146,). Computer Science Department, University of Maryland, College Park.

Boothroyd, G. (1975). *Fundamentals of Metal Machining and Machine Tools.* Scripta, Washington, DC.

Chang, T. C. (1980). *Interfacing CAD and CAM—A study of hole design.* M.S. thesis, Virginia Polytechnic Institute. Blacksburg, VA.

Chang, T. C., & Wysk, R. A. (1985a). *An introduction to automated process planning systems.* Englewood Cliffs, NJ: Prentice–Hall.

Chang, T. C., & Wysk, R. A. (1985). Integrating CAD and CAM through automated process planning. *International Journal of Production Research,* 22:(5).

Chang, T. C., & Wysk, R. A. (1981). An integrated CAD/automated process planning system," *AIIE Transactions,* 13(3).

Davis, R.. Buchanan, B., & Shortliffe, E. (1977). Production rules as a representation for a knowledge-based consultation program, *Artificial Intelligence,* 8(1), 15–45.

Dunn, M. S., Jr., Bertelsen, J. D., Rothauser, C. H., Strickland, W. S., & Milsop, A. C. (1981). *Implementation of computerized production process planning,* (Report R81–945220–14), United Technologies Research Center, East Hartford, CT.

Fikes, R., & Kehler, T. (1985). The role of frame-based representation in reasoning, Communications of the ACM 28(9), 904–920.

Forgy, C. L. (1980). The OPS5 user's manual (Tech. Rep. CMU–CS–81–135), Computer Science Department, Carnegie–Mellon University, Pittsburgh, PA.

Jackson, P. (1986). Introduction to expert systems. Wokingham, England: Addison–Wesley, pp. 142–157.

Link, C. H. (1976). CAPP—CAM-I automated process planning system. Proceedings 13th Numerical Control Society Annual Meeting and Technical Conference, Cincinnati.

Luce, M. work in progress.

Mann, W. S., Jr., Dunn, M. S., & Pflederer, S. J. (1977). Computerized production process planning, Report R77-942625–14, United Technologies Research Center.

Matsushima, K., Okada, N., & Sata, T. (1982). The integration of CAD and CAM by application of artificial-intelligence, CIRP, 329–332.

Mittal, S., Chandrasekaran, B., & Smith, J. (1979). Overview of MDX—A system for medical diagnosis, Proceedings Third Annual Symposium on Computer Applications in Medical Care, Washington, DC.

Nau, D. S., (1983). Issues in spatial reasoning and representation for automated process planning, Proceedings Workshop on Spatial Knowledge Representation and Processing.

Nau, D. S., & Chang, T. C. (1983). Prospects for process selection using artificial intelligence, Computers in Industry 4, 253–263.

Nau, D. S., & Chang, T. C. (1985). A knowledge-based approach to generative process planning, Production Engineering Conference at ASME Winter Annual Meeting, pp. 65–71, Miami Beach, FL.

Nau, D. S., & Chang, T. C. (1986). Hierarchical representation of problem-solving knowledge in a frame-based process planning system, Journal of Intelligent Systems 1(1), 29–44.

Nau, D. S., & Sinha, S. in preparation.

Nau, D. S., Reggia, J. A., Blanks, M. W., Peng, Y., & Sutton, D. (1984). Prospects for knowledge-based computing in automated process planning and shop control (Tech. Report), Computer Science Department, University of Maryland, College Park.

Nilsson, N. J. (1980). Principles of artificial intelligence, Palo Alto, CA: Tioga Press, pp. 350–354.

Ramsey, C., Reggia, J. A., Nau, D. S., & Ferrentino, A. (1986). A comparative analysis of methods for expert systems, International Journal Man-Machine Studies.

Tenenberg, J. (1986). Planning with abstraction, Proceedings AAAI-86, Philadelphia, pp. 76–80.

Sacerdoti, E. (1977). A structure for plans and behavior. New York: American Elsevier.

TNO, (1981). Introduction to MIPLAN. Organization for Industrial Research, Inc., Waltham, MA.

Wolfe, P. M., & Kung, H. K. (1984). Automating process planning using artificial intelligence. *Proceedings 1984 Annual International Industrial Engineering Conference*, Chicago.

Reggia, J. A., Nau, D. S., & Wang, P. Y. (1983). A new inference method for frame-based expert systems. *Proceedings Annual National Conference on Artificial Intelligence*, Washington, DC, pp. 333–337.

Wysk, R. A., (1977). *An automated process planning and selection program: APPAS*. Ph.D. thesis, Purdue University, West Lafayette, IN.

SIX

Direct Manipulation User Interfaces for Expert Systems

James Baroff
Roland Simon
Francie Gilman
Ben Shneiderman

1. Introduction

The emergence of production rules as a programming technique has stimulated the creation of many varieties of expert systems: advisers, consultants, intelligent computer-assisted instruction, oracles, and various decision aids. Applications have ranged from medicine, to computer system configuration, to automobile repair, to financial decision making, and to many other domains (Waterman, 1986).

Production rules have multiple variations, but the central theme is that a system consists of hundreds or thousands of *IF-THEN* rules and a large unstructured set of facts. If the antecedent conditions (IF part) are satisfied by the facts then the rule "fires" and the consequents (THEN part) are carried out. Rules may be written and stored in any order. All rules whose antecedents are satisfied may fire, but the order of firing is unpredictable.

The nonsequential, nonprocedural behaviour and the random firing order are often cited as benefits that free up the programmer to make incremental changes easy. A few rules can be written and the system is quickly working, even though the refinements to make a complete system may take months or years. On the other hand, this approach is sometimes seen as chaotic, unstructured, or undisciplined by those who worry about the difficulties of debugging, error tracing, and predictability.

The unique nature of rule-based programming suggests that special techniques for designing, programming, browsing, debugging, testing, and documenting are necessary for expert systems. This chapter explores some possibilities for programmer and user interface design for expert systems.

Rule-based systems may be well suited for many programming situations, but an interactive system must have a good user interface to succeed. The simple question-and-answer dialogue style (teletype) may be inappropriate for many applications where greater visibility, user control, and user initiative is required. All rule-based systems must provide programmers with good facilities for managing the user interface or provide an exit to a more procedural language with screen manipulation facilities. Rule-based systems are quickly being reshaped to meet the demands of professional system developers. Rule bases are being integrated with data bases, computational tools, communications facilities, graphics manipulation software, etc. The blend of techniques will lead to more powerful systems that ease the programmer's burden and increase the quality of service to the end users.

2. Direct Manipulation

Shneiderman (1983, 1987) describes direct manipulation as the interaction style used in many display editors, the Xerox Star, the Macintosh, video games, etc., in which:

1. The user sees a continuous representation of the "world of action." The objects of interest and the permissible actions are represented on the screen in a visual format that takes into account the user's knowledge of the task domain and taps the human skill for analogical reasoning.
2. Physical actions, such as pointing at a file name in a directory listing, dragging an icon using a mouse, or drawing with a graphics tablet replace typed commands. Selecting from a list reduces memorization, keystrokes, and errors.
3. Actions are rapid, incremental, and reversible. Furthermore, the impact of an action on other objects of interest is shown immediately (the world of action). For example, in a word processor, inserting a word causes text to move right, and line overflows cause subsequent lines to be reformatted automatically.

These design principles lead to several important benefits:

• Users with knowledge of the task domain find the system easy to learn.

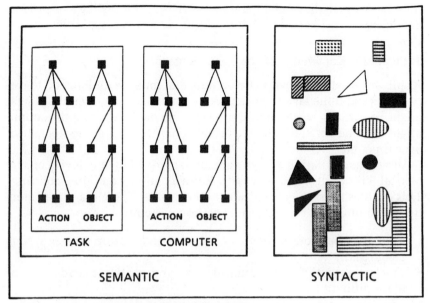

Figure 1. The Syntactic/Semantic Model

- Users must learn only a small number of computer concepts and syntactical rules; therefore they can concentrate on their task (the computer seems to vanish).
- Designers find it convenient to reduce the number of situations in which the users can make errors. Not only are syntax and computer-domain errors reduced, but task-domain errors can also be prevented in many cases.
- Users feel freer to explore novel "what-if" possibilities.
- Retention over time is facilitated.

The syntactical/semantic model of use behavior (Shneiderman, 1987) is helpful in understanding the benefits of direct manipulation. Users must have three kinds of knowledge (Figure 1):

1. Syntactical Knowledge

Device- and system-dependent physical actions, such as typing a string of characters, pressing a function key, or moving a mouse. This knowledge is arbitrary, acquired by rote memorization, and subject to forgetting unless frequently rehearsed.

2. Semantic Knowledge of Computer Concepts

Computer-related objects and actions that must be understood to operate a system, such as hierarchical directories, opening and closing of files, backing up disks, changing access rights, or inserting a record in a data base.

3. Semantic Knowledge of the Task Domain

Application-related objects and actions that must be understood to carry out a task. If the task is stock portfolio management, then the objects might be owners, stock names, prices, trade dates, etc. and the actions might be to buy or sell a stock, evaluate a portfolio, plot the stock price over time. etc.

Direct manipulation systems are characterized by low levels of syntactical knowledge and semantic knowledge of computer concepts. This enables users to concentrate on their tasks. There are some potential difficulties with direct manipulation systems:

- They may be more difficult to program and require greater system resources.
- Tracing execution, recording history, and writing macros may be more difficult.
- Visually impaired users may have a harder time.

Direct manipulation is especially valuable in expert systems applications because the task domains are often complex and it is difficult for users to grasp the implications of changes. By representing the objects and actions of interest on the screen, designers can offer users an exploratory environment where understanding of relationships is increased, exploration of alternatives is facilitated, and the distractions are substantially reduced.

In this chapter we describe our efforts to apply direct manipulation techniques in the design of a Student Advisor experimental expert system. We report on how the software architecture can be shaped to support good user interface design and how such an architecture eases the programmer's work during debugging and testing. Direct manipulation strategies are also a vital part of the programming environment because they facilitate browsing the knowledge base. The resulting Student Advisor was evaluated by 11 subjects, using a thinking-aloud empirical test. The chapter closes with suggestions for further research.

3. Our Experience

In this section we present in some detail our experience in developing and implementing a prototype expert system, and in designing an interactive rule browser (Sec. 3.2).

3.1 The Student Advisor

Introduction to the Student Advisor

Working under a grant from Inference Corporation at the Human-Computer Interaction Laboratory of the University of Maryland, we were tasked with reviewing the input/output interfaces of the software product ART (Automated Reasoning Tool), a data-driven, rule-based shell.

In order to perform this evaluation we decided to develop an experimental expert system, "The Student Advisor," which assists undergraduate computer science students in planning their course schedules. The division of responsibility on the development team was Ms. Sally Heikkenen, domain expert; Roland Simon, knowledge engineer for screen design and mouse-sensitive actions; Jim Baroff, knowledge engineer for domain rules; Francie Gilman, evaluation, and Ben Shneiderman, conceptual designer. The system was implemented on a Symbolics 3600 Lisp Machine. Early in the design process (November 1985), the team agreed on design objectives, which provided guidelines by which to evaluate progress.

Interface lessons learned relating specifically to the Student Advisor and more general benefits of direct manipulation interfaces will be discussed in later sections.

The work on the Student Advisor was motivated by three issues:

1. What interfacing software tools are required to develop an expert system which uses direct manipulation of objects in windows with no keyboard, no user command language, no procedural programming and no hierarchical menus?
2. How difficult is it to build an experimental prototype expert system with a comprehensible and powerful interface, writing entirely in rules, using only a high-order, rule-based language such as ART?
3. Are randomly fired rules a benefit or a detriment in an interactive environment?

A Priori Design Objectives

In order to focus the development work, and emphasize the interactive interface issues, the following guidelines were set out *before* the rule-based programming began:

Objective 1. No direct LISP procedural programming.

ART was being evaluated as a design tool in its own right. The use of LISP statements not implemented under the ART language was to be avoided. We wanted to evaluate ART, not LISP. This objective was met for the problem-domain rules, but slightly relaxed for the interface. Almost no LISP was used, so the "mixed" initiative ART (release 2.0) interface primitives sufficed. No menus or pop-up windows were implemented.

Objective 2.   Minimal use of SALIENCE.

Every ART rule may have a numerical SALIENCE declared which determines its priority of firing on the agenda when many rules are in conflict. Without SALIENCE, the ART programmer cannot predict the order of firing of rules all of whose antecedents are instantiated. Standard rule-based practices, as well as the ART tutorial manual, recommend minimizing the use of SALIENCE. Some delicate use of salience was required for the window management to ensure instant visual feedback.

Objective 3.   Two independently developed rule sets.

The two knowledge engineers agreed early in the project to the structure of just two FACTS: SCHEDULE and DROP-COURSE, but did not confer on methodology, or even discuss system integration until each had completed his part. The first of the two rule sets dealt exclusively with the domain knowledge such as University rules, Computer Science Department rules, prerequisites, credit accumulation, etc.; the second rule set was the interface, dealing only with screen displays, mouse-sensitive areas, and windowing. This objective was successfully met. The 90-rule domain set and the 40-rule interface set were easily integrated.

Objective 4.   Direct manipulation input only.

There would be no use of the keyboard or hierarchical menu selection. The student planning a schedule would be able to "click" on a course, record a grade, or plan a future course and place that course on the schedule by mouse manipulation. There would be no "teletype"-style questions and answers nor menu-driven processes. The user would decide when to schedule and when to drop courses, thereby controlling the sequence of events. The direct manipulation objective was completely satisfied.

Objective 5.   About 100 rules.

It was anticipated that too few rules would not challenge the system, and too many would not be feasible under the 6-month project schedule. A total of 130 rules were ultimately written for the prototype.

Objective 6.   No iterative loops or extensive procedural programming.

The right-hand sides of ART rules can be considered miniprocedures, and so should be kept simple. This was slightly relaxed in the interface rule set.

Objective 7.   Designer-controlled, world-of-action output.

All interaction would take place in a single screen with static, non-overlapping rectangular windows ("tiled" design). This objective was met in the experimental design, but the need was recognized for additional pop-up explanatory windows in a production system.

Objective 8.   No command language required of the user.

This objective was met. The prototype works on pure direct manipulation.

System Description

As illustrated in Figure 2, the student is presented with a complete catalog of courses from which he/she must construct a schedule (right window). Grades may be reported (A,B,C,D) or hypothesized (X). If no grade is selected, the course is considered as part of a future plan. Rules prevent taking courses without prerequisites, discover conflicts, such as failing to report all grades for a given semester, suggest possible alternatives, prompt the user with minimum requirements, etc.

All interactive decisions are handled by clicking on mouse-sensitive regions. The keyboard is neither permitted nor required. Visual feedback is given in two ways. For example, when the mouse is placed on a course on the CATALOG, the course is highlighted. When that course is selected by clicking, the message "Course . . . has been selected" appears at the bottom of the catalog window.

The domain rules were written with such generality that they are transparent to whether a course is scheduled as a result of an automatic rule assertion (such as automatically scheduling a prerequisite for a

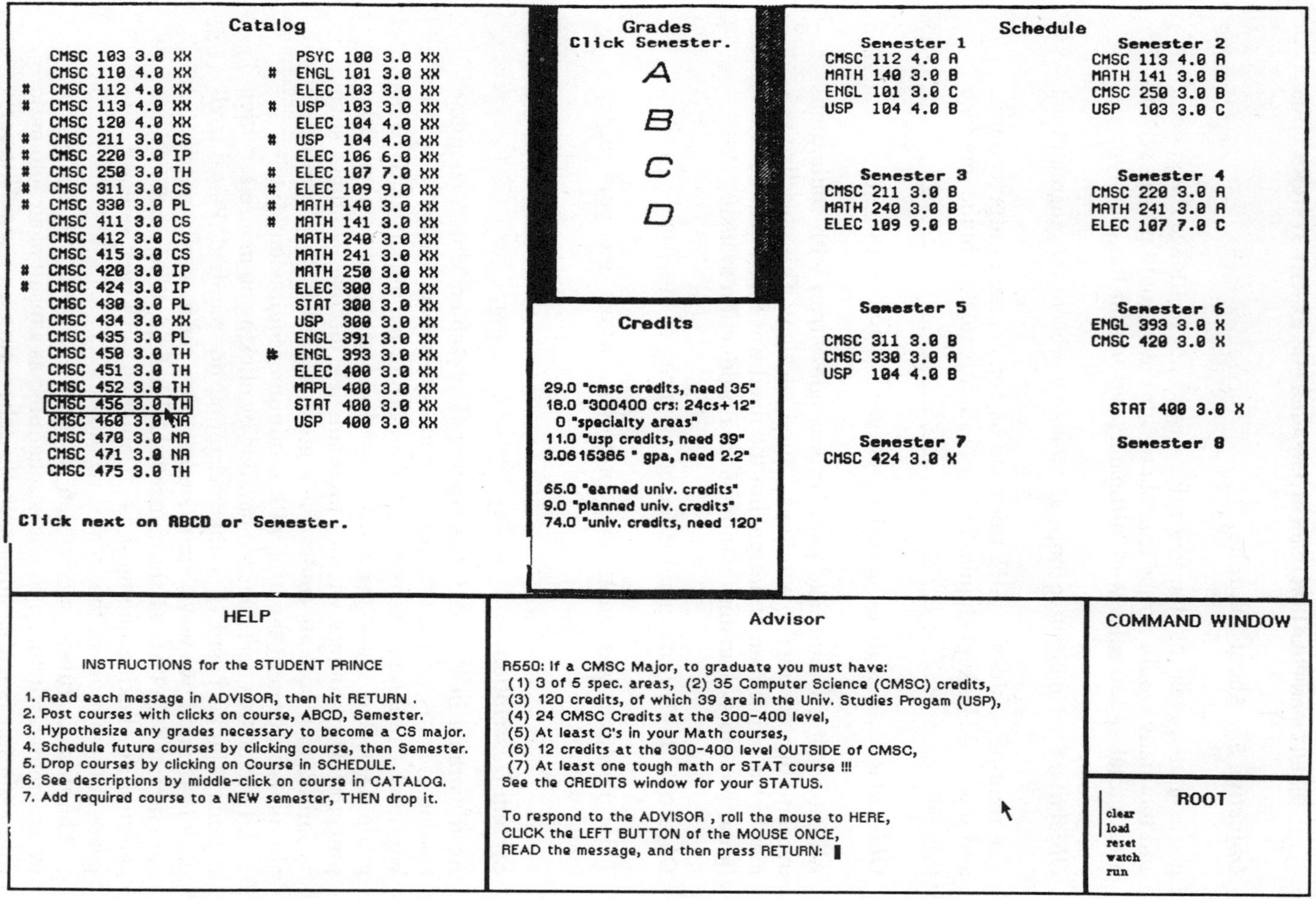

Catalog

	CMSC 103 3.0 XX	PSYC 100 3.0 XX	
	CMSC 110 4.0 XX	ENGL 101 3.0 XX	#
##	CMSC 112 4.0 XX	ELEC 103 3.0 XX	
	CMSC 113 3.0 PL	USP 103 3.0 XX	#
##	CMSC 120 4.0 XX	ELEC 104 4.0 XX	
	CMSC 211 3.0 CS	USP 104 4.0 XX	#
###	CMSC 220 3.0 IP	ELEC 106 6.0 XX	##
##	CMSC 250 3.0 TH	ELEC 107 7.0 XX	
	CMSC 311 3.0 CS	ELEC 109 9.0 XX	
	CMSC 338 3.0 PL	MATH 140 3.0 XX	
	CMSC 411 3.0 CS	MATH 141 3.0 XX	
##	CMSC 412 3.0 CS	MATH 240 3.0 XX	
	CMSC 415 3.0 CS	MATH 241 3.0 XX	
	CMSC 420 3.0 IP	MATH 250 3.0 XX	
	CMSC 424 3.0 IP	ELEC 300 3.0 XX	
	CMSC 430 3.0 PL	STAT 300 3.0 XX	
	CMSC 434 3.0 XX	USP 300 3.0 XX	
	CMSC 435 3.0 PL	ENGL 391 3.0 XX	#
	CMSC 450 3.0 TH	ENGL 393 3.0 XX	
	CMSC 451 3.0 TH	ELEC 400 3.0 XX	
	CMSC 452 3.0 TH	MAPL 400 3.0 XX	
	CMSC 456 3.0 TH	STAT 400 3.0 XX	
	CMSC 460 3.0 NA	USP 400 3.0 XX	
	CMSC 470 3.0 NA		
	CMSC 471 3.0 NA		
	CMSC 475 3.0 TH		

Click next on ABCD or Semester.

Grades

Click Semester.

A

B

C

D

Credits

29.0 "cmsc credits, need 35"
18.0 "300-400 crs: 24cs+12"
0 "specialty areas"
11.0 "usp credits, need 39"
3.06 16385 * gpa, need 2.2"
65.0 "earned univ. credits"
9.0 "planned univ. credits"
74.0 "univ. credits, need 120"

Schedule

Semester 1		Semester 2	
CMSC 112 4.0 A		CMSC 113 4.0 A	
MATH 140 3.0 B		MATH 141 3.0 B	
ENGL 101 3.0 C		CMSC 250 3.0 B	
USP 104 4.0 B		USP 103 3.0 C	

Semester 3		Semester 4	
CMSC 211 3.0 B		CMSC 220 3.0 A	
MATH 240 3.0 B		MATH 241 3.0 B	
ELEC 109 9.0 B		ELEC 107 7.0 C	

Semester 5		Semester 6	
CMSC 311 3.0 B		ENGL 393 3.0 X	
CMSC 338 3.0 A		CMSC 420 3.0 X	
USP 104 4.0 B			

Semester 7		Semester 8	
CMSC 424 3.0 X			
STAT 400 3.0 X			

Advisor

R550: If a CMSC Major, to graduate you must have:
(1) 3 of 5 spec. areas, (2) 35 Computer Science (CMSC) credits,
(3) 120 credits, of which 39 are in the Univ. Studies Progam (USP),
(4) 24 CMSC Credits at the 300-400 level,
(5) At least C's in your Math courses,
(6) 12 credits at the 300-400 level OUTSIDE of CMSC,
(7) At least one tough math or STAT course !!!
See the CREDITS window for your STATUS.

To respond to the ADVISOR , roll the mouse to HERE,
CLICK the LEFT BUTTON of the MOUSE ONCE,
READ the message, and then press RETURN: ▮

HELP

INSTRUCTIONS for the STUDENT PRINCE

1. Read each message in ADVISOR, then hit RETURN.
2. Post courses with clicks on course, ABCD, Semester.
3. Hypothesize any grades necessary to become a CS major.
4. Schedule future courses by clicking course, then Semester.
5. Drop courses by clicking on Course in SCHEDULE.
6. See descriptions by middle-click on course in CATALOG.
7. Add required course to a NEW semester, THEN drop it.

COMMAND WINDOW

clear
load
reset
watch
run

ROOT

Figure 2. Student Advisor Symbolics Screen

106

WINDOW	Current functionality	Planned improvements
ROOT	Standard ART menus	Replace with user menu
COMMAND	Standard ART Interface	Eliminate
CATALOG	List of courses, their credits and specialty areas	Right click on course for pre-requisite tree
	Left click selects course	Right click on white space for explanation.
	Middle click describes course	
GRADES	Left click selects A,B,C,D	Right click for HELP
	Skip for planning (Grade = X)	Allow Grade = F
SCHEDULE	After selecting course, left click on semester stacks course	Scroll if too many courses, or show ellipsis (. . .)
	Left click on course drops course	
CREDITS	Registers credits, GPA, student specialty areas	Right click for HELP Pop-up menu for any line item
HELP	7 fixed instructions	More elaborate explanation
ADVISOR	Advice messages one at a time	Stack all pending "error" messages in pop-up window

student), or by mouse manipulation. The Student Advisor screen has eight windows (Figure 2). In the above chart, window functionality is shown, together with proposed improvements to be implemented in a production version.

Sample ADVISOR Messages

Due to screen space limitations (scrolling being ruled out under the tiled-window design), the advice is necessarily brief, but hopefully clear and constructive. Here are some typical examples:

"To take CMSC220 you need CMSC120 or CMSC113. Schedule one of these courses first."

"A precomputer science major cannot take a 300-level computer science course."

"You must have a C or better in . . . to take . . ."

"To graduate, you need 12 credits in outside 300–400 level courses."

"You are taking . . . , did you think about taking . . . ?"

Coordination Between Two Rule Sets

The domain rules and the screen-manipulation rules were written independently by two programmers. Coordination between the two rule sets was accomplished at system integration time by the writing of only four additional short rules. These interfacing rules send or receive SCHEDULE or DROP-COURSE facts between the domain rules and the interface rules.

3.2 Lessons Learned

Rule-based programming by pattern match forces the programmer to think in concepts quite different from procedural-language counterparts. Following are some lessons learned from the Student Advisor (One cannot generalize from a single case study, but further research might show these conjectures to have general applicability):

1. Arithmetic accumulators are unnatural in ART. For example, in order to accumulate totals, it is necessary to write three rules: initialization, sum assertion, and accumulation.
2. Interacting rules can cause infinite loops. For example, at one point in the development we had a rule which automatically dropped a course that was scheduled in too early a semester, and a second rule, which asserted the same course as a necessary requirement for a student interested in going on to graduate school. The first rule would (automatically) retract the course created by the second rule, which would then reassert it, causing a disastrous infinite loop. The solution was to relax the automatic "DROP" rule and instead present the dilemma to the user to resolve. The user is advised to rearrange the schedule, placing the offending course in an appropriate semester.
3. The number of ART domain rules is about double the number of rules as stated by the human expert. In this application 45 plain-English rules were acquired from the university catalog and the human expert, but it required more than 90 ART rules to implement the details.
4. The multiple window display interface was an extremely valuable tool during debugging. This same window design is close to a production final design.
5. The effect of the advisory messages appearing randomly can be confusing to the knowledge engineer (especially while debugging), but can be a source of comic relief for the user, and shows the difficulty of relinquishing sequential (procedural) control. For example, a rule might advise: "You really ought to consider taking course X if you are thinking about course Y", and a few seconds LATER, course Y appears in the schedule.
6. As in most data-processing development environments, one underestimates the time required to debug the preliminary design

and programs. We had estimated 1 month for debugging, which stretched out over 3. However, the design continued to evolve (and improve) during the entire period due to the concurrent evaluation effort described in a later section.

7. System integration of separately developed rule sets was easier than the corresponding problem in procedural programming. Only four additional rules had to be written for the two rule sets to communicate. The lack of "local facts" in ART meant that some care had to be devoted to naming facts.

8. Minimizing the use of salience (i.e. ignoring rule prioritization, time sequencing and conflict resolution) gives an interactive system an AI "flavor." The sequence with which intermediate results (or messages) appear is unpredictable, but the final results are determined uniquely. As initial data conditions are varied, one is sometimes pleasantly surprised by the sequence of intermediate steps taken by the program to reach what may be a predictable result. This gives the impression that the machine can "think for itself." A slight change in data sometimes has a profound effect on this sequence. In a procedural program one knows in advance what the exact sequence of steps will be, so there are fewer surprises.

9. The use of multiple windows can obviate the need to impose an order to the rules. A series of quickly executing steps APPEAR to be simultaneous on the screen, given the great speed of the compiled LISP on the Symbolics hardware, and the fast refresh cycle of the bit-mapped screen. This would be a problem on slower hardware or screens which refreshed slowly.

10. A great deal of the productivity of the knowledge engineers and their satisfaction in performing this work can be traced to the Symbolics development environment. The multiple windows, file-manager and (ART) incremental compiling allow fast prototyping and testing of rules.

11. In the excitement of developing an application, one may develop a blind spot, which only is discovered in beta test. We forgot to allow students to fail a course! No "F" is included in the mouse-sensitive grading mechanism.

3.3 Rule Browser Design

In 1985 two of the authors (Shneiderman and Simon; cf. Shneiderman et al., 1986b) developed a hierarchical browser for procedural programs. An experiment in which student subjects compared this browser with a simple screen editor proved that the hierarchical browser was faster for answering questions at the same level of programming comprehension.

We have extended these techniques to study the feasibility of developing a prototype of a browser for facts and rules, using Inference Corporation's ART language as a model. The idea is that a knowledge engineer is handed a large rule-based system and has the task of understanding its structure in order to modify and maintain the system. Our effort concentrated on ways to decompose rules for browsing purposes.

The rule decomposition chosen hinges on two specific syntactical features of the rule-based ART language: SALIENCE, and ASSERT/RETRACT facts. In ART, salience is a declared number associated with a rule which determines its order of firing among satisfied rules. Facts are ASSERTED (created) or RETRACTED (deleted). There is no MODIFY FACT construct in ART. Thus the user of the browser can see all rules with a given salience, or a four-way decomposition into subsets of rules which:

- Neither assert nor retract any facts.
- Only assert facts.
- Only retract facts (such as garbage collection).
- Both assert and retract facts within the same rule.

For systems with large numbers of rules (high hundreds) a major problem of this approach is the effective display of the results of the decomposition. Even a list of the names of the rules may be too large to show on one screen. One must also avoid overwhelming the user with too much information.

The proposed solution is to show a small number of rules in each subset, and let the rest of the rule names be scrollable within their windows. This approach does not totally respect the world-of-action principle, since a good deal of information is hidden, and may act as an optical illusion, hiding the true complexity of the underlying rules. However, each subset is labeled with the NUMBER of rules in that subset, and the total number of rules in the entire rule base. For example, if 67 rules have a salience of 1000 and there are 200 rules in the rule base, the heading of the decomposition would include the words:

''67 of 200, Salience 1000'',

even though only 10 of the rule names were displayed. The missing rules are indicated by ellipses: ".....". For an example of the proposed browser decompositions, taken from an ART demonstration on chemical spills, see Figures 3 and 4.

A further element of the proposed browser design is to search only a

4/27 Salience *constraint-salience* 1,000,001	1/27 Salience 999,999	1/27 Salience 10,000
source-of-wrong-material-is-clean source-of-wrong-material-type-is-c... source-of-insufficient-volume-is-cle... contaminated-propagates-downstr...	all-clean-upstream-implies-clean-d...	warn-about-spill-hazards

4/27 Salience 200	12/27 Salience 0	5/27 Salience -1,000
low-pH-implies-acid high-pH-implies-base low-solubility-and-neutral-pH-impl... calculate-volume-of-sill	start-up ask-about-pH ask-about-solubility ask-about-acid-smell ask-about-oil-smell ...	determine-material determine-volume hypothesize-path isolate-source indicate-source

Figure 3.   Salience Browsing

18/27 Assert	6/27 Assert and Retract
start-up	determine-volume ←
determine-material	hypothesize-path
ask-about-pH	isolate-source
ask-about-solubility	promote-necessarily-contaminated-location
low-pH-implies-acid	ask-status-of-suspected-location
...	indicate-source

0/27 Retract	3/27 no (Assert or Retract)
	contaminated-locations-cannot-be-siblings
	tell-user-where-source-is
	warn-about-spill-hazards

Figure 4.   Retract/Assert Browsing

subset of rules which match a given fact pattern in their antecedents. This idea is closely related to the notion of FACT SETS, whereby large knowledge bases are partitioned on the basis of facts rather than rules. A discussion of fact-set theory applied to the ART language is contained in a separate paper (Baroff, Simon, & Shneiderman, 1986).

In any of the browser approaches, direct access to the text of the rules is obtained by clicking the mouse on any rule name. This can clear up ambiguity in the semantics of the rule, and shows the importance of naming rules carefully in the first place to speed up and clarify browsing. An implementation of an actual browser could go one step further and allow in-place editing of the rule text at that point.

4. BENEFITS of DIRECT MANIPULATION for EXPERT SYSTEMS

In this section we discuss the general proposition that the human expert should be heavily involved in the design of the interface as well as in the construction of the rules and acquisition of facts. Some general comments are made concerning interface design, implementation, and the difficult task of testing and debugging.

4.1 Involve the Expert in the Interface Design

An expert system is a computer program with embedded human expert knowledge. What we mean by an expert in this sense is expressed in the following quotation:

> An expert is a person who, because of training and experience, is able to do things the rest of us cannot; experts are not only proficient but also smooth and efficient in the actions they take. Experts know a great many things and have tricks and caveats for applying what they know to problems and tasks; they are also good at plowing through irrelevant information in order to get at basic issues, and they are good at recognizing problems they face as instances of types of problems with which they are familiar. Underlying the behavior of experts is the body of operative knowledge we have termed expertise. It is reasonable to suppose, therefore, that experts are the ones to ask when we wish to represent the expertise that makes their behavior possible. (Johnson, 1983)

The general proposition is that the human domain expert is the one to ask in designing an interface for a rule-based expert system. We shall call this process "INTERFACE ACQUISITION" in analogy with the terminology "Knowledge Acquisition." Knowledge acquisition is to an expert system what INTERFACE acquisition is to an expert interface. The interface acquisition focuses on the symbolic representation of the domain of expertise and the ability to extract relevant data as seen by the human expert. It is just as important for the expert to be involved in the interface design process as it is for him/her to be involved in the development of the facts and rules.

We assume here that the final end user of the expert system is not a naïve user but rather a quite knowledgeable individual, although not in the expert class.

4.2 Design of the Interface

Many "good" interfaces that have achieved success are direct manipulation interfaces. One example is the popular spreadsheet, Lotus 1-2-3, in which the user may "point and paint" to manipulate ranges of data and formulas. Many CAD/CAM graphics tools provide direct manipulation interfaces.

In terms of the semantic/syntactical model (Shneiderman, 1987), we find that good user interface design lies as far away as possible from syntax and as close as possible to semantics. The challenge to produce a good world of action can only be met by careful study and comprehension of the domain semantics, and the involvement of a true expert in this analysis. This properly capitalizes on the symbolic representation appropriate to the problem domain. The human expert has mastered the use of the symbolic tools and is probably a step beyond the conventional "state of the art" in his/her field. This "edge" may be difficult for the expert to express formally and must be revealed during the interface acquisition process.

As an example, one of the authors of this chapter (Baroff) is an expert in the game of backgammon. He reveals that he does not see the backgammon board as average players do, or as portrayed in most "advanced" textbooks on the game. To solve difficult backgammon problems, instead of the usual mental image of four quadrants of 6 points each, with an artificial "bar" dividing the board, he uses a linear model 24 points wide with a sliding window 6 points wide, which may be positioned anywhere along this surface. (In backgammon a major objective is to construct a "prime" of 6 consecutive points.) This kind of "gut feel" of the expert must somehow be captured during the interface design process.

The major problem in designing the interface is fitting the "world of action" onto one screen. When the situation is too complex, there are (at least) two ways of accomplishing this: higher abstraction, and trimming the data.

Common knowledge, state-of-the-art ways of representing a problem diagrammatically is the first level of abstraction. A chessboard is shown as an 8 by 8 matrix; logical circuit boards are shown with the conventional "AND" gate diagram, etc. Experts may want to modify and improve upon the conventional wisdom to accommodate their view of the world. Trimming can be achieved by removing irrelevant data from the state of the system, and also removing relevant data when other visual impact can substitute. One (small) picture might be worth a thousand words!

4.3 Implementation

World-of-action displays must be updated as soon as the knowledge base changes. This is easily realized in data-driven rule based systems, and is almost automatic. Subroutines that one might have to write in a procedural language are unnecessary, since the rules that refresh the screen are ready to fire whenever the data change. The ART language is particularly powerful in this regard as it is "pure" data driven as compared with languages such as KEE or S1, which are hybrid systems.

Strict ordering of the sequence of interaction between the user and the expert system is not easy to control in a rule-based system, in which rules fire "at random" whenever the data exist to match the antecedent of a rule. As long as a succession of rules fire quickly and the refresh-screen hardware mechanism is rapid, the user will not see the exact sequence of firings, and will be satisfied with the final picture of the world. When these timing considerations are met, the rule-based programmer is relieved of the need to control the step-by-step action. When the screen responses are slow, however, this control programming can be difficult. In such a case the advantage of a data-driven system is lost, and an exit from the rule-based language to an external control program may be required.

In some problem domains there may be another complication. Users may be accustomed to expressing their actions in a specific sequence, even when there is no logical reason to do so. People usually give name before address before city, state, and zip in that order. Some procedural control may have to be built into a system to accommodate this structured behavior. The use of fill-in input forms gives the best of both worlds as long as the user has the freedom to move about freely, filling in blanks in any order. The visual representation may be conventional, but the action can suit any user. (Observation shows that when confronted with a new screen, many people scan the form diagonally first, then fill in the easy ones, then proceed sequentially.)

In the design of such fill-in forms, the rule-based system interface designer should make the world of action as easy as possible for the user. For example, if a blank is optional, subquestions that may be triggered by that data should pop up only when needed, avoiding a cluttered screen. Rule-based programming is a natural for this: "IF (data) THEN display subquestions."

4.4 Testing and Debugging

Testing and debugging are often the hardest tasks in developing an expert system. The major problem is managing the numerous changes in the knowledge base. In comparison with procedural languages, rule-based systems are extremely hard to trace. It would be desirable to be able to "reverse" the action as if under instant replay, but these tools are not available. A good world-of-action screen with reversibility would be a great boon to debugging. A change to one piece of data can trigger a large number of rules that have that fact as antecedent. Small changes in the knowledge base trigger intense activity on the agenda, and "irrelevant" rules fire during the trace. Going step by step, firing one rule at a time can be a frustrating experience. The relationships among objects cannot be comprehended by the programmer during such sequential debugging. What a difference the world of action makes. The variety of effects of changing the facts is instantly seen, and the programmer sometimes intuitively knows where the "bug" is without detailed tracing. One's eyes become a debugging tool, taking advantage of one's knowledge of the problem domain. This would suggest that for programmers to be successful in debugging, they had better be near-experts in the problem domain as well.

Direct manipulation interfaces can help because they reflect a higher order of abstraction than the raw facts would suggest. Mathematicians cannot prove a theorem by drawing a diagram, but expertise in finding that proof is often guided by a sketch. That people think in pictures is well known to psychologists. It is impossible to draw a Euclidean geometry "line" with a pencil as a line has no width, but where would the science of geometry be if the abstraction of a line were not used? A good interface will show an error in the rules visually. The problem will "hit you in the eye" and the debugging will flow in a natural, visual way.

Our experience in debugging the Student Advisor is a good example of the benefits of a direct manipulation interface. The interface was developed as a separate rule group independently of the domain rules concerning prerequisites and computer science department requirements. The debugging of the domain rules was proceeding tortuously by displaying facts on the screen, and tracing the logic, using standard

ART debugging tools to browse the knowledge base. For example, accounting for course credits was tedious to verify. Once the interface was integrated with the domain rules, bugs which had been difficult to find were immediately seen and easily resolved. For example, a central window displayed all course credits, and if a loop in the accumulating of credits existed, an out-of-control condition was spotted instantly. The point is that no separate debugging rules had to be written; all of the important results were there at all times. One clicked on a course in a semester to drop a course and it was gone; if not, a bug was apparent. It was not necessary to browse a large number of facts and rules to discover problems.

A difficulty in debugging is to discover that problems still exist. Fixing them is often straightforward. The ability to manipulate objects on the screen and instantly see the "world of action" (or the "world of insanity" when bugs exist) adds a new dimension to debugging technique. We found it very gratifying in our experience with the Student Advisor. This same experience has been borne out by discussions with other developers of complicated rule-based systems.

Finally, the rules that are written to create the interface for the final product are the SAME rules that are used during debugging. One doesn't write the interface twice, once for development and again for production. Procedural programmers who work without appropriate interfaces often write large numbers of subroutines used only during debugging that are later discarded when the system is in production. A well-designed world of action interface serves both purposes.

We conclude this section on debugging with the suggestion that, in fact, the interface should be developed and debugged FIRST and then the domain rules developed and debugged, using the interface as a debugging tool.

5. Evaluation Effort

We conducted individual observations of volunteers to determine the effectiveness of the Student Advisor. We were interested in their deftness with the direct manipulation, in their satisfaction, and with the appropriateness, clarity, and ease of use of all input/output methods. Several specific questions intrigued us: How quickly would the students become comfortable with the mouse? Would using both the mouse and the keyboard cause confusion? (**Note:** At the time of the evaluation, the keyboard had not yet been totally eliminated as an input device.) How helpful was each of the windows?

It had been our intention to test the Student Advisor only with students, since they were the proposed end users; but in order to get a wider sample, we invited several more experienced computer professionals to try it out as well. This led to an interesting divergence of opinion that can be usefully contrasted—students naïve to expert systems vs. the more knowledgeable professionals.

Pilot Test

A pilot test of the system with one student led to several interface findings that would reappear later in the observations:

- Frequent confusion between "Return" and "Click."
- Use of mouse judged highly appropriate.
- Inaccurate tally in CREDITS window.
- ADVISOR window messages not context-sensitive.
- HELP window not very helpful.
- Window size and placement good.

Actions taken on the basis of the pilot test included:

1. Changes to the questionnaire.
2. More verbal help given to the participants.
3. Scheduling beginning at the junior year to give more time with a partly filled-in SCHEDULE.
4. CREDITS window arithmetic bugs fixed.

Subjects

Student participation was open to computer science juniors, seniors, and graduate students, assuring a minimum level of familiarity with courses and requirements. The six students who participated were told that the observations were to test the effectiveness of an experimental interactive, mouse-driven, rule-based system, and that it was the system being evaluated, not their own performance. One student had taken a course in artificial intelligence. Two were women. All were taking a course entitled "Human Factors in Computer and Information Systems." We asked each to spend a total of 1 hour, and to fill out a questionnaire at the end of the session.

To expand the evaluation, we invited five computer professionals to try the system. They brought higher expectations and different perspectives, which provided an interesting contrast to the attitudes of the students. Only one had extensive experience with expert systems.

SCALE: 1 LOW
2 FAIRLY LOW
3 MODERATE
4 FAIRLY HIGH
5 HIGH

	EASE of USE		APPROPRIATENESS		CLARITY	
	Student ($N = 6$)	Observer ($N = 5$)	Student ($N = 6$)	Observer ($N = 5$)	Student ($N = 6$)	Observer ($N = 5$)
ıput Devices						
[OUSE	3.7	4.0	3.8	5.0	not asked	
EYBOARD	4.3	4.0	2.8	1.0	not asked	
ʼindows						
DVISOR	3.0	2.0	3.3	2.0	3.2	3.0
ATALOG	4.7	4.0	not asked		3.7	3.0
REDITS	not asked		3.5*	3.0*	3.5	2.0
CHEDULE	4.2	3.0	not asked		4.5	5.0
ELP ($N = 3$)	2.0	1.0	not asked		2.3	1.0
REREQ's	3.7	2.0	not asked		2.6	1.0

*These scores relate to a question of ACCURACY of response, rather than APPROPRIATENESS

eneral Issues

	STUDENTS ($N = 6$)	OBSERVERS ($N = 5$)
esponse time	4.0	3.0
ıse of learning	4.0	3.0
verall ease of use	4.2	3.0
verall satisfaction	3.2	2.0

igure 5.   Evaluation Summary

Results of the Evaluation of the Student Advisor

The opinions of the students and independent observers on selected features of the Student Advisor are summarized in Figure 5. While the responses of the students were tabulated from their questionnaires, the responses of the observers were gleaned from their oral comments while on-line.

It is immediately apparent that the students' reactions were universally more positive than those of the independent observers, whose experience and expertise led them to expect more, even from a fledgling system. Most of the students enjoyed using the mouse and became fairly proficient. While the students could in most cases only guess at the appropriateness of using both the mouse and the keyboard, the observers, like the design team, quickly recognized the flaw in using both. (Use of the keyboard was eliminated in July, 1986.)

Both groups felt the need for more and better on-line help. This was an acknowledged weakness in the system, the more so because the HELP window was virtually jettisoned to make way for an improvement to the system—a list of course prerequisites. Since the designers were aware of their decision to exclude explanation and justification, the low results on the HELP window provide some measure of the evaluation reliability.

The CATALOG window was a success with the students, since it was instantly recognizable as a COMPLETE list of familiar courses. After they had learned to maneuver the mouse, it was a simple matter to "point and click" and fill up the SCHEDULE, keeping track of the chosen courses by the pound signs. (Feedback on selected courses is shown by a # symbol.) The observers, on the other hand, mourned the inability to "drag" courses from the CATALOG window to the SCHEDULE.

Finally, none of the students took control of the system to the extent the observers did. There was an absence of a sense of "owning" the system. Instead there was an amazed "awe," gratifying to us, but not when contrasted to the observers' more caustic, constructive comments.

Student comments were directed more at the accuracy of the operations (the TASK domain), while those of the observers considered the entire environment (COMPUTER domain).

Here are some suggested improvements from both groups:

- On-line tutorial with novice/expert levels.
- Ability to choose between using the mouse or keyboard.
- Many context-sensitive HELP windows (Explanation).
- Course prerequisites and postrequisites tree in a pop-up window.
- CREDITS window accurately showing "have" and "need" status.
- Ability to drag courses around the screen.
- Leave no guesswork, just choices.
- An easy way to undo the last command(s).
- Give users the feeling they are in control.

On Conducting Evaluation Observations

Under normal circumstances in product development, one establishes certain product standards in order to know when beta testing should begin. However, if one is conducting an early evaluation, to explore the nature of the product development process itself, the need for specific standards is frustrated. In our case, exploration was the purpose, and there were no measurable standards to be met. If the goal had been to create a finished product, the development process and the testing and evaluation would have been different.

General Considerations for Evaluation Research

1. Have two groups look at the product—one composed of future users and the other of people who are interested but objective frequent users of similar products. Start with small groups and gradually expand to larger groups as the bugs are worked out of the product.
2. Observations are best when done on a one-to-one basis.
3. If it becomes obvious that the product is not ready even for informal evaluation, stop testing; you may wear out your welcome.
4. The evaluation researcher should have the user population in mind at all times rather than the programming difficulties in making improvements or corrections.
5. It helps if the researcher has some idea of, if not experience in, what the programmer(s) have accomplished and how they went about designing and developing the program. Sitting through some debugging sessions is helpful for both parties.
6. Know the assumptions that the designers of the system made about the users—their knowledge and experience level, interests, etc.

6. Summary

Based on our experience in developing an experimental expert system, the Student Advisor, we conclude that Direct Manipulation is an appropriate style for designing a visual interface for an expert system.

A multiple-window system is an abstraction which emphasizes the task domain. It is designer-designed and is compatible with the type of random rule firings common to rule-based programming.

This "World of Action" also serves as an effective debugging tool in which valid and invalid states are easily recognized. Because of its value during debugging, we recommend that the interface be written *before* the domain rules.

An interactive conceptual design of a rule browser was introduced, which itself takes advantage of direct manipulation techniques.

The process of actively involving the human domain expert in the interface design for a rule-based expert system we call "Interface Acquisition."

A useful hands-on evaluation of the interface was carried out during development. Even a modest evaluation effort can be valuable in discovering weaknesses in the design, especially if the subjects include potential users as well as expert observers. The results of the evaluation were used in refining the design and assisted in the debugging effort.

7. Research Directions

There is a wealth of opportunity for research into the programmer/user interfaces for expert systems. Empirical studies will be helpful in understanding how opposing strategies influence ease of learning, speed of performance on benchmark tasks, rate and distribution of errors, subjective satisfaction with the system and results, and ease of human retention of the operation of the system over time.

Thinking aloud and observational studies, data collection from monitoring users, and surveys are helpful at early stages of research for formulating hypotheses and spotting unusual performance. Then more controlled experiments can establish causality and document the impact of individual factors.

General user interface issues include:

- Screen size, layout, and readability;
- Use of color and windows;
- Input devices: keyboard, mouse, touchscreen, etc.;
- Interaction styles: commands, menus, fill-in, direct manipulation;
- Response time impacts;
- Error messages, handling, and prevention;
- On-line help, manuals, demos, and tutorials;
- Printed user manuals and tutorials. (Shneiderman, 1986a)

Many researchers are pursuing these issues in applications, ranging from expert systems, to air traffic control, to educational packages, to office automation, etc. Clearer guidelines for designers are emerging, but much work remains.

There are many interesting problems that are specific to expert systems, because expert systems deal with complex knowledge domains and a particular kind of interaction. The users of expert systems usually have a specific decision to make in a complex domain. Their task is to establish the known conditions and explore possible resolutions. This situation leads to several intriguing research problems.

Locus of Control: User-centered vs. Computer-directed

In many expert systems the computer asks a sequence of multiple-choice or fill-in questions that the user is expected to respond to. Changing or reviewing responses may be difficult and the sequence of questions is computer-controlled. Then the expert system produces possible resolutions with the opportunity for the user to trace back the sequence of rule firings that led to the result. This computer-directed style may be appropriate in some cases, especially with novice users, but many users may prefer a user-centered style of interaction that puts them in command, entering information in the sequence that suits them, changing values to explore interactions among variables, and developing an understanding of the underlying model. This latter style puts the locus of control in the user's hands and is more in harmony with the spirit of direct manipulation systems. Researchers could help develop guidelines based on empirical data for choosing between these possibilities.

Window Layout: Designer-designed Coordination vs. User-managed

Modern high-resolution, bit-mapped displays offer users the opportunity to display large amounts of information on the screen. There are occasions when one large display is helpful, but often several windows with differing information is more beneficial. In some systems the user is responsible for managing the placement, size, and contents of windows. Some designers and product salespeople promote the "cluttered desk" approach in which windows can be overlaid in arbitrary patterns, supposedly reflecting the creative ways in which paper documents are spread out on a desk. This approach offers the greatest flexibility and power, but in many applications it puts an unnecessary and substantial burden on the users.

An alternative is for designers to lay out a set of windows, usually in a tiled format to cover the available screen space, as a function of the users' tasks. If a medical diagnosis situation requires information from a patient history data base, from laboratory tests, and from the current hospital record, then the designer should arrange that all three windows appear with the proper information in a reasonable layout. The user can revise the layout, but most of the time the designer's choice will be acceptable. Coordination among windows may ensure that if the report of a previous hospitalization is displayed, then relevant lab tests would appear automatically (a strategy we call synchronized scrolling). Furthermore, by pointing at the name of a lab test shown on the screen, the user can bring up a window that describes the lab test and normal ranges (a strategy we call direct selection). Empirical tests of these strategies might reveal conditions under which each is superior (Bly & Rosenberg, 1986).

Browsing Complex Displays

Rule-based systems record information about complex relationships that are often conveniently represented by graphical displays of networks (Poltrock, Steiner, & Tarlton, 1986; Richer & Clancey, 1985). In realistic applications, the entire network cannot be shown on the screen at once. Is modular decomposition necessary, or can browsers support sufficiently rapid display as the users move the window? Does zooming work?

Hierarchical Browsing: Multiple Levels vs. Fisheye

Many kinds of information are organized into multiple levels; e.g. books have a table of contents of the chapters, and each chapter may have a table of contents of the sections. Similarly maps or networks may have a high-level view with more details at lower levels. In these cases there are at least two strategies for browsing. The fisheye approach (Furnas, 1986) would remove some of the higher-level information and give greater detail from the lower levels at the point of interest, e.g. in a table of contents when a user points at a chapter title, the chapter text would replace it, displacing some of the chapter titles. The multiple level approach (Shneiderman, Shafer, Simon, & Weldon, 1986) would show two windows containing the higher- and lower-level views; e.g. pointing at a chapter title would produce the contents in a separate window, enabling the user to continue seeing two levels of detail. An understanding of when the fisheye or multiple-level approach is preferred would be useful.

References

Baroff, J., Simon, R., & Shneiderman, B. (1986). *Fact sets: A remedy for rule-based clutter.* Paper presented at the June 17–18 Conference on "Expert Systems: The User Interfaces," University of Maryland Institute for Advanced Computer Studies College Park, MD.

Bly, S., & Rosenberg. J. (1986). A comparison of tiled and overlapping windows. In M. Mantei & P. Orbeton, (Eds.), *Proceedings CHI 86 Human Factors in Computing Systems*, ACM, New York, pp. 101–106.

Furnas, G. (1986). Generalized fisheye views. In M. Mantei & P. Orbeton (Eds.), *Proceedings CHI 86 Human Factors in Computing Systems,* ACM, New York, pp. 16–23.

Johnson, P. E. (1983). What kind of expert should a system be? *Journal of Medicine and Philosophy, 8,* 77–97.

Poltrock, S., Steiner, D., & Tarlton, P. N. (1986). Graphics interfaces for knowledge-based system development. In M. Mantei, & P. Orbeton, (Eds.), *Proceedings CHI 86 Human Factors in Computing Systems,* ACM, New York, pp. 9–15.

Richer, M., & Clancey, W. J. (1985). GUIDON-WATCH: A graphic interface for viewing a knowledge-based system. *IEEE Computer Graphics and Applications, 5*(11), 51–64.

Shneiderman, B. (1983). Direct manipulation: A step beyond programming languages. *IEEE Computer, 16*(8), 57–69.

Shneiderman, B. (1987). *Designing the user interface: Strategies for effective human-computer interaction.* Reading, MA: Addison–Wesley.

Shneiderman, B. (1986a). Seven plus or minus two central issues in human-computer interaction. In M. Mantei, & P. Orbeton, (Eds.), *Proceedings CHI 86 Human Factors in Computing Systems,* ACM, New York, pp. 343–349.

Shneiderman, B., Shafer, P., Simon, R., & Weldon, L. (1986b). Display strategies for program browsing: Concepts and experiment. *IEEE Software 3,* (May), 7–15.

Waterman, D. (1986). *A guide to expert systems,* Addison–Wesley. Reading, MA.

SEVEN

Development Tools for Rule-based Systems

Stephen Fickas
University of Oregon

Abstract

We report on our efforts to construct a development environment for a
rule-based language, describing first the language and then the environment. We introduce our design goals and present a small development
scenario. Finally, we discuss our attempts to extend the environment by
moving into more speculative research areas.

1. Introduction

Over the past four years, a group of faculty and students at the University of Oregon has been working on an environment for a rule-based
language. This chapter reports on these efforts. Our work on rule-based
programming started with the Hearsay III system developed at Information Sciences Institute (Erman, London, & Fickas, 1981). It progressed
to incorporate programming in OPS5 (Forgy, 1981), and then YAPS
(Allen, 1983). Minor detours were taken through ROSIE (Fain et al.,
1981) and PROLOG. Each of these languages gave us insight into what
is needed in a good rule-based programming environment. Since 1983,
we have been working on our own rule-based system called ORBS
(Oregon Rule-based System). For the most part, this chapter is based on
our experience constructing and using ORBS (see also Fickas, Novick,
& Reesor, 1985).

It is often difficult in a system such as ORBS to separate language
from environment, or even the ORBS environment from the Lisp en-

vironment on which it rests. Further, while we use the term *rule-based* to describe ORBS, an ORBS program may make use of flavor-based and procedural languages in carrying out a computation. Complicating matters further, an ORBS program may be embedded in a program written in any of these other languages. Some of the newer AI language efforts argue (see, for instance, LOOPS [Loops, 1982]) that this is just right: Complex problems often do not fit into a single language, but instead will need a variety of representations. We support this argument (although we continue to worry about the type of environment needed to support programming in such a language salad). Our discussion in this chapter then has less to do with "expert systems" per se, and more to do with the view of rule-based languages as just another computational paradigm, often included under the same roof with other nonrule-based languages. Just as environment research has progressed for non-rule-based languages, we would like to build more powerful environments in the rule-based world.

Finally, we note that we are taking a specific view of the term *interface* in this book. In particular, our major concern has been supporting the programmer of a rule-based system (A.K.A the knowledge engineer). Thus, our interface issues revolve around the environment and language as opposed to end user support. We also note that our recent work, discussed in a later section, has found us moving toward a more traditional development model of analysis, specification, design, and implementation.

The layout of the chapter is as follows: first, a section presenting a description of our design goals; second, an introduction to the language; third, a discussion of the environment by way of a scenario; finally, a discussion of our current efforts to extend the environment, using ideas from the software engineering and expert system fields.

2. Design Goals

We have found that a lack of design goals during either language or environment construction leads to ad hoc and "feature-prone" systems. If the language and environment designers do not have a clear idea of how the language will be used, nor who will use it, then resulting systems do not attract a user following. In designing both the ORBS language and its environment, we have attempted to keep our goals clearly in mind. They are as follows:

1. ORBS programs should be able to be built quickly. Although at first glance this appears to be a platitude, it has led to hard design decisions in the definition of the language and environment.

2. We wished to produce a general-purpose language. Hence, language components tied to particular problem domains (e.g., a hard-wired control strategy for modeling human memory) were to be avoided.
3. ORBS programs should be able to be tested even if in incomplete form, i.e., incremental, interactive development of prototypes should be supported.
4. ORBS programs should be able to be tested even if in buggy form, i.e., errors should not cause system seizure.
5. Competency and performance concerns should be separated. That is, the user should be able to concentrate on the design of rules and data base while holding control issues in abeyance.
6. We would like to reuse past efforts when possible. Thus, our model is more of load-and-tailor than build-from-scratch.

Our discussion of ORBS development tools in the remainder of this chapter must be viewed in light of the above goals. Different goals, e.g., the nonprototyping goals of Hearsay III or the noninteractive, nonincremental development model of the OPS family, can clearly lead to different tools and different languages. For further discussion of the interaction of language, environment, and development model, see the ORBS design rationale in Fickas (1985).

3. An Introduction to the Language

In the following sections we will describe the ORBS language. Before doing so, we note that ORBS falls in the class of rule-based systems that often is categorized as forward-chaining or data-driven. Other systems in this category include OPS5, YAPS, and all of the Hearsay family. What is often taken as the inverse of this set are the backward-chaining or goal-directed languages, such as EMYCIN (Van Melle, 1981) or PROLOG. Arguments for and against the forward and backward approaches have been made many times elsewhere (see, e.g., Buchanan & Duda, 1983), and we will not address the issue further in this chapter.[1] While we believe that many of the arguments we make for the design of ORBS are applicable to rule-based systems in general, any further reference to the term *rule-based system* should be taken in light of the above classification.

---

[1] Many modern systems have attempted to combine aspects of both.

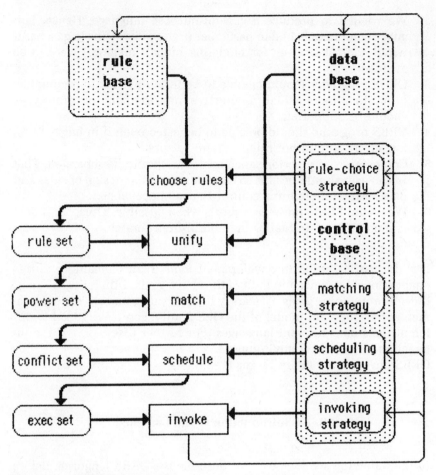

Figure 1. ORBS Components

3.1. The ORBS Database

A program written in ORBS contains a set of tuples in a data base, a set of rules that match on those tuples, and a set of control strategies that determine which rules will be executed. Figure 1 conveys this graphically. A cycle starts by executing the *choose rules* box. It takes as input components of two permanent data stores (denoted by dotted, rounded boxes), the *rule base* and the *control base*. It produces an intermediate data store (denoted by clear, rounded boxes), the *rule set*. A cycle ends by executing the *invoke* box. Invocation can cause changes (denoted by thin lines) to any of the permanent stores. We will discuss each of the three permanent stores in more detail in the remainder of this section.

The ORBS data base consists of zero or more tuples, also called *facts* for historical reasons. Each fact can take as arguments either Lisp objects or Flavor objects.[2] For example, three data base facts are given below:

```
(location susan office)
(actions (go stop continue))
(hit {person} {person})
```

The notation {name} represents an *instance* of a flavor object of type name.

Because ORBS itself is implemented as a single flavor object, multiple instantiations of the ORBS system are possible, allowing separate ORBS systems to be inserted into a larger application program. For instance, one ORBS system can reside in the data base of another ORBS system (as an argument of a fact). Thus we can have something like the following:

```
(subproblem-solver decide-route {orbs})
(subproblem-solver decide-day {orbs})
```

where two different ORBS systems have been constructed by the user to solve subproblems in a travel agent system, each of which appears in the data base of yet a third ORBS system. Each of the three systems have their own relations, rules, and control.

Relations have *optional* declarations, which take the following form:[3]

```
(relation ⟨name⟩ (⟨arg1⟩ ⟨arg2⟩ . . . ⟨argk⟩)
    (type ⟨arg1⟩ ⟨datatype⟩)
    (type ⟨arg2⟩ ⟨datatype⟩)
    . . .
    (type ⟨argk⟩ ⟨datatype⟩)
)
```

A ⟨datatype⟩ is either *integer, integer range, atom, list, flavor, enumerated set*, or a *user-defined* type checking function (written in Lisp). If the type field of an argument is omitted, ORBS gives the argument type *entity*, which will match any value.

Because of our interactive, incremental development goal, the typing machinery does not cause an interruption in processing. Instead, if an undeclared relation is used, a warning is given. If a relation is used that

---

[2] *Flavors* add an object-oriented capability to Lisp. (The interested reader should see Weinreb & Moon, 1981.)

[3] There are actually several other types of information that can be associated with a relation other than what we show here, e.g., key, count, print-form, who-can-add, who-can-delete.

disagrees with its declaration, a warning is given. Finally, the system gives a warning if pattern clauses will not unify according to type. Type unification is determined by attaching the associated type with each pattern variable, and then looking for consistent usage. As an example, if -x is used in two places, one an integer argument and one a list argument, we know that no value can be bound to -x that will meet both type requirements; i.e., its types cannot be unified.

To add facts to the data base, the fact statement is used:

```
(fact location susan office)
(fact actions (go stop continue))
(fact hit ^(make-instance person . . .)
          ^(make-instance person . . .))
```

As can be seen above, the fact function expects its arguments to be literal unless preceded by a hat (^).

3.2. Rules

An ORBS rule is made up of zero or more LHS (Left Hand Side) pattern clauses, zero or more Lisp test predicates, one or more RHS action statements, and zero or more rule attributes. An example rule is given below that determines whether a player should play the queen of spades on a trick in the card game Hearts. We assume that the relations *player*, *owns-card*, *suit-to-follow*, and *choice* have been previously declared, and that -p will be bound to a flavor instance (as specified in the declaration of the *player* relation).

```
(defrule play-the-queen
     (player -p)
     (owns-card -p spade queen)
     (suit-to-follow-on-trick -s)        ;This and the not-clause
                                          determine
     (~(owns-card -p -s -))              ;whether player -p can slough a
                                          card.
 test
     (((send -p ':current-points) 13)   ;A naïve test for shooting the
                                          moon.
 -->
     (fact choice -p spade queen)        ;Choice is to play queen of
                                          spades.
 :::
     (status: 'on)
     (author: 'fickas))
```

Above, the LHS consists of four clauses, the last of which is a not-clause, designated be a tilde (~). A not-clause will block a match if any fact matches its pattern. Pattern variables in a clause will match any object (subject to unification); they are distinguished from literals by a prepended hyphen.

The (optional) keyword *test* marks the beginning of the filtering predicates. In this case, we assume that -p has been bound to a player object. Each Lisp predicate is evaluated in turn (there is only one such predicate in the example above). If a nil is returned by any predicate, the match fails. Note the use of message passing in the test predicate to retrieve a slot-value of a player, in this case *current-points*. This is typical programming style in ORBS: bind flavor instances in the clauses, and examine their slot-values in the test. Practical use of ORBS has led us to believe that this separation is less useful than one that allows direct access to slot-values within a clause; we are currently attempting to define a syntax that will allow such access. While we still believe that it is useful, in general, to separate out Lisp predicates from clauses, it seems clear that some inclusion of Lisp-like code can profitably be used within clauses. This argument over separation of concerns is discussed more fully by Fickas (1985).

The "--)" marks the beginning of the RHS (Right Hand Side) actions. Each action is a lisp expression. Actions are evaluated sequentially, and for their side-effects. In the above example, the RHS adds a fact to the data base.

The ":::" marks the beginning of rule attributes. There are predefined system attributes, such as status and author. The user may also define new attributes to suit the problem domain. An attribute value may be read or written at any time during program execution.

3.3. Control Strategies

There are at least four decision points that arise in a rule-based system such as ORBS: rule selection, rule matching, conflict resolution, rule execution. We define a control strategy to be a means of choosing among alternatives at a decision point.

Different applications may require different control strategies to determine what rules to select for matching, how to match those rules against the data base, how to resolve conflicts among the rules, and how to handle the execution of the rules chosen. Further, these strategies may need to be changed to meet new conditions during program execution; i.e., the same application program may need more than one selection, matching, resolution, or execution strategy as it runs. Existing rule-based systems generally provide hard-wire strategies for each of these decision points; the user cannot change them, nor can they be changed dynamically. While it is sometimes possible to implement different control strategies using a fixed strategy by clever encoding of control knowledge in domain knowledge terms, the resulting system is cumbersome to develop, debug, and maintain. In general, an entirely new control model must be simulated atop the old. Though some languages make this simulation process easier than others, we argue that this is the wrong approach.

Instead, we have attempted to explicate the implicit decision points in a rule-based system, and to make them accessible to and modifiable by the user or application program. As shown below, ORBS follows a rule-gathering/match/resolve-conflict/execute cycle. Each step in this cycle can be tailored to fit the application at hand.

1. Gather all of the rules together that will participate in this cycle. Rules are selected according to a user-defined selection strategy. For instance, selection may be on a rule set, or on some particular rule attribute. The default strategy is to select all rules that have status "on."

2. Match each rule generated from the previous step against the data base. For a single rule, separate *activations* are created for each different match. An activation is the record of data base tuple to LHS clause bindings. Activations generated from this step are collectively known as the *conflict set.*

    The matching process itself is determined by a user-defined matching strategy. For instance, the user can specify that certain LHS clauses are supportive, and should not be taken into consideration when determining match success or failure, or that the test predicates should be ignored for now (possibly for efficiency sake). The default strategy is for all clauses and test predicates to participate in matching.

3. The conflict set[4] is passed to a user-defined conflict resolution strategy. This strategy prunes and orders activations according to domain specific constraints and heuristics. The default conflict resolution strategy, MANUAL, is discussed further in subsequent paragraphs.

    The outcome of this step is an *execution set* containing zero or more activations to be executed.

4. The execution set is passed through a user-defined execution strategy. The default strategy is simply to execute the RHS actions of

---

[4] This is a historical name that is no longer entirely accurate. Specifically, in ORBS there need not exist any conflict within the set: All activations may be executable on the current cycle.

each activation in the execution set in the order given. However, this can be overridden by a strategy more suited to the problem domain. For instance, activations can be reordered to meet dependency constraints. It is also here that the system can be halted, for example in the case of an empty execution set (the default is to keep cycling until a specific halt is called for by a RHS action or the user at a breakpoint; in Fickas and Novick (1985) we argue why this default seems more appropriate than the traditional halt-on-empty-conflict strategy).

5. The cycle repeats until explicitly halted by either a RHS action, as part of the execution strategy, or by the user.

As can be seen, each step in the cycle involves a user-defined strategy. Each such strategy has a default that can be overridden by installing a new strategy. Installation can come on any cycle, i.e., any strategy can change at the beginning of any cycle. Installation of a new strategy can be brought about by the user at a break point, by a RHS action during execution, or even by a currently installed strategy replacing itself or another strategy.

Although each strategy has different concerns, all have been designed to have a uniform appearance to the user, i.e., a directed acyclic graph with control functions as nodes. We will describe one specific strategy, that of conflict resolution in step 3, in more detail, and note the similarities in the rule selection, matching and execution strategies along the way.

The user defines a conflict resolution strategy by piecing together *scheduling functions*.[5] The conflict resolution strategy is used to choose among competing solutions or tasks, and consists of a directed acyclic graph with scheduling functions as nodes. Each function is a packaged Lisp procedure. The strategy is carried out by passing the conflict set along arcs and through nodes. Each scheduling function takes as input a set S of rule activations, and returns none, some or all of S. Generally, a function either removes or orders one or more activations. The new set is in turn passed along arcs to other scheduling functions. The process completes when the last scheduling function (as designated by the user) returns zero or more activations for execution. In Figure 2, we see two separate strategies for two separate ORBS systems, both of which are part of some larger application program. The bottom strategy is currently active, and has reached the merge step

---

[5] The other strategies have *selection functions, matching functions,* and *execution functions* as nodes.

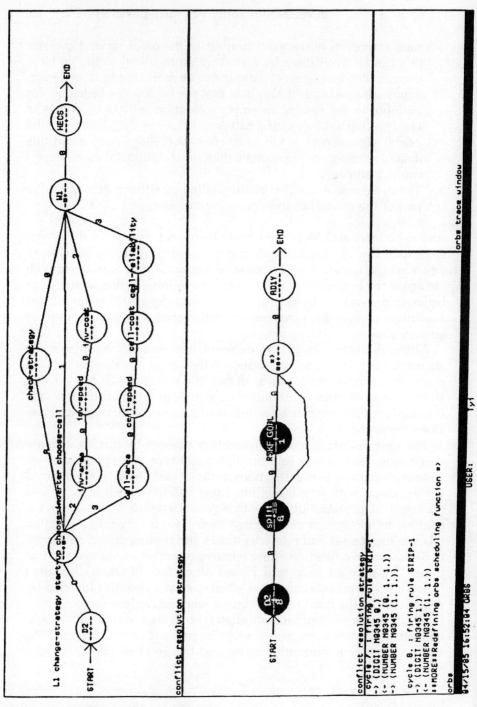

Figure 2. Conflict-resolution Strategies

(denoted by "$\Longrightarrow$)"); a blackened step signifies that the step has been executed. The top strategy is part of a currently suspended ORBS. Note that this strategy sets up separate but parallel lines of analysis. The W1 node coordinates collection of results from each line. The system also catalogs complete control strategies that have been found useful across domains. For instance, both the OPS5 and YAPS strategies are available to the user in precanned form. The function *set-strategy* is used to load a complete strategy, e.g.,

```
(set-strategy 'conflict-resolution 'OPS5)
```

Other control strategies are constructed and loaded in a similar fashion. This ends our introduction to the ORBS language. We now turn to the environment that supports the development of ORBS programs.

4. The ORBS Development Environment

The ORBS environment provides the following components:

- A suite of editors for the various components of the system. Thus, we have a rule editor, a flavor editor, a data-base editor, and a control strategy editor (used to build conflict resolution, rule selection, matching, and execution strategies). The flavor editor and control strategy editor are graphic. For instance, the strategies in Figure 2 were produced by editor commands for building acyclic graphs from both predefined and custom components. The flavor editor, shown in Figure 3, allows a graph to be built from class and instance nodes, and inheritance links.
- A break package that supports incremental development. This will be discussed in more detail below.
- A catalog of useful domain objects that can be melded together to build new programs. This is integrated with the flavor editor to allow the user to peruse the catalog, and splice in pieces that are useful (see Figure 3). Actually identifying new pieces, generalizing them for inclusion in the catalog, and finally placing them in the catalog are all still manual processes.
- In ORBS, a control strategy is user-defined: the user must (1) define a set of functions, and (2) define how those functions are to be combined to form a control strategy, i.e., define the arcs of the graph. ORBS maintains a catalog of scheduling components found useful in previous systems. These components can range from individual functions to larger pieces of control strategies for rule selection, matching, conflict resolution, and execution. The catalog is inte-

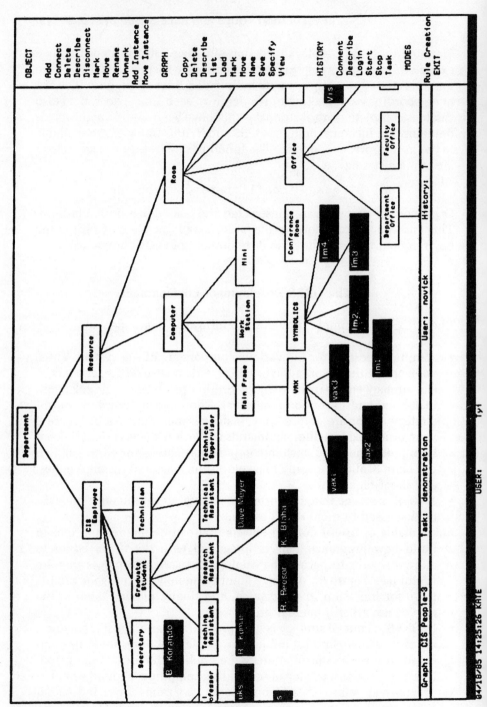

Figure 3. Flavor Editor

138

grated with the control strategy editor to allow the user to peruse the catalog, and splice in pieces that are useful.

We can see how these components work together by following a small example of a programmer building an ORBS program.

4.1. A Development Scenario

Suppose that a user, Jane, wished to build an ORBS program that laid out lab, office, and storage space in a computer science department. Jane's first step would be to identify the components of the problem. One goal of the ORBS environment is to allow an ORBS program to be built by a combination of component reuse and tailoring. By calling in the flavor editor, Jane can begin to define the objects of the domain. The flavor editor has access to a catalog of domains that we have worked on in the past. Assume that Jane finds CS-Dept-World and Circuit-Design-World as two entries in the catalog. The first contains objects (Faculty, Staff, Student, Office) dealing with department life. The second contains, among other things, objects associated with layout (Minimum-Distance, Communication-Link, Area-Requirement). As is typical, we want some from each entry. Using the editor, Jane loads both.

Once loaded, unwanted pieces can be trimmed (e.g., much of the Circuit-Design-World objects), other pieces can be tailored (e.g., Circuit-Design-World layout components mapped to office layout components), and missing pieces can be added (e.g., additional space planning concepts unique to office layout). While our current research effort is aimed at supplying these editing operations at the level at which they are stated above (meld, tailor, trim), the flavor editor currently allows only primitive addition, deletion, and modification actions. Thus it is up to the user to add, delete, rename, and splice objects on an object by object basis.

Once the objects are defined, Jane must define procedural and constraint knowledge in the form of rules. ORBS provides an editor for constructing such rules. The editor is tailored to rule definition. It has a primitive, built-in model of the way rules are constructed and the type of errors that occur when defining rules. Since it appears that rules are rarely written from scratch or in isolation, the editor supports the copying of rules with designated changes. It also allows a user to build his or her relation definitions incrementally in tandem with rule definitions, and thus supports our incremental development goal.

After defining a core set of rules, Jane is ready to test the program. She will use the ORBS break package to do tracing and as a platform from which to patch bugs. The break package allows Jane to set breaks on all ORBS actions, e.g., data-base transactions, matching, rule execution, scheduling. Because this is the first test of her program, Jane will cautiously place a break at the beginning of every cycle, and view various components during execution. She will also turn on undo-history, which tells ORBS to keep an undoable history of all processing. Because maintaining this history tends to lessen execution speed, it is made switchable in ORBS.

Jane is now ready to go except for one major detail: She has yet to define the various control strategies she will need. For most application problems, the system defaults for three of the four strategies—rule selection, matching, execution—will suffice initially. This leaves the conflict resolution strategy. Our experience tells us that this is not the proper time to define this strategy. It is better to watch how the rules interact for several cycles before attempting to translate general conflict resolution goals into concrete scheduling functions. To support this model, the initial conflict resolution strategy consists of a single, pre-defined (i.e., cataloged) scheduling function called MANUAL, which simply presents the entire conflict set to the user, and asks him or her to choose none, some, or all of the activations for execution.[6] MANUAL also allows the user to call a subordinate break, or further inspect the activations in the set.

Jane starts ORBS running, and the system begins to execute the first cycle. The rule selection and matching strategies will complete, and MANUAL will call upon Jane to select activations for execution. Given that this is a first prototype, there likely will be activations in the conflict set that do not belong, and others that do belong will be missing. We will assume that both are true in this scenario.

First, let's assume that rule R1 has been matched unexpectedly. The easy part is asking MANUAL to remove the unwanted activation; a single key stroke will do the job. The harder part is fixing the bug that allowed R1 to match in the first place. The first step will be to reach the break package so that the data base and rules can be inspected. MANUAL allows the user to push to the break package from conflict resolution. One tool that we find is required at this point is a "micro matcher," i.e., a matcher that gives a minute, blow-by-blow account of generating an instantiation. In ORBS, this is implemented as a simulation tool that takes a rule and a subset of the data base as input. The output is a transcript of the system's attempts to match each clause, each not-clause, and each test predicate, along with a summary of

---

[6] As discussed in section 3.3, this default can be overridden by simply loading another strategy. Thus, if the user knows that she wants to use the YAPS strategy, then the set-strategy function is called before the first cycle commences.

match failure for each, and a list of the instantiations generated. After using this and other tools, Jane may discover that R1 is buggy, the data base is buggy, or both.[7] Jane may edit R1 and/or the data base to fix the problem. When satisfied, she pops from the break back to MANUAL.

Let's also assume that an activation of a rule, say R2, should have been produced (i.e., R2 should have matched), but no such activation exists in the conflict set. This is a much harder problem to deal with, at least from the system's viewpoint, than the extraneous appearance of an activation. First, Jane must find why the rule failed to produce an activation. ORBS allows a user to ask why a rule did not fire in cycle k. The answer is the name of the control function that eliminated the rule, e.g., "⟨rule⟩ was eliminated during rule selection by . . .", "⟨rule⟩ was selected, but did not match", "⟨rule⟩ was matched, but eliminated during conflict resolution by . . .". After narrowing the focus to one of the control strategies, other tools can be used to further refine the bug, e.g., the micro matcher discussed in the previous paragraph can be used to detect failure-to-match bugs.

Once the problem is found and repaired, we'd like to be able to force a rematch of R2 so as to include the missing activation in the current conflict set. The approach in ORBS is to provide a general backup/undo facility that allows the state of the system to be returned to some previous cycle, given the setting of the undo-history. Here, Jane wants to back up one cycle (to cycle 0), fix the bug, and then start the matching process again. Using the break package, she does exactly this.

At some point Jane will have repaired all matching bugs for this cycle. She must then determine what activations to let through or throw out given a problem-specific control strategy (residing for now in her head). In our example domain, suppose we may have a rule that places the chairman in the biggest office available, and another rule that attempts to pack as many graduate students as possible into the biggest office available. Suppose further that both have matched, and MANUAL is calling for a decision by Jane. Jane will likely make this decision, based on a number of factors, including rank and amount of space remaining. Whatever choice is made, MANUAL can be used to trim out the losers and finally pass on the winners for execution. The default execution strategy simply invokes RHS actions in the order received.

One execution cycle has now been completed. Before the next cycle begins, the break set previously (break every cycle) will be called. From here Jane can examine the effects produced by the rules that fired. If

---

[7] Section 5.2 discusses the possible problems that can lead to matching bugs.

bugs are detected, rules and data base can be edited. If necessary, she can also use the backup facility to return to an earlier state.

To summarize, we have attempted to build an environment based on a specific set of design goals. We have a particular model of how ORBS rule based programs can most effectively be built, and we have used this to construct development tools that support the model.

After using our environment for an extended time, we found the need for a further set of tools that would require much more knowledge than is currently available in ORBS. The next section discusses our current work to extend the ORBS environment along these lines.

5. The Next Generation of Development Tools

The ORBS environment discussed in the last section is operational, and has been in use over a range of projects for more than 3 years. The experience gained has pointed to further needs. Our current research is tied to meeting these needs, which can be stated as follows:

1. We need machine support in replacing the manual scheduler (i.e., the user) with a problem-specific conflict resolution strategy after the data base and rules have been debugged.
2. We need to capture the rationalization of our rules and relations. Without a picture of the role rules and relations are playing in larger structures, it is difficult to see how better tools can be built.
3. We need to address programming-in-the-large (PITL) issues. We would like a sophisticated version control tool. We would like to be able to partition a problem into semiindependent "modules" and parcel them out to different programmers.
4. We need a better model of how interacting rule-based systems can be effectively used, and how to develop and debug them. Our tools to date (and the development model from which they derive) have been restricted to analyzing and debugging a single ORBS system at a time.

We have done enough work on the first two to be able to report some limited results in the next two sections. For the third, we have done some preliminary work on connecting separate *but complete* ORBS systems together; the context of this work is discussed in Fickas (1985). As discussed in section 3.1, we have also encapsulated ORBS to allow multiple ORBS systems to be extant simultaneously. However, we have not dealt, in general, with the problem of PITL in relation to building a single ORBS system. This problem, and the fourth, support for developing interacting (possibly distributed) ORBS systems, remain open issues.

5.1. A Control Assistant

The use of the MANUAL scheduling function allows domain objects and rules to be defined and debugged before worrying about control knowledge. It requires that the user "simulate" the conflict resolution strategy he or she expects the system to follow eventually.[8] Initially, the manual scheduler forces the user to make all decisions (i.e., to select the activations from the conflict set to be invoked). As time passes, the user may add in scheduling functions, but still remain in the control loop. Eventually, the complete graph will be built, forming a coherent strategy. At this point, the user has been completely removed from the loop.

We have found that it is often difficult for a user, when attempting to build a conflict resolution strategy using MANUAL, to recall each decision made at each cycle. Even with perfect recall, the user is left with mapping abstract strategy onto concrete scheduling functions. In response to these problems, we have been exploring the use of a machine-based assistant that would aid the user in setting up a control strategy. Our long-term goal is for a system that would watch over the user's shoulder as he or she makes control decisions, and build a hypothesis of the control strategy being used. Once confirmed by the user, the assistant would find appropriate scheduling functions in the catalog, and replace MANUAL with the corresponding conflict resolution strategy. We view this problem as a specific instance of the more general problem of concept recognition in the learning field.

The information available to the assistant would be a cycle-by-cycle history of the state of conflict resolution. This would include a snapshot of the data base on each cycle (already kept by ORBS), a snapshot of the conflict set on each cycle, and a history of user control decisions using MANUAL. The assistant will also require knowledge of the type of scheduling functions available to build control strategies.

We are currently working on an assistant that offers help on a simple conflict resolution problem: rules are assumed to have a partial ordering based on a fixed priority (as opposed, for instance, to PROLOG which gives a linear and lexicographical ordering). By watching the user's choices, the assistant discovers the ordering, selects scheduling

---

[8] For the final time we will note that there is no requirement that the user must employ the MANUAL strategy initially; he or she is free to choose a predefined strategy or install a tailor made strategy.

functions that implement it, and replaces MANUAL with the corresponding control strategy. There are two things to note about this simple assistant. First, not a small percentage of control problems seem to be based exactly on the notion of rule priority, hence the assistant can be of real help if it can automate this process. Second, our assistant makes no attempt to represent the reasons why the priorities hold; rules are treated at the level of set elements and the ordering is unvarying. Thus, if priorities change or are computed according to a function on the current state, the assistant will be of no help to us; it cannot discover the underlying rationale for prioritization. To handle this more sophisticated type of control problem will almost certainly require the assistant to have knowledge of the problem domain.[9] As we discuss in the next section, we are working on tying domain knowledge into the rule base for completely separate reasons. However, we believe that this representation of domain knowledge, and its availability to the assistant, will allow us to build more sophisticated control assistants as well.

Finally we note that work by Cohen (1983) and Swartout (1983a) in testing formal specifications might have some relevance here. Their approach is to execute a specification (symbolically) while keeping a trace, and then use a knowledge-based tool to help decipher what happened (e.g., point out interesting events, trim away boring details). If one views the conflict resolution history as such a trace, then a tool that presents the trace in some coherent manner might allow the user to design the right strategy more easily. While this approach moves away from the automation provided by the assistant described earlier, it may be more realistic to rely on the user to generate the strategy given that the key information has been extracted from the heap of raw data, and presented in an understandable fashion.

5.2. Beyond Rules and Relations

Others have argued that rules alone provide a weak representation for *explanation* (Clancey, 1983; Swartout, 1983b). We have come to regard unadorned rules (and relations) as weak from a *development* viewpoint as well. We have come to this view by paying attention to the bugs that crop up in our ORBS programs, and by dutifully asking ourselves what type of knowledge would be necessary to mechanize their discovery and eradication. Many of the bugs succumb to syntactical analysis. However, others require more extensive knowledge. It is this latter set

---

[9] As an exception, the BB1 project is attempting to use a structured, but domain independent model of control to learn control heuristics [18].

that we are interested in. Listed below is the specific set we are currently working with.[10]

> A LHS clause may be syntactically correct, but semantically incor-
> rect. Thus, the wrong relation may be used, a literal value may
> be wrong, the wrong pattern variable may be used.
>
> A test predicate may be wrong, e.g., too lenient, too strong, plain
> wrong.
>
> The LHS may contain too many clauses, i.e., be too restrictive.
>
> The LHS may contain too few clauses, i.e., be too general.
>
> There may be too many test predicates, i.e., too restrictive.
>
> There may be too few test predicates, i.e., too general.
>
> The LHS may contain a pattern variable where a literal should be,
> i.e., be too general.
>
> The LHS may contain a literal where a pattern variable should be,
> i.e., be too restrictive.
>
> An existing rule does not belong (e.g., it's redundant, irrelevant,
> wrong).
>
> A rule may be missing altogether.
>
> An existing fact does not belong (e.g., it's redundant, irrelevant,
> wrong).
>
> A fact may be missing from the data base.

To help detect and correct these bugs will require tools with access to
much more information than that which is now available in ORBS. For
instance, it is clear that relations are used to represent complex, domain-specific structures. We are not capturing these structures in any
way that is useful to our tools. Hearsay III, also based on a relational
representation, takes notice that relations are used to model aggregate
structures, and it is these structures that we want to debug. Hence,
Hearsay III provides (1) specially defined relations to build aggregates,
and (2) analysis routines to verify that these aggregate structures meet
system-defined and user-defined constraints.[11]

The same problem arises in rules as primitive objects: we lack a
model of our rules in larger terms. For instance, a rule could be one

---

[10] The reader will note that the set does not include control errors. While we would
like to extend our control assistant to include a debugging package, we now have nothing
in the way of a control debugger, beyond the graphical editor and animator discussed in
section 4.

[11] Unfortunately, the Hearsay III structuring constructs are difficult to build and
debug, and fail to meet our design goals of a fast prototyping environment that supports
incremental development.

member of a "decision set," i.e., a collection of mutually exclusive rules for making a single decision. A rule could be part of some higher-level computational entity such as a loop. We might expect a loop to have a looping component (a generator), a body, and a halting condition. One or more rules could fill each of these components. A rule could be part of a "task set," i.e., a collection of rules, all of which must be executed. Typically there is a partial ordering associated with such a set. Various mutations and combinations of each of the above seem possible as well.

We thus came to believe that a better development environment for ORBS must rest on a richer representation than that afforded by our rules and relations alone. We have found two different viewpoints useful in tackling this problem. The first might be called the software engineering viewpoint. It comes from viewing rule-based languages in the same way we view Lisp, Fortran, and ADA, i.e., as a target language for building systems. With this view, we can use ideas from modern development environments that encompass specification, design, and even testing tools. Thus, we may be able to tie rules and relations to the specification of domain objects and operations, and record the design steps that produced them.

The second viewpoint might be called the Expert System viewpoint. Clancey (1983) and Swartout (1983), among others, have argued that we need a knowledge representation in expert systems that can tie components in running programs to the domain concepts and design steps from which they sprung. In Swartout's work, this means using various languages for different jobs, i.e., a language (NIKL [Kaczmarek, Bates, & Robins, 1986]) for representing domain concepts, a problem-solving language for creating a rationalization and building the system, and finally Lisp as the target language. In a similar fashion, Clancey argues for a four-tier representation that can produce levels of explanation.

Although they address different goals, both viewpoints argue for a formal representation of specifications or domain concepts, and a formal representation of the design process that maps specification to target program. We have taken this as the starting point of a system that assists a user in incrementally mapping from a problem specification to an ORBS program. We are pursuing this work along two fronts. First, we are experimenting with the use of an existing specification language, Gist (London, et al.) as our problem description language. We have built a small set of tools that help a user transform a Gist specification into an ORBS program. We have had some success with this approach, although too much of the process remains unmechanized, and hence unanalyzable. Progress here seems linked to progress in the transformational implementation field in general (Balzer gives a good

overview of the problems in the field in (Balzer, 1985), and also discusses attempts to use AP5 (Cohen, 1985), a language that has some
similarity to ORBS, as the target for a transformational style development).

Our second approach has been to define a more limited, domain-
specific problem description language from which we can hope to automate design and code generation. Like Swartout's EXPERT system, we
use a language (again NIKL [Kaczmarek, Bates, & Robins, 1986]) ror
representing the objects and operations in a domain. The domain we
have chosen is resource management. Particular problems that we have
looked at in this domain include course registration, library management, conference organization, and floor layout in an academic department. Our goal is to transform such problem descriptions automatically
into ORBS components (relations, flavors, rules, control strategy). Our
efforts thus far have focused on the definition of the problem description language and an editor that allows a user to build a description
graphically. Figure 4 shows a snapshot of the editor, called OZ, while
building a description of a course registration system.[12] Once this work
is completed, our next task is the construction of a transformation
system from problem description to rule-based program. We note that
our approach here is similar to that of Barstow's PHI-NIX system (1985)
and Irvine's DRACO system (Neighbors, 1984), both of which attempt
to use domain specific components (e.g., languages, design rules) to
automate software development.

5.3. A Model of Typicality

Davis (1982) describes an extension to the rule representation of
MYCINthat includes *rule models*. Each rule in Davis's system is associated with a single-rule model. Each model is indexed according to a
particular conclusion (relation), and includes statistics on all rules that
assert that conclusion. The main contribution is to provide a measure
of typicality over this rule set, e.g., "most rules that conclude C in their
RHS reference property P in their LHS." In this way, the system can
check additions or modifications to rules that conclude C, and warn the
user if a new or modified rule does not match the statistical norm, e.g.,
contain a reference to P.

We also believe some notion of typicality is important in developing
rule-based systems. While Davis's rule models are based on domain

---

[11] OZ attempts to formalize some of the design notions introduced by both Goldman
(1983) and Feather (1985). For the purposes of this paper, it can be viewed as a development editor supporting systems analysis using Data Flow Diagrams (Page–Jones, 1980).

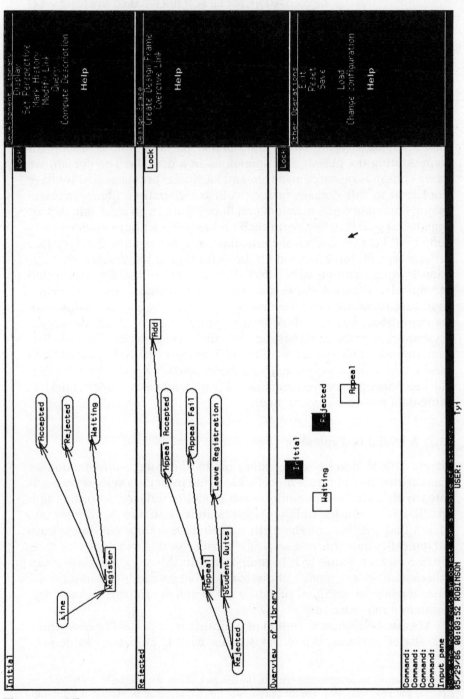

Figure 4. OZ

independent, syntactical evidence, and are targeted at rules, we are attempting to build a model of typicality at the domain level, and make it available to a problem description critic. As with Davis's system, this critic would warn the user of nontypical components. However, the explanation takes the form of domain-specific information, e.g. "You have introduced classes of students (e.g., major, senior, grad) without defining an ordering on them. Most registration systems give priority to one group over another." This critic is part of a more ambitious effort to build an assistant to a software systems analyst. It is based on having a rich model of a specific domain, a model that we hope to exploit in our rule-base programming environment as well. (For a detailed description of the work see Fickas, 1987.)

6. Summary

We have presented an environment for building rule-based systems. The environment is based on a development model that we have tried to make explicit in the chapter. Both our language and environment are directed toward the application programmer. In this vein, we share many of the traditional programming environment concerns, but must address them in a nontraditional programming paradigm. Using a scenario, we have attempted to show how the various tools in the environment meet our development goals.

After using the system for some time, we found a need for more sophisticated development tools. Our two major efforts in this area are (1) building a control assistant, and (2) capturing more of the design process. For the first, we have built a successful, but limited, program that will aid a user in formalizing a partial ordering on a rule set. For the second, we have experimented with mapping from a specification or requirements language to a rule-based program. Again, we have had limited success. In both efforts it appears that much hard work lies ahead before industrial-grade tools become part of our environment.

The ORBS language and environment is in use on Vaxen, Symbolics, and Tektronix work stations, all using a Common Lisp implementation.

Acknowledgments

Many people have contributed to the ORBS project. One valuable group has been the users willing to try the system and diligently report on its good and bad points. In some sense, they have been the designers of the system; it is their comments that have led to major changes in the language and environment. Others have spent long hard hours coding and maintaining the system. Others still have built experimental versions for testing and evaluation. We would be exaggerating only slightly to include all of the CIS graduate students at the University of Oregon over the last 3 years as contributors to the system. We would like to thank them collectively for their interest and effort. We also thank Bill Bregar of the Tektronix AI Lab for his participation and support in the project, and the National Science Foundation, Tektronix, the University of Oregon and Oregon State University for their funding of the work.

References

Allen, E. (1983). *YAPS: Yet another production system* (Tech. Rep.), Computer Science Department, University of Maryland.

Balzer, R. (1985). A 15-year perspective on automatic programming. *IEEE Transactions on Software Engineering, 11*(11).

Barstow, D. (1985). Domain-specific automatic programming. *IEEE Transactions on Software Engineering 11*(11).

Buchanan, B., & Duda, R. (1983). Principles of rule-based expert systems. In M. Yovits (Ed.), *Advances in computers.* New York: Academic Press.

Clancey, W. (1983). The epistemology of a rule-based expert system: A framework for explanation. *Artificial Intelligence 20*(3).

Cohen, D. (1985). *AP5 Manual,* Information Sciences Institute, Marina Del Rey, CA.

Cohen, D. (1983). Symbolic execution of the Gist specification language. *Proceedings of the 8th International Conference on AI.*

Davis, R. (1982). Applications of meta level knowledge to the construction, maintenance, and use of large knowledge bases. In R. Davis & D. Lenant (Eds.), *Knowledge-based systems in artificial intelligence.* New York, McGraw–Hill.

Dietterich, T., & Michalski, R. (1983). A Comparative Review of Selected Methods for Learning from Examples. In R. Michalski, J. Carbonell, & T. Mitchell (Eds.), *Machine Learning.* Tioga Press.

Erman, L., London, P., & Fickas, S. (1981). The design and example use of Hearsay III. *Seventh International Joint Conference on AI,* Vancouver.

Fain, J., Gorlin, D., Hayes–Roth, F., Rosenschein, S., Sowizral, H., Waterman, D. (1981). The ROSIE Language Reference Manual, Rand Note N-1647.

Feather, M. (1985). Language support for the specification and development of composite systems, Information Sciences Institute, Marina Del Ray, CA.

Fickas, S. (1985). Design Issues in a Rule Based System, In *ACM Symposium on Programming Languages and Programming Environments,* Seattle.

Fickas, S. (1987). Automating Analysis: An Example. In *Proceedings of the 4th International Conference on Software Specification and Design,* Monterey, CA., April.

Fickas, S., & Novick, D. (1985). Control in rule based systems: relaxing restrictive assumptions, In *5th International Conference on Expert Systems and Their Applications.*

Fickas, S., Novick, D., & Reesor, R. (1985). An environment for building rule based systems, In *3rd Annual Conference on Intelligent Systems and Machines.*

Forgy, C. (1981). OPS5 User's Manual, Tech Report, Computer Science Dept., CMU.

Goldman, N. (1983). Three Dimensions of Design, In *Proceedings of the Third Annual National Conference on Artificial Intelligence,* AAAI, Washington, D.C.

Hayes–Roth, B., & Hewett, M. (1985). *Learning Control Heuristics in BB1,* STAN-CS-85-1036, Department of Computer Science, Stanford University.

Kaczmarek, T., Bates, R., & Robins, G. (1986). Recent Developments in NIKL, In *Proceedings of AAAI-86,* Philadelphia.

London, P., & Feather, M. (1982). Implementing specification freedoms, *Science of Computer Programming,* No. 2.

LOOPS Reference Manual, (1983) Xerox PARC, Palo Alto, CA.

Neighbors, J. (1984). The DRACO approach to constructing software form reusable components. *IEEE Transactions on Software Engineering,* 10(9).

Page–Jones, M. (1980). *The Practical Guide to Structured Systems Design.* Yourdon Press.

Swartout, W. (1983a). The Gist behavior explainer. *Proceedings of the National Conference on AI.*

Swartout, W. (1983b). XPLAIN: A system for creating and explaining expert consulting programs. *Artificial Intelligence,* 21(3).

Van Melle, W. (1981). *EMYCIN: A domain-independent system that aids in constructing knowledge-based Consultation Programs.* Pergamon–Infotech, New York.

Weinreb, D., & Moon, D. (1981). Objects, Message Passing, and Flavors, *Lisp Machine Manual,* Ch. 20. Symbolics, Inc.

EIGHT

Using a Knowledge Base to Drive an Expert System Interface with a Natural Language Component

Philip J. Hayes

Carnegie Group, Inc.
Pittsburgh

Abstract

Expert systems are typically driven by an extensive knowledge base specific to the domain and task of the system. This knowledge base contains much of the information needed to provide an effective end user interface to the expert system. This chapter presents a style of knowledge base organization suitable for driving interfaces to a broad class of knowledge-based systems. It also describes an interface support framework that allows direct-manipulation interfaces with an optional natural language component to be driven from a knowledge base organized in such a fashion. The description focuses particularly on issues involved in integrating the natural language component with the direct manipulation component. The chapter also examines the question of whether a knowledge base organized for inference purposes might typically satisfy the criteria established for driving the knowledge base. It concludes that this is generally not the case, and recommends separate, but linked, knowledge base representations for interface and inferencing purposes.

1. Introduction

Expert systems are typically driven by an extensive knowledge base specific to the domain and task of the system. The primary use of this knowledge is to put the expertise into the expert system, i.e. to drive the inferential mechanisms of the expert system to perform the diagnosis, scheduling, simulation, or whatever other task the system is expert in. However, the knowledge can also be useful in driving the interaction between the system and its user. For instance, if a knowledge-based system needs to display a graphical representation of a complicated situation it is working with, all the structural and current state information it needs is probably already in the knowledge base. Again, if natural language is being used, the system may be able to employ a description of the current task state contained in its knowledge base to resolve a pronoun reference or an ambiguity.

This chapter examines some of the issues involved in driving the interaction with a knowledge-based system directly from its knowledge base. The chapter concentrates on the interaction of such systems with their end users, but many of the conclusions may also be applicable to interaction with domain experts during knowledge acquisition. First, we describe a style of knowledge base organization that can be used to drive a user interface to an expert system. Knowledge bases organized in this way can be used to drive graphically oriented direct manipulation interfaces with an optional integrated natural language component. We look at issues in driving both the direct manipulation and the natural language parts of the interaction, but concentrate particularly on the natural language component and its integration with the direct manipulation component. The result is a framework currently under development[1] at Carnegie Group for creating interfaces to knowledge-based systems. This interface support framework can be seen as a kind of User Interface Management System (UIMS). UIMSs are currently a major research topic in the field of computer-human interaction as a whole (Hayes, Szekely, & Lerner, 1985; Jacob, 1984; Mark, 1981; Tanner & Buxton, 1983; Wasserman & Shewmake, 1984; Yunten & Hartson, 1984).

The style of interface and knowledge base organization we discuss is of wide applicability to knowledge-based systems. It is particularly well suited to systems for planning, scheduling, or simulation, but less well suited to systems for diagnosis. We attempt to characterize more generally the kind of system to which the style is applicable.

In addition to driving a user interface, the knowledge base of an expert system must also support the system's inferencing needs. The chapter goes on to look at some problems that can arise from the differing demands placed on knowledge representation by interfaces and

---

[1] The framework is still at the design stage. Nothing in what follows should be interpreted as a commitment to nor an announcement of specific product enhancements by Carnegie Group Inc.

underlying inference methods. If the needs of the underlying inference methods are not met by the level of representation required to drive the user interface, then it suggests that two separate, but coordinated, representations are indicated. The chapter ends by discussing ways in which the coordination can be accomplished.

2. Knowledge Base Organization to Drive an Interface

This section describes a style of knowledge base organization. This style of organization is required by the interface support framework that we are developing for driving integrated graphical and natural language interfaces to a class of expert systems from their knowledge bases. The defining characteristic of this class of expert systems is that they support the user in the exploration and modification of a simulated world. The internal coherence and consistency of the world in the face of changes by the user (or other external inputs) is maintained by the system. Examples of such systems include knowledge-based simulation, planning, or scheduling systems (e.g., Fox et al., 1983; Sathi, Morton, & Roth, 1985). Diagnosis systems in the tradition of MYCIN (Shortliffe, 1976) with their emphasis on directed dialogue do not fit this model as well.

This class of expert systems is further defined and discussed by Hayes (1987). That paper views the interfaces concerned as generalizations of numerical spreadsheets because they allow their users to make alterations to the simulated world and immediately see the consequences of their actions. With suitable low-level interaction details the interfaces can thus also be cast naturally as direct manipulation interfaces (Hutchins, Hollan, & Norman, 1986; Shneiderman, 1981). Our interface framework allows the interfaces to operate both through direct manipulation and through natural language interaction.

In addition to supporting the mechanics of these kinds of interaction, the style of knowledge base organization required by our framework also incorporates a model of the domain. Such a domain model is in any case required to support the world simulation mentioned above. For the interaction to feel natural to the user, this model should be the same as his own mental model of the domain (Norman, 1986). Section 6 discusses potential conflicts between the user's and system's requirements on the domain model.

The style of knowledge base organization required by our interface support framework can be expressed as a joint set of requirements on the task and knowledge base.

- The user's mental model of the task domain is oriented around a collection of entities and relationships;
- The knowledge base contains schemas (or frames) for each entity and relationship in the user's model;
- The user's model has a notion of "current state" which can be modified by user actions or domain events across time;
- The state is represented by the entities in the user's model, together with their relations to other entities and their attributes;
- There is a mapping from the domain entities into one or more visual representations (for display in a graphical interface);
- There is a mapping of relations into visible links between the entities they relate and/or into relative positions of the entities on the display;
- There are general facilities for interrogating/altering the current state of the system by examining/editing the attributes of the displayed entities—these facilities have a strong direct manipulation flavor, based around property sheet editing (Smith et al., 1982);

In addition, if the interface is to have a natural language component, the requirements also include

- A domain-specific caseframe grammar (see Section 4.1) that provides syntactic and semantic information about the language a user would employ in talking about the domain, and thus allows analysis of natural language input from the user about the domain;
- A set of mappings from the resulting linguistic analysis of natural language input into schemas representing the underlying domain objects.

To make this abstract set of requirements more concrete, let us look at some example domains that fit the requirements and examine the appearance and behavior of interfaces in those domains that can be supported from our framework.

Consider a factory simulation system for a flexible manufacturing system. The domain entities from a user's point of view include the machines available to perform operations (either a fixed set of them if the goal is to simulate an existing factory or a set of machine types with a variable number of instances if the goal is to design a new factory), plus the orders that circulate around the machines, plus perhaps a more abstract set of operations that must be done to the orders (but whose mapping onto machines is not one to one). Important relations in this domain from the user's point of view are the physical proximity of machines, plus the possibility and means for transporting orders

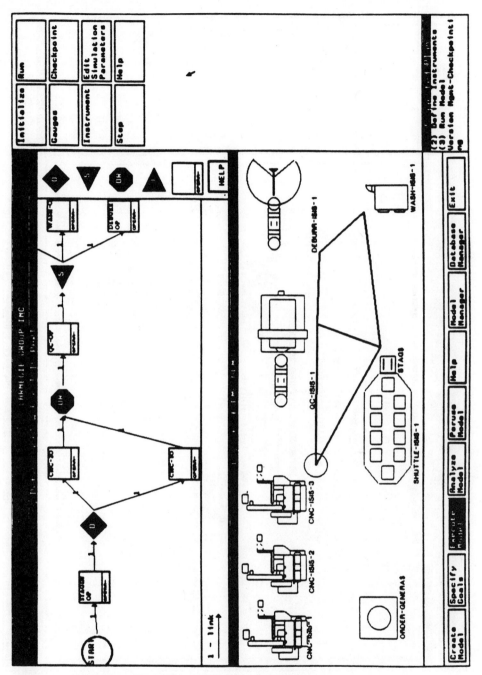

Figure 1.   Snapshot of Interface to Factory Simulation System

157

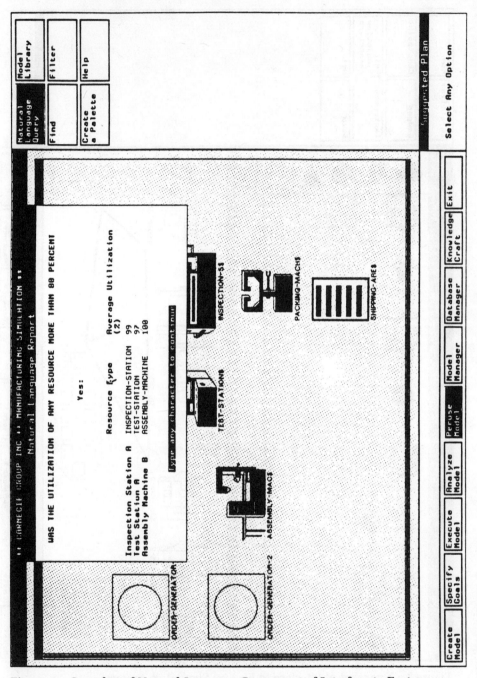

Figure 2. Snapshot of Natural Language Component of Interface to Factory Simulation System

between machines, the association of queues of orders with machines, the sequencing relations between operations to achieve the processing of given orders, and the mapping from operations to the machines that realize them.

A snapshot of the kind of interface to such a system that our framework could support is shown in Figure 1. The figure shows an actual interface to a prototype factory simulation system currently under development at Carnegie Group. The interface was not developed using the interface support framework described in this chapter. However, it has served as the basis of many of the ideas that appear in the framework and is a prime example of the kind of interface whose development would be much easier through the framework.

The lower left window in Figure 1 shows a set of specific machines. Their screen position shows their physical proximity and graphical links between them show the ways in which orders can flow between them. A second window shows the operation flow for a specific order or set of orders. The mapping from operations to machines is not visible. The elements of the state of the simulation not visible in this display are available for inspection and editing on property sheets associated with the icons representing the various entities. For instance, each machine icon has an associated property sheet containing fields for such information as next scheduled maintenance time, mean uptime between failures average queue length over a given period, etc., while the property sheet of an operation icon contains references to which machine or machines that operation is currently assigned, and what kinds of machines are capable of performing that operation.

A direct manipulation interface is highly appropriate for examining/editing information which can conveniently be distributed in this manner, and for laying out such graphical interfaces initially. However, certain queries or commands are expressed much better in propositional form, and in such circumstances, a natural language component of the interface is appropriate. As Figure 2 shows, this component can be provided through a separate window in which a natural language dialogue takes place. Again, the figure is a snapshot of a real interface that was not developed through the interface support framework described in this chapter, but which was influential in the design of the framework and could be supported by the framework. The figure shows an example of the kind of query for which a propositional form of interaction is appropriate ("Was the utilization of any resource [i.e. machine] more than 80%?"). This information could be determined by examining the property sheet of each machine individually. However, by expressing the question propositionally, the search involved can be taken over by the machine, rather than being left to the user. As we will see in Section 4, a natural language dialogue of this kind can be integrated with the graphical component of the interaction by allowing the user to point to specific machines, rather than typing in their names ("Can this machine ⟨click⟩ be used to replace this one ⟨click⟩?"); by interpreting descriptions with respect to the visual context ("the milling machine" means the one currently shown on the screen); and by using the display to provide feedback indicating the system's understanding of the natural language input.

The overall feel of the kind of interface supported by the task and knowledge base requirements outlined in this section is intended to be one of a conversation around a blackboard, with natural language input mixed with pointing. However, the blackboard itself is active and can rearrange and change itself in response to direct manipulation input. The following two sections give some details of the way our interface support framework actually drives such interfaces given a knowledge base organized in the way outlined above. The two sections deal with the areas of direct manipulation and natural language interaction respectively. The details provided for natural language interaction are considerably more complete than those provided for interaction by direct manipulation.

3. Driving a Direct Manipulation Interface from a Knowledge Base

To drive a direct manipulation interface from the kind of knowledge base outlined above, one needs facilities to display the schema-based representations of domain entities and relations plus facilities for the user to examine and edit the attributes of such entities and relations and the layout and appearance of their graphical representations. Our facilities in this area will be built on top of Knowledge Craft™, Carnegie Group's knowledge-engineering tool.

Knowledge Craft provides an excellent base for such developments. It already contains all the features necessary to build the underlying knowledge-based system, plus substantial existing facilities for display of items from the knowledge base. In particular, it is organized around a schema-based knowledge representation language, called CRL™, with powerful facilities for default reasoning through a programmer-controllable inheritance mechanism. CRL is fully integrated with OPS and Prolog-like languages for inferential reasoning. Knowledge Craft's graphics system allows graphical representations of items from the underlying konwledge base to be displayed on a conceptually infinite canvas, which can then be displayed to the user through one or more windows. Each such view of the canvas can be transformed by scaling and rotation with respect to arbitrary axes. Some graphical representations of entities are editable. Changes made to such representations are reflected in the underlying knowledge base.

The extensions to current Knowledge Craft facilities needed for our interface support framework include:

- **Automatic selection of display format appropriate to detail level:** The framework will provide ways of specifying multiple display formats for a domain entity, appropriate to different levels of detail. The correct format for mapping the entity onto the display canvas will then be automatically selected according to the current zoom level. For instance, a machine shop might be represented as a single icon in a picture of a complete factory, but could be represented as a box, containing several individual machines at a finer level of detail.

- **Coordinate mappings from entities to world display:** For tasks such as geological exploration or communication network management, the domain entities have real positions (and extents) in some coordinate system appropriate to the domain. The framework will provide a convenient method of mapping this position information (which may well be used by the inferential part of the application) into appropriate canvas coordinates.

- **Logical mappings from entities to world display:** In other applications, such as job-shop scheduling, the actual location of objects may be unknown or less important for display purposes than their groupings or other logical positional relationships (such as above, below, left-of, etc.). Such logical positional relationships are often used to denote logical relationships of the entities involved (e.g. left-of could mean that one machine is used before another in a machining process). To support displays of this kind, the framework will map logical positional relationships of this kind into canvas positions for the entities involved in a way appropriate for the current level of detail.

- **Mapping of relations into links:** In addition to mapping relations into relative positions, it may also be appropriate to map some relations, such as a transport relation between two machines, into explicit graphical representations. These graphical links would have the same valency as the underlying relationships they represent. For instance, two machines feeding into a third might result in a three-pronged link.

- **Detail level manipulation:** Once a mapping has been specified from domain entities to canvas, the framework will support the basic operation of displaying a given domain coordinate area or collection of domain entities in a given window area. This will be used by commands available to the end user of the interface to change the area of the application world visible through a window, to change the level of detail visible through a window, and to change the number of windows currently viewing the world.

- **Graphical layout editor:** This will allow the user to specify a domain model from menus of representations of entities and relations. The editor will perform the inverse of the coordinate and logical mappings described above, so that the appropriate relations will be inferred from the links and relative positionings between entities as selected by the user. A user could employ such an editor to construct or alter a factory floor layout by creating or moving machines and transport connections between them.

- **Attribute editor:** This will provide a pop-up property sheet through which the user can view and/or edit attributes of the entities and relations visible on the display. The editor will support pop-up and explicit menus of values for attributes when appropriate. Such an editor could be used to view/edit the attributes of a particular machine or the transport mechanism between two machines in a factory layout. Some of the attributes may affect the appearance of the entities, so this can also be viewed as a secondary way of editing the display.

With the above components of the interface support framework in place, the implementer of a knowledge-based application satisfying the knowledge base organizational requirements described in Section 2 will only need to specify the graphical representations, coordinate or logical mappings, and the set of entities currently making up the domain world. The interface framework will be able to use this information to provide a direct manipulation interface to the simulated world thus defined. In this way, the interface framework can be viewed as a user interface management system for the appropriate class of knowledge-based applications.

4. Adding a Natural Language Interface

While direct manipulation interfaces are highly effective when appropriate, there are some circumstances when they are not appropriate and a more propositional form of interaction, such as through natural language, is needed. In particular, direct manipulation interfaces are less convenient:

- When there is a large range of options to choose between, especially when the options can be composed in a combinatorially explosive kind of way;
- When there is no convenient way to distribute the information in a two-dimensional space;
- When a suitable spatial distribution exists, but the resulting space of information is so large that only a small fraction of it can be presented to the user at any one time;
- When the user is looking for information that is distributed across several spatially distinct items, so that retrieval of the information by direct manipulation would require iterative examination of each of the relevant interface components.

These conditions are not true for most interactive situations, so we expect natural language interaction to be a secondary mode of interaction for most interfaces developed using our interface support framework. However, it can provide important added functionality in those circumstances where it is appropriate.

Formal command languages are a more common method than natural language of propositionally specifying commands or queries to computers. However, natural language has significant advantages over command languages in terms of learnability and expressiveness. Its disadvantages, including computational expense and potential ambiguity, are likely to be less troublesome in the context of a knowledge-based system than in a more conventional architecture. In particular, the knowledge already in the knowledge base can be used to help resolve many of the ambiguities that might otherwise arise. A secondary disadvantage of natural language is its relative verbosity and the correspondingly greater number of keystrokes it requires compared with typical command languages. For this reason, expert users may prefer command languages over natural language. However, most knowledge-based systems of the kind we are discussing are targeted at users who are not computer experts, so natural language remains the preferred form of propositional interaction for our interface support framework.

The natural language capability of our interface framework is based on Carnegie Group's existing Language Craft™ product. Language Craft is an environment for developing natural language interfaces to a wide variety of application systems. The interfaces it produces are robust in the face of user errors (an important characteristic when dealing with spontaneously generated dialogue). Language Craft also provides ways to incorporate various methods of resolving communication problems into its interfaces. For instance, it can generate paraphrases of its understanding of an input, and these paraphrases can be used as confirming feedback. This paraphrase facility can also be used in interactive resolution of inputs it finds ambiguous, by asking the user to select between paraphrases of the alternatives. Language Craft does not currently contain all the facilities necessary to drive interfaces directly from a knowledge base. In the remainder of this section, we briefly describe how Language Craft operates. We then cover in more detail some of the features necessary to drive a Language Craft-based interface from a knowledge base so that it integrates well with a direct-manipulation interface driven from the same knowledge base.

4.1. Current Language Craft Operation

Language Craft interfaces derive their robustness from Language Craft's parsing technique: semantic caseframe instantiation. Semantic caseframe instantiation is a technique for parsing natural language in a semantically well-defined domain, such as a command or query interface to a software system, a data-base manager, a factory simulation system, or other interfaces to specific software systems. The grammar defining a Language Craft interface is organized around definitions, called caseframes, of the objects and operations relevant to the application domain. The grammar writer constructs caseframes to specify the structure of the domain objects and operations, the words and phrases used to refer to them, and the grammatical roles of these words and phrases. All the syntactic and morphological knowledge necessary to recognize an end user's input is supplied automatically by Language Craft. For instance, the grammar for a Language Craft interface to a meeting scheduling application might contain caseframes for meetings, rooms, meeting scheduling actions, and room reservation actions. These objects and actions might have components (or *cases*) as follows:

```
meeting
    participants (list of employees)
    start-time (a time)
    end-time (a time)
    meeting-date (a date)
    meeting-room (a room)
room
    room-number (an integer)
    room-name (an employee - occupant if room is an
    office)
schedule
    meeting-to-schedule (a meeting)
    scheduler (an employee)
```

```
reserve
  room-to-reserve (a room)
  reserver (an employee)
  meeting-in-room (a meeting - the one to be held in
  the reserved room)
```

In addition to structural information of this kind, a grammar contains lexical information (e.g. "schedule" or "set up" refers to the scheduling action) and syntactic role information (e.g. meeting is the direct object of schedule).

The robustness of caseframe instantiation derives from the high level of abstraction at which caseframes define a domain-oriented language. Only the grammatical roles and semantic categories of the relevant words and phrases are specified. It is up to the case frame parser to map these roles onto the input. Caseframe instantiation is thus highly interpretive. It can use the information in a caseframe to map it onto the input in several quite different ways. If the grammatical constituent it is looking for does not appear in the place it is supposed to be, a caseframe parser is free to look elsewhere in the input. In fact, there is nothing to stop a caseframe parser from putting grammatical constituents together on purely semantic grounds in the absence of good syntactic cues. This kind of approach allows Language Craft to deal with constituents that are out of order, missing, or interspersed with spurious phrases (e.g. "In room 5 the meeting please schedule for Tuesday 2 pm.").

4.2. Dialogue Management

The most challenging and interesting area for integration between natural language and direct-manipulation interfaces, and the one that can benefit most from use of the underlying knowledge base is natural language dialogue management. Dialogue management is also very important for the naturalness of interaction through natural language.

When people engage in a dialogue, they share a context of past events, objects and events mentioned in the conversation, mutual assumptions about each other's goals and motivations, etc.. This shared context allows them to communicate intelligently with each other: by resolving pronouns or other abbreviated forms of reference into objects just mentioned, by completing elliptical questions by analogy with previous utterances, by recognizing that a statement is inconsistent with the speaker's assumed goals or beliefs and (internally) correcting it so it is consistent, etc.. For a machine to appear to communicate intelligently with a person, it needs to share context in a similar kind of way. Moreover, an ability to deal with anaphora and ellipsis allows the natural language input to be much more terse. It is much quicker to say or type "it" or "the machine" than always to have to say "grinding machine number 4."

The dialogue management facilities of our interface support framework are currently restricted to support for anaphora and reformulation ellipsis, though we hope in the future also to add more sophisticated facilities driven by a representation of the user's goals. This chapter focuses on the way we deal with anaphora, i.e. the way we use context to interpret abbreviated descriptions of domain entities. Given the integration of graphical and natural language modalities in our interface model, we need to use two kinds of context to resolve anaphoric references:

- **Dialogue context:** the set of entities mentioned or implied by the recent dialogue.
- **Visual context:** the set of entities visible on the screen, plus perhaps other entities closely associated with them.

Moreover, the two modalities allow two kinds of anaphoric reference:

- Standard natural language anaphora (pronouns, definite noun phrases, etc.)
- Reference to objects by pointing at their images on the screen. Naturally, this kind of reference is resolved only against (a localized subset of) the visual context.

The following two subsections describe how each of these kinds of anaphor are handled by our interface support framework.

4.3. Natural Language Anaphora

In this section, we turn to the anaphoric interpretation capabilities we have designed as an extension to Language Craft. There is already a substantial body of work on the resolution of anaphora with respect to dialogue context (Charniak, 1972; Grosz, 1977; Hayes, 1981; Sidner, 1979). Our approach does not represent a significant departure from this tradition. It uses techniques developed in the previous work to produce an anaphora capability suitable for restricted domain interfaces, rather than one that is completely general. In particular, we expect to make maximum use of the restricted domain semantics and not to use any techniques that would lead to noticeable (by the interface user) processing times. The novel aspects of our approach relate to the addition of visual context (see, however, Bolt, 1980; Grosz, 1977).

Many current treatments of dialogue anaphora (e.g. Grosz, 1977; Sidner, 1979) use the concept of a set of entities that are in the immediate *focus* of the context, plus others that are outside the immediate focus, but may become focused. The focus may change through nesting (subtopics or digressions) or by moving to related topics. Entities in the immediate focus may be referred to by pronouns. Entities that are outside the immediate focus may be referred to by abbreviated descriptions. We have adopted this kind of approach. The focus of the dialogue context is represented as a set of domain world entities. These entities may be referenced by pronouns or other abbreviated descriptions. There is a second set of entities, those related to the focussed entities by one of a (domain-specific) class of relationships, that may also be referenced by definite noun phrases, but not by pronouns. These entities form the *potential focus* (Sidner, 1979). Referring to an entity in the potential focus adds it the focus.

We can see how this works in the following dialogue fragment with a hypothetical factory scheduling system:

User:	*Do any grinding machines have less than 80% utilization?*
System:	*Yes, grinding machine 4 has only 65% utilization.*
User:	*Has it had unscheduled downtime since Monday?*
System:	No.
User:	*Preventive maintenance?*
System:	No. It is not scheduled until Friday.
User:	*Who is the maintainer?*
System:	*Albert Smith.*
User:	*Ask him to do the preventive maintenance today.*

Here the grinding machine mentioned by the system becomes part of the focus and is referred to via the pronoun "it" by the user (and the system) in the question about utilization. The next question relies on Language Craft's current ability to handle reformulation ellipsis (Carbonell & Hayes, 1984). The system uses the context of the previous question to interpret the user's input as though he had said "Has it had preventive maintenance since Monday?". The user then goes on to refer to an entity that has not been mentioned in the dialogue so far, but is in the potential focus, viz. the maintainer of grinding machine 4, by the incomplete description "the maintainer" (the system would presumably know about lots of maintainers). There is only one maintainer in the potential focus, so the anaphoric noun phrase can be resolved correctly and unambiguously. Mentioning the maintainer entity adds it to the focus, so that the "him" in the next input can be interpreted correctly.

Integration between Language Craft and Knowledge Craft is important for the implementation of this anaphora mechanism. We represent the dialogue focus as a set of domain entities represented as Knowledge Craft schemas. The process of resolving an anaphoric referent against such a context involves integrating the constraints provided by the pronoun (e.g. "he" is a male person, "there" is a location) or noun phrase ("maintainer" is an entity in a maintaining relationship with some other entity) with the constraints provided by sentential context (e.g. in "ask him to do the preventive maintenance today," "him" must be an entity that can be asked to do maintenance—a maintenance employee), and then finding items in the context that match the integrated description. Both the integration and the matching require the support of an inheritance mechanism which Knowledge Craft provides. For instance, in the above example, "him" has the constraint of being a male person inherent in the pronoun, and the constraint of being a maintenance employee from the sentential context. These two constraints are consistent since a maintenance employee ISA person and may be either gender. So the integrated description is a male maintenance employee. In the dialogue given above, this description would match (again through an inheritance process) with the focused entity representing Albert Smith.

Knowledge Craft inheritance is also useful in specifying the relationships which define the potential focus (e.g. the relationship between a machine and its maintainer). Knowledge Craft relations are represented by user definable and modifiable schemas. This makes it convenient to attach such information to the relations.

The kind of interface we are considering here is unusual for natural language in that it has a representation of the world separate from the dialogue itself. This allows us to provide some interesting capabilities that have only been touched on in earlier work, in particular the work by Grosz (1977) on task-oriented dialogues and Bolt (1980) on an integrated natural language/graphical interface. First, we allow the user to refer to any entity visible in the world display by the minimum description necessary to distinguish it. For instance, if only one milling machine is shown on the display at any given time, the user can refer to it by "the milling machine" rather than by typing its full name. The entities in the world display thus play a similar role to the potential focus and are treated in the same way by the anaphora resolution mechanism. In other words, the system will look for referents for definite noun phrase descriptions both among the entities in the potential focus and among the entities currently displayed on the screen.

The second useful capability opened up by the existence of the world display is an explicit representation of the dialogue focus through highlighting on the display. This allows the user to be clear at all times on what is the system's focus of attention, and helps prevent the kind of reference problems that could arise if the user thinks he has made a shift of focus, but the system fails to pick up on it. An even more intriguing possibility is to allow the user to edit the dialogue context explicitly. In this way, he could make up for any deficiencies in the system's focus tracking. He could also, as a part of browsing through the world display, explicitly set up the dialogue focus. For instance, if he set the focus of attention to include only a particular machine, then on the next natural language input, he would be able to refer to that machine by "it." The human factors of such an interface feature have never been examined and are hard to predict in advance. We, therefore, plan to determine its usefulness empirically.

In order to maintain a visual representation of the dialogue focus, the interface system will, when necessary, adjust the domain display in such a way that the dialogue focus remains a subset of the visual context. For instance, in the above dialogue example, when the user starts to ask about details of the grinding machine (utilization, unscheduled downtime, preventive maintenance, maintainer), the display of the machine (which we will assume was a named icon) is expanded to or overlaid by a display of its attributes. The attributes that the user focuses on are highlighted appropriately. Again, this is breaking largely unexplored ground from a human factors point of view. And we anticipate changes to the design based on experience with an implementation. The obvious danger is that the user might become confused or annoyed by changes to the display that he did not request directly. In addition, there is the potential for overly cluttered displays if this mechanism only ever displays additional entities and never removes any. The issue of when a defocused entity can safely be removed from the display is a tricky one, involving unresolved research issues in dialogue management. Our current design does not address it.

4.4. Anaphora by Pointing

One of the most interesting capabilities opened up by the kind of interface we are discussing is intermixing natural language input with pointing input. This will allow the user of a factory scheduling system to input, for instance, "Can this machine ⟨point at one machine⟩ take over the orders scheduled for that ⟨point at other machine⟩", where the pointing was done to the world display. We will call this kind of pointing *natural language pointing* and treat it as a kind of anaphoric reference. Natural language pointing is extremely useful in combination with speech input, allowing a very efficient combination of gesture and speech—the most natural way for people to communicate. Its effectiveness in an interface has already been demonstrated by work at MIT (Bolt, 1980; Negronponte, 1981). It is somewhat less attractive for typed input because of the overhead involved in moving the hand from keyboard to pointing device and back again. However, work on the Scholar project (Carbonell, 1971) has shown that pointing can be used effectively with typed input in the context of maps in geography lessons.

Natural language pointing can be more efficient than speech alone because it is often faster to point at something than to identify it verbally (particularly when it is not in the immediate focus of the dialogue and so cannot be referred to by a pronoun). Moreover, pointing is a more direct form of identification than speech, so that its processing is likely to be faster and less error-prone, considerably reducing the need for clarification dialogues, and hence enhancing communication efficiency. There are even some circumstances where pointing can communicate information that is very difficult to communicate through speech. For instance, pointing at a position on a map is very much easier and probably more accurate than trying to give the same information by speaking map coordinates into the system. In such circumstances, natural language pointing is also convenient to use with typed input, particularly if all the pointing can be done after the entire sentence has been entered.

Though there are numerous advantages to natural language pointing, there are several issues which make its inclusion in an interface less than straightforward. In particular, it is necessary to:

- Determine when pointing events are natural language pointing events;
- Determine where the entities pointed at fit within the overall interpretation of the natural language input;
- Identify which entity was actually pointed to (an issue when the visual representations of entities are nested within each other on the screen).

The difficulty of identifying pointing events as natural language pointing events stems both from ambiguity inherent in the use of the pointing device and in ambiguity in natural language as to whether a given phrase implies that a natural language pointing event will occur. In the kind of interface we are discussing, the pointing device will have other uses besides natural language pointing. In particular, it will figure prominently in the interface that allows the user to navigate around the world display. Pointing events are then potentially ambiguous between natural language pointing and these other uses of pointing. There are several potential solutions, none of which seems ideal:

- Make natural language pointing events identifiably different from others, for instance, by dedicating one mouse button (assuming there are several) to natural language pointing. This has the advantage of being clear, but the disadvantages of being fragile and difficult to learn (use of the wrong mouse button could produce highly unexpected and unintuitive results), and of reducing the options available for the world navigation interface.
- Overload some kind of neutral pointing event from the navigation interface—one that does some kind of selection without causing any specific action to happen. This has the same disadvantages in being fragile and hard to learn, and has the additional disadvantage of not being totally unambiguous, but the constraints it places on the navigation interface are different.
- Poll for the position of the pointing device when a deictic phrase is used. This avoids the disadvantages of the other alternatives, but runs into serious trouble because it is not always possible to identify deictic references in natural language just from the words involved. For instance, "there" may indicate a deictic reference or be a reference to an item in the dialogue context ("Order 17 is the queue for grinding machine 4." "How long has it been there?"). It also reduces the freedom of the user in terms of the relative ordering of pointing and the deictic reference.
- Assume that all pointing events during (or close to, see below) natural language input are natural language pointing events. This has the advantages of simplicity, robustness, and lack of ambiguity. Its main disadvantage is making world navigation impossible during natural language input (even during a pause for thought during type in).

Our interface framework will initially use the final alternative, but we regard the choice as an empirical matter and expect to experiment with several possibilities.

Once we have determined that a pointing event is a natural language pointing event, there is still the problem of matching it up with a phrase or hole in the natural language input. The co-occurrence of words and pointing events is useful information here, but does not give the whole story. All of the following examples and many other possibilities are plausible:

```
Can this machine ⟨point at one machine⟩ take over the
orders scheduled for that one ⟨point at other machine⟩?
```

Can this ⟨point at one machine⟩ machine take over the
orders scheduled for that ⟨point at other machine⟩ one?

Can this machine take over the orders scheduled for
that one ⟨point at one machine⟩ ⟨point at other
machine⟩?

The last of these is most likely in a typed input situation where the user
wishes to cut down on the overhead of moving between keyboard and
pointing device. The only real invariant seems to be that the natural
language pointing events will occur in the same order as the phrases (or
holes[2]) in the natural language input to which they correspond. Moreover, the pointing events usually come during or immediately before or
after the corresponding phrase. This latter fact means that information
on the start and end time of words in the natural language input is
required for the analysis of natural language pointing input. As part of
the development of our interface support framework, we will extend
Language Craft to make it produce that information.

There are thus two kinds of indication, neither of them conclusive,
that a phrase in the natural language input corresponds to a natural
language pointing event: the temporal co-occurrence of the phrase with
the pointing event, and the actual form of the phrase itself. For instance, phrases with a demonstrative determiner ("this machine") are
more likely to correspond to natural language pointing than phrases
with a definite determiner ("the machine"). Once a candidate correspondence has been established between a phrase and a pointing event,
it must be verified that the two are compatible. This process is very
similar to anaphoric reference determination, except that the candidate
referent is known in advance. It involves determining the constraints
on the candidate phrase both instrinsically ("this machine" must be a
machine) and from the sentential context (in the above examples "that
one" must be a machine since orders are scheduled for it), and then
checking if the entity pointed at met those constraints.

Since there is no conclusive way to determine which phrases in the
natural language input correspond to pointing events, we have designed the following heuristic procedure for finding the correspondence.

---

[2] Our current design requires some form of deictic expression and does not allow the
user just to leave a gap in the input corresponding to the pointing event as in "Can ⟨point
at one machine⟩ take over the orders scheduled for ⟨point at other machine⟩". The semantic caseframe approach used by Language Craft is already quite capable of skipping over
gaps and producing a partial analysis of the input. The additional ability required to
match up gaps with natural language pointing would be for Language Craft explicitly to
recognize that there is a gap in the input and to determine where in the input that gap is.

1. list in left to right order all schemas representing phrases in the input that could potentially correspond to natural language pointing events;
2. list in left to right order all natural language pointing events;
3. form all lists of pairings between schemas and pointing events, such that:
   a. the left to right ordering is preserved for both schemas and pointing events;
   b. paired schemas and pointing events are compatible in the way described above;
4. if more than one list of pairings remains, choose those with the maximum number of schemas that correspond to phrases that are linguistically likely to be deictic (including all pronouns and noun phrases with demonstrative determiners);
5. if more than one list of pairings still remains, choose those with the shortest time mismatch between the pointing events and the phrases corresponding to the schemas;
6. if there is still more than one, ask the user to decide.

In the example above, little of the complexity of this algorithm is needed. There are only two pointing events and three schemas (corresponding to "this machine," "the orders," and "that one"), and hence there are three possible list of pairings, of which only the correct one satisfies all the constraints. More complex sentences could require all the steps in the algorithm to find the correct pairings.

The last major issue in dealing with natural language pointing is that there can even be uncertainty as to which entity is being pointed to. In particular, if one entity has some kind of containment or subset relation with another, then the graphical representation of the contained entity may be nested within the graphical representation of the containing entity, so that pointing at the contained entity would be ambiguous between the two. For instance, an icon representing an individual machine may be graphically contained within an area which represents the factory shop of which it is a part, so that pointing at the machine icon might mean the machine or the shop. Sometimes, the corresponding natural language phrase or its sentential context can disambiguate. For instance, if the corresponding phrase was "this machine," there would be no confusion. If such disambiguation is impossible, then the system must query the user to resolve the issue. Modifying the above algorithm to use this approach means creating, for each potentially ambiguous natural language pointing event, copies of the pairing lists which differ only in the entity referred to by the ambiguous pointing event. There would be as many copies as there were alternative interpretations.

A final complication arises if the user desires to identify a group of objects or an area of the display through natural language pointing. For instance, he might want to ask about the average utilization of a group of machines. Conventional graphics applications provide ways of making group selections by incremental selection or selection by (usually rectangular) area. A similar approach could be used for natural language pointing, but it would eliminate some of the naturalness that we hope to achieve. Instead, our interface framework will allow freehand area designation by closed curves. In addition to being natural, this allows arbitrarily shaped areas to be designated as well as being able to select groups of individual entities. As in ordinary natural language pointing, all such line drawing during or temporally close to a natural language input will be interpreted as a natural language pointing event corresponding to some deictic phrase in the input.

5. Problems in Using a Knowledge Base to Drive an Interface

As discussed earlier, to communicate effectively with an end user, an interactive system needs to present a coherent domain or problem model to the user. For most systems, this model is implicit. An electronic calculator, for instance, might have a model based on a stack of numbers and operands (Young, 1981), or a spreadsheet program might have a model based on a set of registers plus a set of equations constraining their values. In such examples the system typically does not have an explicit representation of this model that it can reason with or manipulate. The situation for expert systems is potentially quite different. An expert system, by definition, does have some kind of explicit model of its problem domain. A factory simulation and scheduling system would have an explicit model of process flows through the factory; a vehicle fault diagnosis system would have an explicit model of faults and symptoms. Given the description in earlier sections of driving an interface from a knowledge base organized in a certain way, it is now natural to raise the question: Can this explicit model that the expert system already needs to behave in an expert way also be used to drive the user interface to the system? In other words, will it generally be the case that the underlying knowledge base of an expert system is organized in the style we specified earlier?

The advantages of being able to use the expert system knowledge base to drive the end user interface in this way are significant. They include:

- Reduction in interface design time—the user's model of the system is constructed during design of the underlying expert system, so that effort is saved at interface design time;
- Guaranteed consistency between the system's internal view of the problem and the view that is presented to the user;
- No need explicitly to program updates to the user's view; if the user's view is driven from the underlying knowledge base, changes to the underlying model will be reflected automatically.

Unfortunately, it appears that this promise is seldom realized in reality. Examination of several real expert systems developed at Carnegie Group revealed problem models that were quite unsuitable as bases for a user's mental model of the problem. The inferencing techniques used by the expert systems turned out to place quite different demands on the problem representation than those imposed by the goal of human comprehensibility. A recurrent problem was the level of detail of the underlying representation. The knowledge bases we looked at often turned out to contain either too much detail or not enough detail to be appropriate for human mental models. In no case was the level of detail ideal for the end users.

One of the systems we looked at was a prototype factory simulation system. An important component of this system is a model of the flow of operations or processes in a factory. Operations can be linked together in various ways. The simplest linkage is that one operation follow another (first put the engine in the car and then put on the wheels). A more complex linkage is for one operation to be followed by one of several others, each with a separate probability of occurrence (first assemble the car body, and then paint it green with a probability of 60% or red with a probability of 40%). The way such linkages are presented to the user is shown in Figures 3 and 4. Unfortunately, the underlying representation required by the underlying expert system is quite different from this visually intuitive model. It is based on a state and action model. In this model, actions never follow each other directly, but may only transform one state into another. This means that the internal representation of Figure 3 looks like Figure 5 in which the operations have initial and terminating states. The internal representation of Fig-

Figure 3.   User's View of Simple Two Operation Sequence

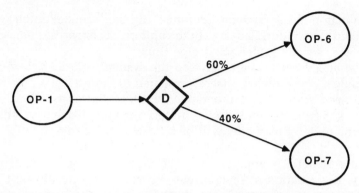

Figure 4.   User's View of Probabilistic Operation Sequence Branching

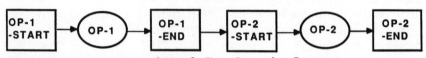

Figure 5.   System's View of Simple Two Operation Sequence

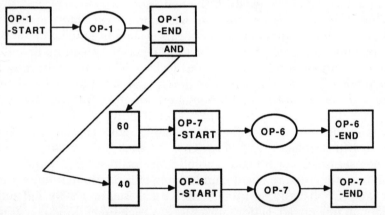

Figure 6.   System's View of Probabilistic Operation Sequence Branching

ure 4 as shown in Figure 6 is even worse. Not only is there considerable extra detail, but there is no single item corresponding to the decision link from the first to the second and third operations. Instead, the probabilistic decision link is encoded in a pattern of five connected states. Clearly, in this system, the underlying representation is much too detailed to form the basis of a good model of presentation to the user.

Instead of too much detail, an underlying system can also contain too little detail. A good example of this showed up in a motor vehicle diagnosis system. The system we looked at was organized around faults (battery is dead) and tests (does engine turn over when key is turned). The goal is, of course, to predict faults from tests and to recommend further tests to pin down faults that are ambiguous on the basis of existing tests. The problem from an interface view is that concepts that are primitive from the underlying system's point of view (battery-is-dead) are composite from the user's point of view. For instance, the underlying representation does not contain the concept of a battery separately from the fault battery-is-dead. This makes it inconvenient for the user to inquire about the status of the battery, or to assert that the battery has just been charged. If such a system were to try to support natural language interaction,[3] the underlying representation would thus be inadequate. It would have to be supplemented by primitive concepts more in line with the user's view of the world.

We can summarize the lessons learned in looking at these systems as follows. If the representation and primitives used in an expert system are selected on the basis of its convenience for the underlying inference processes, it is unlikely that they will also be suitable for driving the end user interface to the expert system. To get a representation that is suitable for both purposes requires that both the needs of the underlying inferencing mechanism and the way the user thinks about the problem must be taken into account. In practice, what we observed was an original design which took into account only the needs of the underlying inferencing mechanism, followed by a set of modifications and additions to ameliorate the poor user interface which resulted.

6. Reconciling the Differing Needs of Inference Mechanisms and Users

Given that the interface and inference mechanisms each place their own demands on the problem representation, there are two obvious approaches to setting up the knowledge base of an expert system so that it can be used to drive the interface to that system:

1.   Design the representation in such a way that it can satisfy both sets of demands;
2.   Provide two separate representations: one for the interface and the

---

[3] The system we examined did not try to support natural language interaction and instead relied on menus for input, thus exploiting its user's ability to recognize composite concepts rather than having to generate or think in terms of them.

other for the inference mechanism and provide a mapping between them.

This section discusses both of these alternatives and comes out in favor of the second.

The primary problems in designing a representation which is fully adequate for both interface and inferencing needs are pragmatic, rather than conceptual. Since a poor interface is likely to result if the user is asked to distort his intuitive view of the application domain to accommodate underlying system needs, the form of the representation must follow the user's intuitions. The representation may contain extra detail that is not shown to the user, but in structure it must conform to the user's view. Since all necessary information can be accommodated in this way, such a representation can always be concocted. The question is whether the underlying expert system can use it and still produce an acceptably efficient performance. For instance, in our vehicle diagnosis example, the reason for using faults, rather than vehicle components, as primitives was the more efficient processing that can be achieved. Since a component may have several fault states and several tests, separating these out as primitive items, rather than as attributes of a component involves less structure manipulation. Moreover, including components as primitives in addition to faults and tests could considerably increase the amount of storage required for the system (a vehicle may have several thousand components) and thus decrease efficiency of operation in that way. Again, in our simulation example, the underlying representation was designed to provide explicit state objects for manipulation by the underlying expert system and to provide explicit hooks to hold temporary information generated during the performance of the simulation. The same goals could probably be achieved by a representation which allows the kind of direct operation to operation linking that typifies the user's view of the problem, but only at the cost of considerably increased programming complexity.

While the problems of concocting a representation adequate for both interface and inferencing purposes are pragmatic, there are deeper issues involved in constructing separate representations for interface and inferencing purposes with a mapping between them. These issues concern the way the mapping works, and its reversibility. This chapter falls well short of proposing a complete solution to this mapping problem, but the remainder of this section examines some of the issues.

If we view the interface and inferencing representations as being rearrangements of the same information, then the mapping between them involves specifying how the information is rearranged. For instance, in our vehicle diagnosis system, the battery-is-dead fault might be represented by the following frame or schema:[4]

```
[[ battery-is-dead
      STATUS:
            ⟨range: true false unknown⟩ ]]
```

The precise details of the notation are not directly relevant to our current purposes. It should be read as a schema with one slot, STATUS, that can take values out of the set: true, false, or unknown, with the obvious semantics. The interface representation might contain a battery schema:

```
[[ battery
      CHARGE:
            ⟨range: charged discharged⟩ ]]
```

The mapping so far is straightforward: the CHARGE of battery is charged iff the STATUS of battery-is-dead is false and similarly for values of uncharged and true. A mapping of this kind can easily be implemented through demons (procedures which are invoked when the value of the slot is changed) on the two slots involved.

How would the user interface use this information? Suppose the interface had a natural language component and was trying to respond the question: "What is the condition of the battery?". Assuming a suitable natural language interpretation facility, it would be straightforward to translate this query into an appropriate query on the CHARGE slot of the battery schema.

The advantages of using a battery schema for user interface purposes are clearer if we introduce a second fault, called battery-is-disconnected:

```
[[ battery-is-disconnected
      STATUS:
            ⟨range: true false⟩ ]]
```

and change the battery schema to:

```
[[ battery
      CHARGE:
            ⟨range: charged discharged⟩
      CONNECTION:
            ⟨range: connected disconnected⟩ ]]
```

---

[4] The formalism is that of the schema-based CRL representation language of Carnegie Group's Knowledge Craft knowledge engineering tool.

with appropriate mappings between its connection slot and the bat-tery-is-disconnected fault schema. The battery schema now serves as a central repository for all the information about the battery, so that the natural language question above can be mapped onto a query involving both slots of battery. It would be much harder to organize such a query without the benefit of a schema in which all the informa-tion about the battery was grouped together. If the natural language interface goes beyond simple status queries and tries to answer ques-tions such as "what can go wrong with a battery?", a centralized bat-tery schema is essential.

The advantages of such information grouping are not confined to natural language interfaces. A graphically oriented interface to the di-agnosis system might also allow the user to find out the status of a particular component (say, by clicking on an icon representing that component). An interface of that kind also needs a battery schema so that all the information can be grouped for presentation.

The mapping problem is much harder when there are major struc-tural differences involved. Going back to our factory scheduling exam-ple, consider the issues involved in mapping between the represent-ations shown in Figures 3 and 5. During a simulation, the information related to a particular operation is accumulated in its enabling and terminating states, so that questions about how many times an opera-tion has been performed, for instance, would have to be mapped onto queries on slots of the states. More problematic is the issue of establish-ing the correspondence between the pattern of schemas used to repre-sent the probabilistic decision link in Figure 6 and the single schema used in Figure 4. The information shared between these schemas can be transferred through demons as before, but the specification of just what schemas should be established in the underlying model when the user edits a process flow to introduce a new decision link is quite complex, and would be hard to specify declaratively.

In summary, the maintenance of two different, but consistent, repre-sentations for interface and inference purposes appears to be a tractable problem, but the task of specifying the mapping is not straightforward, and may be hard to accomplish without extensive ad hoc programming.

7. Conclusion

This chapter has examined the problem of using the knowledge base of an expert system to drive its end user interface. It presented a style of knowledge base organization suitable for driving interfaces to a broad class of knowledge-based systems. It went on to describe an interface support framework that allows direct manipulation interfaces with an optional natural language component to be driven from a knowledge base organized in such a fashion. The description of the framework focused particularly on issues involved in integrating the natural language component with the direct manipulation component.

The chapter also examined the question of whether a knowledge base organized for inference purposes might typically satisfy the criteria established for driving the knowledge base. It concluded that in general this would not be the case, and went on to recommend separate, but linked, knowledge base representations for interface and inferencing purposes.

Interfaces to intelligent systems are currently not nearly as intelligent and responsive as the underlying systems themselves. This severely limits the utility of such systems. We believe that the way around this problem is to use the knowledge already in the knowledge base to help drive the appearance and behavior of the interface. The interface support framework presented above represents a small step toward that goal.

References

Bolt, R. A. (1980). "Put-That-There": Voice and gesture at the graphics interface. Computer Graphics, 14(3), 262–270.

Carbonell, J. R. (1971). Mixed-initiative man-computer dialogues. Cambridge, MA: Bolt, Beranek, & Newman, Inc.

Carbonell, J. G., & Hayes, P. J. (1984). Recovery strategies for parsing extragrammatical language. Computational Linguistics 10.

Charniak, E. C. (1972). Toward a model of children's story comprehension. TR–266, MIT AI Laboratory, Cambridge, MA.

Fox, M. S., Allen, B. P., Smith, S. F., & Strohm, G. A. (1983). ISIS: A Constraint-directed reasoning approach to job shop scheduling. (Tech. Rep. No. CMU–RI–TR–83–8). Robotics Institute, Carnegie–Mellon University, Pittsburgh.

Grosz, B. J. (1977). The representation and use of focus in a system for understanding dialogues. Proceedings Fifth International Joint Conference on Artificial Intelligence, MIT, Cambridge, MA, pp. 67–76.

Hayes, P. J. (1981). Anaphora for limited domain systems. Proceedings Seventh International Joint Conference on Artificial Intelligence, Vancouver, pp. 416–422.

Hayes, P. J. (1987). Intelligent interfaces to expert systems. In T. Bernold (Ed.), User interfaces, gateway or bottleneck? North Holland.

Hayes, P. J., Szekely, P. A., & Lerner, R. A. (1985). Design alternatives for user interface management systems based on experience with Cousin. Proceedings of CHI85, San Francisco.

Hutchins, E. L., Hollan, J. D., & Norman, D. A. (1986). Direct manipulation interfaces. In D. A. Norman & S. W. Draper (Eds.), *User centered system design*, Hillsdale, NJ: Erlbaum, pp. 87–124.

Jacob, R. J. K. (1984). An executable specification technique for describing human-computer interaction. In H. R. Hartson (Ed.), *Advances in human-computer interaction*. Norwood, NJ: Ablex.

Mark, W. (1981). Representation and inference in the consul system. *Proceedings Seventh International Joint Conference on Artificial Intelligence*, Vancouver, pp. 375–381.

Negronponte, N. (1981). Media room. *Proceedings of the Society for Information Display*, 22(2), 109–113.

Norman, D. A. (1986). Cognitive engineering. In D. A. Norman & S. W. Draper (Eds.), *User centered system design*, Hillsdale, NJ: Erlbaum, pp. 31–65.

Sathi, A., Morton, T. E., & Roth, S. (1985). *Callisto: An intelligent project management system*. ISL, Robotics Institute, Carnegie-Mellon University.

Shneiderman, B. (1981). Direct manipulation: A step beyond programming languages. *Computer*, 16(8), 57–69.

Shortliffe, E. H. (1976). *Computer-based medical consultations: MYCIN*. New York: American Elsevier.

Sidner, C. L. (1979). *Towards a computational theory of definite anaphora comprehension in English Discourse*. TR–537, MIT AI Lab, Cambridge, MA.

Smith, D. C., Irby, C., Kimball, R., Verplank, W., & Harslem, E. (1982). Designing the Star user interface. *Byte*, 7 (4, April), 242–282.

Tanner, P., & Buxton, W. (1983). *Some issues in future user interface management system (UIMS) development*. IFIP Working Group 5.2 Workshop on User Interface Management, Seeheim, West Germany.

Wasserman, A. I., & Shewmake, D. T. (1984). The role of prototypes in the user software engineering (USE) methodology. In H. R. Hartson (Ed.), *Advances in Human-Computer Interaction*. Norwood, NJ: Ablex.

Young, R. M. (1981). The machine inside the machine: Users' models of pocket calculators. *International Journal of Man-Machine Studies*, 15, 51–85.

Yunten, T., & Hartson, H. R. (1984). A supervisory methodology and notation (SUPERMAN) for human-computer system development. In H. R. Hartson (Ed.), *Advances in human-computer interaction*, Norwood, NJ: Ablex.

NINE

A UIMS for Building Metaphoric User Interfaces

Ross Faneuf
Steven Kirk

Digital Equipment Corp.

Abstract

The OASIS User Interface Management System (UIMS) is being developed to create high-quality interfaces for a diverse set of applications, including expert systems in Digital's manufacturing organization. The design of OASIS was shaped by three objectives: to support familiar interface styles (e.g., menus, direct manipulation and forms), to facilitate experimentation with new interface styles, and to separate clearly the semantics of user interfaces from the semantics of their applications. The resulting system permits user interfaces to be specified by a simple declarative description. This interface description determines how objects are presented to the user and how the user may manipulate them. The only communication between the application and OASIS is the creation, deletion, and modification of objects which have semantic value to the application. OASIS is particularly well suited for building metaphoric interfaces, where the exact details of the presentation are not important to the application.

1. Introduction

This article discusses the conception and implementation of the Object-oriented Adaptable Sapient Interface System (OASIS), chiefly from the viewpoint of the interface designer who uses OASIS to design and build human–computer interfaces. Our goal is to motivate and explain the design, capabilities, and use of OASIS by these designers. Accordingly, we include: the factors which motivated us to build a User Interface Management System (UIMS); the issues which OASIS tackles and those which it does not; the conceptual model on which OASIS is built; the implementation of that model; and some simple examples of interfaces built with OASIS.

1.1. Background

In the fall of 1985, our group had several expert system development projects beginning or in progress. These projects covered a diverse set of domains, including CAD, cooperative work, and manufacturing process simulation. These systems were being developed in an equally diverse set of AI programming environments (LISP, production rule systems like OPS5, and a frame-based knowledge representation system). Yet despite these differences, these projects were encountering similar problems developing graphic user interfaces. All of them shared these complaints:

- Interface development was consuming a great part of the efforts of expert system developers and represented a significant proportion of the resulting code—as much as 60%.
- Expert systems developers were usually inexperienced at interface design, and generally had no interest in becoming experts in low-level graphics or other interface tools.
- There was no consistency of interfaces across applications.
- It was difficult to provide multiple interfaces to applications running on different classes of machines. Applications running on both VAXstations and character-cell terminals were typically limited to interface styles for the terminals.
- A lack of powerful tools inhibited experimentation with new visual metaphors and interface styles for expert systems.
- There were no tools to support both local and distributed interfaces (i.e. for both local applications and remote ones accessible over a network).

1.2. Objectives

To support these diverse systems and to deal with the issues they raised, the OASIS project was started to create an interface building tool. It was designed to make high-quality interfaces less expensive to construct, and to test new, experimental interface styles. We established these objectives for the project:

- It must support a wide variety of interface styles for a conventional work station (VAXstation).
- It must support several different application programming language environments. This precluded embedding the interface system deeply in any one environment.
- It must support both localized and distributed interfaces. This implied a separate interface system (probably as a separate process), and also implied a low-bandwidth interface between the interface controller and the application.
- It should simplify rapid prototyping of interfaces, provide powerful and easily modifiable interface styles and support experimentation with new styles. These implied a multiple-level open architecture— that is, one in which any of several architectural levels are accessible, documented, and modifiable.
- Performance and resource consumption were important but secondary issues.

We judged that a user interface management system (UIMS) was most likely to be successful in meeting these objectives.[1]

1.3. Scope

User Interface Management Systems have been described in recent literature (Buxton et al., 1983; Hayes, Lerner, & Szekely, 1985; Olsen, Dempsey, & Rogge, 1985; Schulert, Rogers, & Hamilton, 1985; Sibert et al., 1986; Tanner & Buxton, 1985). We will not review the basic concepts here. However, the term, UIMS, has referred to a wide range of systems from simple window- and menu-building libraries to intelligent interface systems that adapt to the changing experience level and habits of their users. The theme of all such systems is the separation of the details of the user interface from the rest of the application, with various resulting benefits.

Most of these UIMS systems described are not "complete" interface systems; such a system is simply too ambitious. A "complete" interface system would include dialogue management, direct manipulation, automated assistance, powerful presentation capabilities, user-accessible customization facilities, and natural language input. Instead, most systems tackle the features that are important to the applications they are intended to serve, and other features of a hypothetical complete system are left out or minimally developed.

---

[1] A list of benefits typically promised for a UIMS can be found in Olsen, Buxton, and Ehrich (1984).

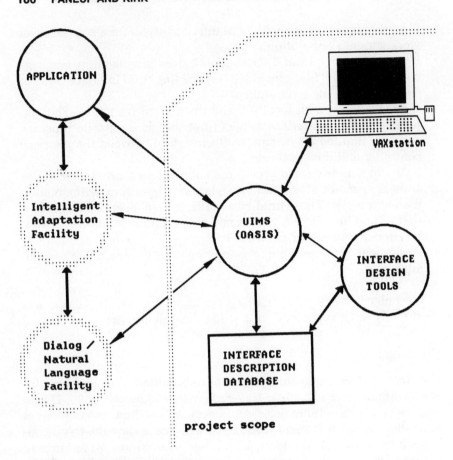

Figure 1.   The Scope of OASIS

OASIS likewise does not attempt to be a complete interface system. Figure 1 indicates the scope of OASIS, and suggests several components which might appear in a more fully developed interface system.

In OASIS, the most important user interface requirement is the presentation of highly complex interrelated data. The manipulations performed on that data are comparatively straightforward. As a result, most of the effort to develop OASIS has been spent creating a powerful presentation engine. The input-processing engine is only complex enough to handle simple direct manipulation and text interaction. Currently OASIS does not have powerful dialogue management, natural language, or adaptation facilities.

1.4. Metaphoric Interfaces

In addition to acknowledging what OASIS does and does not address, we should describe what OASIS was designed specifically to do well. To do so, we need to distinguish between two basic classes of user interfaces. OASIS' principal interface environment is the VAXstation, which is characterized by high-quality raster graphics and pointing devices. We locate application interfaces for this environment on a spectrum between two end points:

- **Pictorial Interfaces:** in which the application is intimately concerned with the pictorial aspects of the presentation. Examples include drawing systems, WYSIWYG editors, and layout systems.
- **Metaphoric Interfaces:** in which the application is primarily concerned with the information which is provided to users and received from them via the interface rather than the pictorial details of presentation. Examples include data-base systems, operating systems, simulation systems, and many expert systems.

This distinction is easily seen by comparing an electronic schematic editor and a VLSI layout system. The layout system is concerned with the exact position and size of all objects because the product of the system is a photographic mask used to create chips. If two objects are placed too close together they prevent the proper operation of the entire chip. This concern is directly reflected in the interface, which is a pictorial metaphor for the layout. In a schematic system, however, the position of a particular gate within the diagram is not important; the important details are the electrical relationships between the logical components (which gates are connected to which). The interface is then a logical metaphor for these relationships. (The positions may be important to the user; but that information is not required for a logical analysis of the circuit one is designing.)

We don't mean to imply that the user interface is unimportant in metaphoric interfaces; an appropriate and usable interface is vital for the success of both types of interfaces. Instead, saying that an application is "not concerned" with the details of presentation implies that its particular presentation was just one out of a set of possible presentations that could have been used. For example, in a file manager, it makes no difference whether directory files are shown pictorially as folder icons or as text by their path name. Each presentation is useful, but which form is most appropriate depends on the situation.

Applications at the metaphoric end of the spectrum may benefit from separating interface processing from the application. Their core functionality is independent of the details of the interface. Thus, their metaphoric properties make them natural targets for UIMS-supported interfaces. Pictorial applications are probably not natural targets; too much detail would be replicated in both application and UIMS, since their presentation is intrinsic to the application.

OASIS was designed specifically to build rich and powerful metaphoric interfaces. All of its initial applications are metaphoric; we feel that most expert systems are similarly metaphoric. OASIS can support pictorial interfaces, but at some cost in performance and duplicated information. Supporting primarily metaphoric interfaces made the development of OASIS much simpler in several important ways. When an application does not need to know specifically how information is presented to the user, it is much easier to separate the semantics of the user interface from the rest of the application. This makes a highly abstract interface description possible. It also becomes much easier to limit the bandwidth of the communication between the application and OASIS so that it is reasonable to place them in separate processes. Finally, less powerful graphics capabilities are typically required for metaphoric interfaces than pictorial ones.

These factors plus the requirement to support multiple application implementation languages led us to develop a UIMS with an extremely narrow interface to the application, and a complementary high level of abstraction at that interface. In OASIS, only data objects pass through that interface, and OASIS is responsible for all presentation operations. Here are our design principles:

- An application communicates data at a high level of abstraction to OASIS. It knows nothing about how that data are presented.
- All interface semantics, including those which reflect the application semantics, are created by the designer and embodied in an interface description.
- OASIS only knows how to present and accept data. It can create arbitrarily rich presentations and manipulations of data. However, that presentation knowledge is generic and contains no application semantics.

2. Conceptual Model

The conceptual model for OASIS organizes the ideas in OASIS. It explains the process by which OASIS presents an interface to a user of an application, and how the user and application communicate through

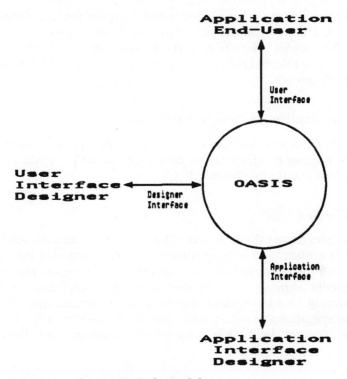

Figure 2.   The OASIS Role Model

the interface. This conceptual model underlies the OASIS implementation, which it predates and inspired.

The model has the following components:

- The roles of people dealing with OASIS.
- The application interface model.
- The presentation model.
- The user interface model.
- The designer interface model (interface design tool kit).

2.1. Roles

By separating the semantics of the user interface from the rest of the application we have introduced several distinct roles among people dealing with OASIS.

As shown in Figure 2, OASIS makes a distinction between an application interface designer, a user interface designer, and the end user of an application. These roles are analogous to the roles for printing a book. The author of the book collects and develops the knowledge to be presented. The publisher decides how this knowledge should be presented. The reader interacts with the final product. A person may fill more than one role, but the tasks and knowledge required by these roles are very different.

2.1.1. The Application Interface Designer

The application interface designer defines what types of information the end user may manipulate or access. He does NOT describe how this information should be presented.

2.1.2. The End User

The end user (here called the user) of a specific application built upon OASIS can interact with the application without knowing that OASIS handles all his communications. The interface he or she sees has its own conceptual model based on the tasks that the application program is performing. One simply sees objects on the screen, manipulates them with the operations provided, and observes the results of these manipulations. To map clearly these user actions to operations is the role of the user interface designer.

2.1.3. The User Interface Designer

The user interface designer (here termed the interface designer) is the only role which requires knowledge about the inner details of OASIS. He or she is responsible for the development of a specific user interface for a specific application. This task includes defining how the application data should be presented to the user and how the user's actions should affect the application data. Tools and defaults provided with OASIS make this easier.

2.1.4. Viewpoint

The interfaces between OASIS and these three roles each relay different types of information. Our description of these interfaces is biased toward the viewpoint of the interface designer.

2.2. Application Interface

The application interface is by far the simplest of the three interfaces. Application and interface semantics are separate; the only information

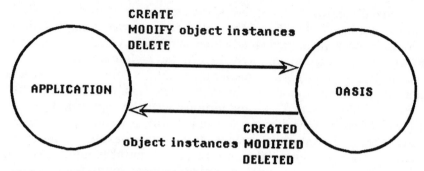

Figure 3.   The Application Interface

which passes through this interface is application data. The application program has some information which it wants to present to the user so that he or she can manipulate it. The application program, however, knows nothing about how this information is presented or how it is manipulated. The only information the application needs to provide to OASIS is the data to be manipulated. Similarly, the only information it receives from OASIS is data which have been created or modified by the user. OASIS thus has no semantic knowledge about the application data; the interface semantics are supplied by the interface designer, who chooses appropriate visual metaphors and manipulation mechanisms.

OASIS uses an object-oriented paradigm. Accordingly, the information which passes through the application interface is modeled as data object instances. As part of the OASIS/application separation, object classes are defined in the OASIS interface definition, and only requests to create, modify, and delete data object instances pass through the application interface.

This interface model, shown in Figure 3, loosely couples the application and OASIS. They are expected to be asynchronous independent processes with an appropriate internal control structure. OASIS is event-driven, and applications may be either event driven or perform polling. There are no mechanisms for the application to represent control information explicitly at the interface. Instead, some of the object classes defined in the OASIS interface will function as interface controls through methods defined by the interface designer, and the application must imply control operations by creating/modifying/deleting instances of these object classes. In the same way, OASIS can communicate control information back to the application.

Tanner and Buxton (1985) and Hayes, Lerner, and Szekely (1985), have identified three control structures for UIMSs: internal, external, and mixed control. In these terms, the control structure for OASIS is closest to mixed rather than either internal or external. However, these categories were developed largely for synchronous UIMS architectures. Since the application and OASIS can be performing tasks simultaneously, it is more correct to refer to the OASIS control structure as a fourth type, asynchronous. In a mixed control metaphor, control is like a token which is passed back and forth between the application and the UIMS. No such control token is needed with asynchronous control. This permits the interface designer to determine explicitly the granularity of the operations at the interface, and to build an interface using whichever of the four control metaphors is most appropriate.

The interface and application designers must cooperate closely in designing the objects which pass through this interface. The objects must have clearly understood semantics for driving or responding to the interface which OASIS presents. In particular, these objects relate to the semantics of the interface rather than to the application kernel. They will usually be similar or identical to data structures within the application kernel, but their semantic content is that of the interface. When the internal model of the application differs from the metaphor used to represent the application, the objects at the application/OASIS interface will reflect the interface and its control rather than the application kernel.

2.3. The Presentation Model

A major responsibility of OASIS is to map application data objects into an interface presentation at any level of desired pictorial richness. This is done by a series of transformations through several information levels, as shown in Figure 4. The information created by these transformations can be described in a hierarchy which should be intelligible to an interface designer. Nearly all the operations available to him modify these transformations.

2.3.1. Data

Data are the basic units of information communicated to and from the application program. This level includes definitions of data object classes and specific instances of these classes, called application data objects or ADOs.

2.3.2. Representation

A representation is a specific way of looking at an application data object. Any given ADO may have several possible representations. For example, an ADO may have a text representation and several different

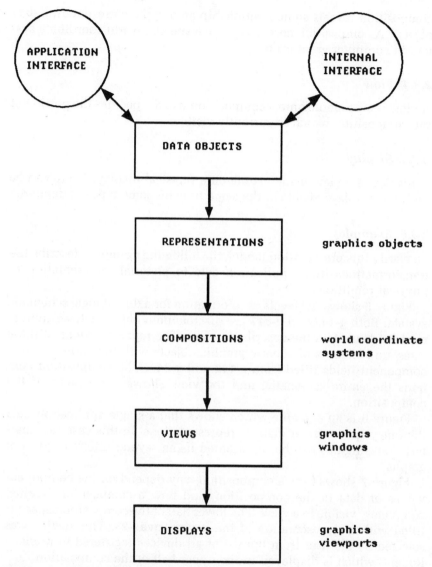

Figure 4.   The OASIS Information Levels

graphics representations. Representations can contain simple, conditional, complex, and compound subrepresentations.

2.3.3. *Composition*

A composition is a collection of representations which appear together in a single "space." How thse representations are combined into a composition reveals some relationship among the corresponding data objects. A composition corresponds to a specific world coordinate system in computer graphics terms.

2.3.4. View

A view is a peephole onto a composition which specifies the portion of the composition which is currently visible.

2.3.5. Display

A display is a view made visible on a physical display; There can be multiple displays visible at the same time on some types of devices.

2.3.6. Examples

To clarify this presentation model, the following examples describe the transformations from application data to pictorial representation to physical rendition.

Figure 5 shows the levels of information for a digital logic schematic system. Both **g-142** and **g-347** are discrete *data objects* whose component fields contain the described values. The *representations* of these gates are instances of generic graphic objects with the corresponding component fields filled from **g-142** and **g-347**. The *composition* contains the entire schematic, and the *view* shows some piece of the composition.

Figure 6 is an example which shows that a single application data item may have several distinct representations. In this case the quarterly sales figures can be represented using several different types of graphs.

Figure 7 shows how a composition may depend on the component values of data in the composition, and how a composition is often completely visible in a view. The lower half of the composition space is filled with a representation of the device, **uvax-23**. This device was selected by the user from the list of all devices registered to Michael Rodent, which is displayed in the upper half of the composition.

2.3.7. Mappings Between Levels

As these examples show, any object or set of objects on one level can map into one or more objects on the next level. These mapping operations can be fairly complex combinations of the supplied primitive mapping operations at each level. In practice, these mappings or transformations are the most powerful components of OASIS.

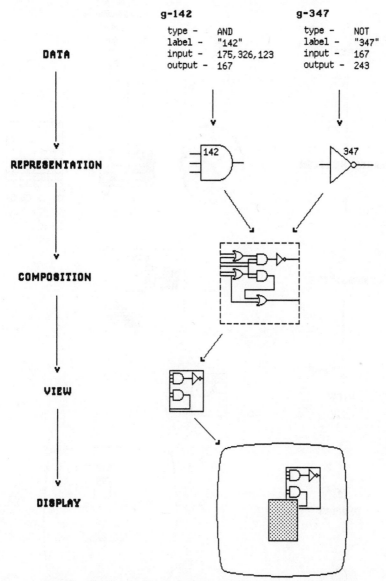

Figure 5.   Information Levels in an Electronics Application

2.3.8. Relationship with Graphics Systems

This model bears some obvious analogies with some of the levels and transformations of conventional graphics systems (e.g. GKS). A composition is analogous to a world coordinate system; a view is analogous

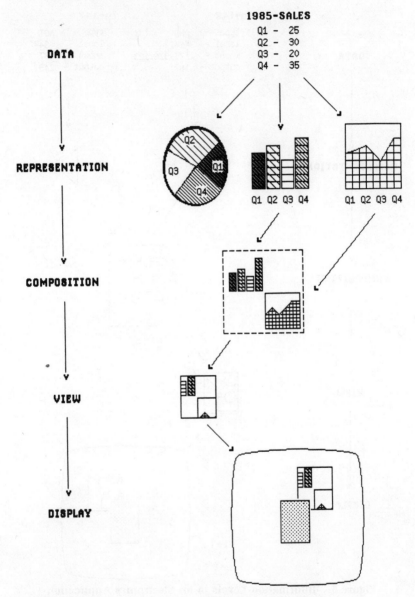

Figure 6.   Information Levels in an Sales Application

to a window, and a display is analogous to a viewport (although these analogies should not be pushed to the limit). However, this model does not describe a graphics system in the usual sense. It is pictorially more limited; this system is not intended to support sophisticated graphics features such as model clipping, perspective, etc. It only has sufficient

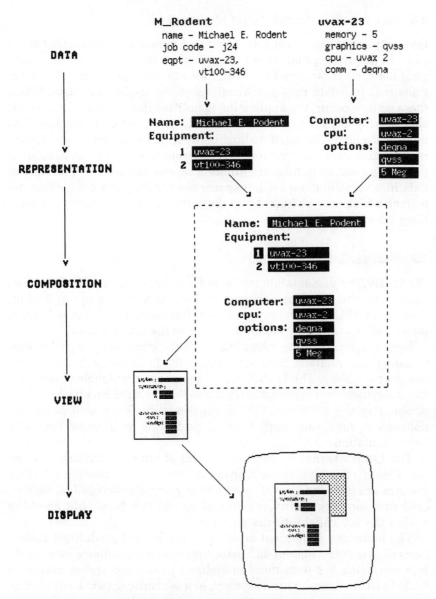

Figure 7.   Information Levels in a Business Application

pictorial expressiveness to represent metaphoric interfaces, in which icons and simple graphics are usually adequate. OASIS also has some of the features of a window manager in allowing multiple views with arbitrary content. OASIS differs from most graphics or window systems in having a single presentation system which integrates these features.

2.4. User Interface Model (Input Mapping)

User actions, such as keyboard input and mouse selection, also have a place in this conceptual model. The interface designer specifies a mapping between these low-level input events and operations. Some actions will translate into modifications of the application data. When these actions occur, the application is notified that a piece of the data it shares with OASIS has been modified. Other actions translate into modifications of the relationships between information levels. Examples include panning the view to a different piece of the composition, deleting a view, switching to a different representation for some class of data in a specific composition space, etc. OASIS restricts neither the actions which may be bound, nor the primitive data or mapping operations which may be used.

2.5. Designer Interface Model

Obviously, the presentation methods for a particular application must come from the interface designer. There is a mapping of application data to specific presentations and a similar mapping of user actions to modifications of the application data or of the presentation.

Both the presentation mappings and the input mappings are provided by the interface designer through the tools which make up the designer interface. The OASIS model includes three levels of designer interface; these levels reflect several possible levels of involvement by a designer in the details of OASIS functionality. They also provide a convenient migration path from a prototype to a more complete implementation.

The OASIS kernel is the lowest level at which interfaces may be specified. At this level there is no commitment to any specific interface features or style, and the full power of the kernel is accessible. Significant programming ability is required to use this level, but anything within OASIS' capabilities is possible.[2]

The enhanced functional layer provides several predefined collections of data object classes and mappings which are conventional interface templates. We term these predefined collections styles; examples include basic menus, a forms system, or a semantic network editor. The interface designer can use these templates as they are, modify and extend them or change their presentation, or use them as a springboard to create completely new styles. This layer can be elaborated indefinitely either by the OASIS developers or by interface designers. The

---

[2] The object-oriented design and the LISP environment used to create OASIS make it relatively easy to add features to this kernel level when an interface designer wants something unanticipated.

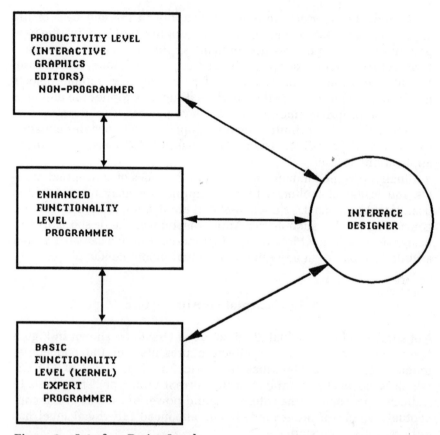

Figure 8.   Interface Design Levels

programming ability required to use this level is significantly less than
for the kernel. The productivity layer is a set of interactive tools for
interface design. These tools are a current research topic; they include
representation editors or interface layout editors. These tools are implemented in OASIS, and require less programming ability than the lower
architectural levels. At each successive layer, there is less expressive
power available to the interface designer; but there is also less effort to
define a working interface.

2.6. Benefits of this Conceptual Model

This system model has several useful features: First, the communication channel between the application program and OASIS is narrowed
to the creation, deletion, and modification of application data objects.
This narrowness encourages strict separation of the application from
the presentation. In addition, it simplifies many implementation issues
within OASIS.

Second, the interface designer can supply to the end user of his application any of the capabilities of the supplied tool kit. Creating new graphics objects is unnecessary for many applications. But for schematic layout system, for example, this is an important feature. In this case, the interface designer makes the tool for creating new graphics objects available to the user. Thus the interface designer supplies the end user with the appropriate amount of expressive power.

Third, collecting primitive mapping operations into styles expands the library of predefined styles. This makes OASIS easier for future applications to use.

Finally, this model does not constrain the types of conceptual models and visual metaphors which the application may present to the user. If the interface developer wants his application to have a desk-top conceptual model, such as the Apple Macintosh,[3] he or she is free to design an interface which follows that model. But one can also design an interface based on any other conceptual model he/she pleases.

3. Implementation Architecture

Not surprisingly, the actual architecture of OASIS, as shown in Figure 9, closely resembles the architecture presented in the conceptual model. This section describes the basic functional level of OASIS, which is reasonably complete in the current prototype. The goal is to indicate how some of the interesting and powerful aspects of the conceptual model are implemented. The enhanced functional level has only recently been started.

Both the OASIS kernel and the interface descriptions created by interface designers are object-oriented. OASIS was designed and built on Digital's VAXstation, using the VMS operating system and Digital's VAX LISP/VMS. OASIS is implemented in a simple object-oriented LISP-based system which supports an arbitrary number of object slots and single-line inheritance of methods, instance variables, and default values. This makes it very natural to describe the implementation in terms of the object classes and their functions.[4] To reduce confusion, the types of objects that can be received from the application will always be referred to as ADOs to distinguish them from all the other types of objects which exist inside OASIS.

---

[3] Macintosh is a trademark licensed to Apple Computer, Inc.

[4] An excellent introduction to object-oriented programming for a UIMS which attacks a different part of the interface system problem space may be found in Sibert, Hurley, and Bleser (1986).

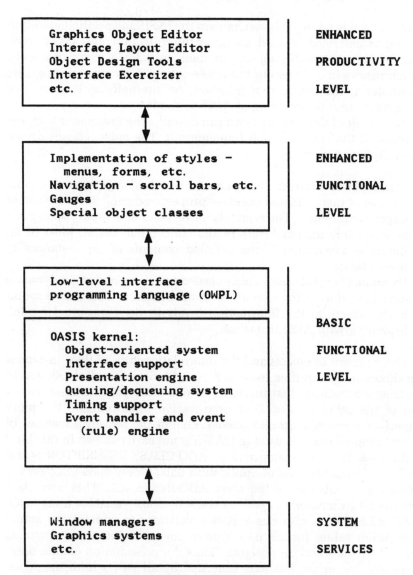

Figure 9. OASIS Presentation Architecture

4. The Presentation Engine

The presentation engine in OASIS uses an unusual approach. The narrow application interface suggested a presentation engine that was data-driven, in a manner similar to forward chaining inference engines or to the *active values* of CommonLoops (Stefik, Bobrow, & Kahn,

1986). There is no explicit mechanism in OASIS to specify that output should be generated. Instead, changing the collection of ADOs by creating, deleting, or modifying one of them initiates a chain of events, which results in a change in the presentation. A change can originate externally at the application interface, or internally as the result of some user input or the firing of ADO methods.

As a result of this approach we can describe the presentation engine in terms of the objects which implement it. The object classes divide naturally into two types:

- Static Object Classes: Those classes which always have the same number of instances and the same properties during the execution of a specific interface. These largely correspond to mapping operations between information levels in the conceptual model. Most of an interface description is the detailed contents of the instances of these classes.
- Dynamic Object Classes: Those classes which represent the dynamic data base during the execution of an interface. These correspond fairly closely to the information levels in the conceptual model, beginning with ADO instances.

These classes of objects and the interrelationships of their instances are shown in a simplified form in Figure 10. Structural links shown in the diagram indicate that instances of one class point to instances of one of the other classes. Data or directive links indicate the more important types of messages passed. One of the powerful features of object-oriented systems used in OASIS is not easily shown in this kind of diagram. When an instance of an ADO-CLASS-DESCRIPTOR is created to represent a class of application data, a new class of objects is defined as a subclass of the class ADO-INSTANCE. This new class inherits all its methods as well as some instance variables from ADO-INSTANCE, but it also has instance variables to contain the actual application values for the new type of object, and any new methods defined by the interface designer. Thus the presentation engine operates only due to the methods inherited by all ADOs from the ADO-INSTANCE class. The properties described below for ADO-INSTANCE objects are thus true for all ADOs.

4.1. Dynamic Objects

Dynamic objects store information about the current state of the interface presentation. Most of their properties can be inferred from the conceptual model.

STATIC OBJECTS   DYNAMIC OBJECTS

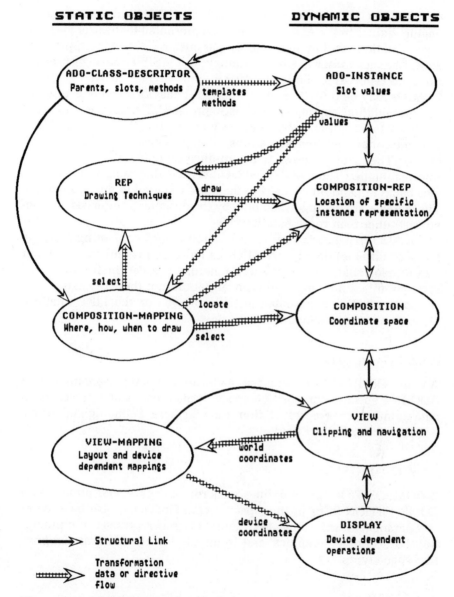

Figure 10.   OASIS Presentation Engine

4.1.1. ADO-INSTANCE

An ADO-INSTANCE may be created either by the application or by procedural components internal to the interface description. Each instance is created with the slots and default values specified by its ADO-

CLASS-DESCRIPTOR. Any change to an ADO fires the presentation engine. Values in the ADO's slots may be presented to the user via some representation, or they may supply parameter values to mapping objects. Changes to ADOs which originate in OASIS because of user actions are reported to the application.

ADOs may be used to control interface behavior as well as to drive the presentation engine. Control is expressed as side-effects of ADO methods; for example, to create a new view or other ADOs. These ADOs will often have no representations, or representations which do not change. They will be known to the application only if they pass control information between it and OASIS. Otherwise, they simply affect interface behavior, and no changes to them are reported to the application. These ADOs are distinguished only by the designer's emphasis on side-effects rather than representations.

An ADO instance is similar to a scalar record containing multiple fields of different data types. ADOs can also be instantiated as one or two dimensional vectors of these records. The cardinality of an instantiation is a property of the instantiation, not the ADO class. This supports repetitive presentations, like menus or the LIFT interface given as an example below.

4.1.2. COMPOSITION-REP

A COMPOSITION-REP describes the location of a representation of an ADO in a specific composition space. It also retains any presentation data unique to that representation, e.g. whether it is highlighted, or the editing status of a text field.

4.1.3. COMPOSITION

A COMPOSITION object defines a coordinate space, and points to all COMPOSITION-REPs in that space. COMPOSITIONs also have types and parameters which specify different classes of presentation properties. For example, 'graphics' and 'scrolled text' are different composition space types.

4.1.4. VIEW

A VIEW object specifies the viewing (clipping) rectangle for a composition. A VIEW can pan across or zoom into a composition. All dynamic objects, from ADO-INSTANCEs to VIEWs (but excluding DISPLAYs) describe virtual rather than device-dependent coordinate spaces.

4.1.5. DISPLAY

A DISPLAY object maps one-to-one with a single VIEW. It is always device-dependent, and contains all necessary information and methods to map a view and its operations to a particular device.

4.2. Static Objects

The bulk of an interface description data base defines static objects. They represent most of the power of the presentation engine. Their number is usually fixed by the interface description, although it is possible for the procedures included in the description to create more.

The power which is not in static objects is found in the procedures which the interface designer can provide with the interface definition. Most of this procedural information is embedded in the methods defined for ADO classes, either for the built-in CREATE, MODIFY, or DELETE methods, or methods written and fired by the designer. Procedural information can also be embedded in mapping objects themselves, since their defining parameters can be either constants or values computed while an interface is running.

4.2.1. ADO-CLASS-DESCRIPTOR

An ADO-CLASS-DESCRIPTOR describes an ADO class. An ADO class can inherit slots and methods from superclasses of ADOs just as all the other object classes used to implement OASIS can. The class descriptor specifies instance variables and their default values. All ADO classes have three built-in methods: CREATE, MODIFY, and DELETE. These are automatically fired by the presentation engine whenever instances are created, modified, or deleted. These methods are the principal procedural hook associated with ADOs, but the interface designer can also provide additional methods, which can be fired by any procedural information in the interface description.

4.2.2. REP

A REP object specifies how an object should be represented graphically. In essence a REP is a static mapping object which describes how an ADO should be mapped into some presentable entity. It may specify a primitive representation, e.g., a vector, arc, or text, or it may describe a composite of simpler representations. Composite REPs can create arbitrarily complex graphic representations by allowing the interface designer to specify transformations to be applied to components of a REP before they are drawn. All REPs support translation, rotation, and scaling transformations. In addition to transformations, all the parameters which describe REPs (e.g. transformation parameters or text to be displayed) can be set from slot values in the ADO being represented. The interface designer can also supply arbitrary procedural information to compute parameter values.

This modeling of representation as hierarchies of REPS nested arbitrarily deep, with transformation or value substitution possible at each level, provides the interface designer with a powerful and flexible set of graphics and text operations.

4.2.3. COMPOSITION-MAPPING

A COMPOSITION-MAPPING object specifies how and where ADO instances are represented in some composition space. COMPOSITION-MAPPING objects are associated with ADO classes, and apply to all ADO instances in that class. Its mapping transformation can be stated as:

Map <u>ADO–CLASS</u> into <u>composition</u> at <u>location</u> using <u>rep</u>
when <u>condition</u>

The composition mappings for a class are applied whenever an instance of the class is changes. The result of executing this transformation is to create a single representation of an ADO instance in a single composition space. (A COMPOSITION-REP object is instantiated). *Composition* and *location* name the composition space and location for the ADO representation. *Rep* names the REP object which will draw the representation. *Condition* is a boolean which controls whether the representation appears. The designer supplies multiple composition mappings if she wants multiple representations. The ADO-CLASS is a fixed value naming the associated class; all other parameters of this mapping may be constant, supplied by ADO slot values or computed by arbitrary procedures.

Executing this transformation may remove a representation from a composition space. This occurs when the value of *condition* becomes false when it was previously true. (ADO deletion removes all representations of that instance without invoking this mapping transformation.) An ADO-class may have no composition mappings, in which case it must be a control class which exists for its side-effects. No presentation can occur without a composition mapping.

4.2.4. VIEW-MAPPING

A VIEW-MAPPING object supplies parameters to map a view into some device via a display (a DISPLAY object is instantiated). The mapping supplies location and sizing parameters in device dependent units. Multiple view mappings must be specified to map views onto different types of devices. This mapping object is much less powerful than either a REP or COMPOSITION-MAPPING, but its parameters may be supplied in the same way (constants, ADO slot values, or procedures).

4.3. OPERATION

The presentation engine is fired by any change to an ADO instance. It invokes each composition mapping defined for the ADO's class and executes any presentation changes which the mapping specifies. This may create or delete COMPOSITION-REPs corresponding to each ADO presentation in a composition space. The necessary COMPOSITION, VIEW, and DISPLAY objects usually already exist. They are typically defined by the CREATE method of some ADO accessible to the application. ADO changes which trigger the engine may originate either in the application, or in input mappings which handle user input. These cases differ in that user-generated changes are reported back to the application.

5. The Input Mapping Engine

As stated earlier, the input processing capabilities provided to interface designers are relatively simple. These capabilities were designed to achieve three objectives:

- It must do anything realizable on the physical device(s).
- It must be easy for the interface designer to implement direct manipulation and simple textual interfaces.
- The commitment of OASIS computing resources (and project development resources) should be lower than for the presentation system (since the presentation system is more critical for our group's interfaces).

The last requirement precluded a powerful dialogue manager and the second requirement precluded a simple-minded one. We chose simple input-processing specification over powerful dialogue management.

This choice led us to extend the simple input-handling in programmable text editors. Our input engine is designed around a synchronized stream of events, which are supplied to an input queue by a low-level event handler. An event can be physical, such as a mouse button click; temporal, like a timer expiration; or logical, created within some procedural element in the interface description.

The interface designer can specify an action to occur whenever a specific type of event occurs. This is similar to the binding of keys to actions which has been so successful in programmable editors. Some programmable editors, such as EMACS, allow these bindings to be collected into a key-map structure and applied to specific text buffers rather than all buffers. OASIS provides an analogous structure to collect the mappings from events into actions, and to specify the contexts where they apply.

5.1. Events

The input engine distinguishes between two classes of input events.

- Global Events: which have no relation to a specific view (window). OASIS currently supports two: timer events and logical events.
- View Events: which apply to a specific view. These include mouse button clicks, mouse tracking, and keyboard input.

A further distinction can be made between these two classes of events. All view events correspond to input received when the user performs some physical activity. In contrast, all global events are generated by the execution of procedural portions of the interface description, and do not correspond directly to any physical actions of the end user. If facilities are added for handling additional physical input devices,[5] then this distinction will no longer be true.

5.2. Actions

Input processing takes place through actions associated with events by the interface designer. Whenever an event is received, it is placed at the end of an event queue. Events are processed in order from the front of the queue. Any action associated with the event by the interface designer is then executed; the event is ignored if there is no associated action.

---

[5] Adding simultaneous input from multiple devices should be easy to implement, given this event stream design.

Actions are encoded as procedural descriptions. This allows the full capabilities of LISP to be used if the interface designer feels it is necessary. However, most of the time the actions involve only a small set of operations. These common operations include:

- Creating, deleting, or modifying an ADO (e.g., dragging an object on the screen is equivalent to modifying an ADO).
- Sending a message (such as SELECTION) to an ADO.
- Storing or retrieving some state value.
- Generating a logical event or starting a timer event.

In theory, nearly all desired actions could be encoded as conditional or sequential combinations of these operations. However, in some cases, especially where the speed of interaction is critical, this general mechanism is too slow. For these situations we added to the OASIS kernel a second level of operations which can respond much faster. These second-level operations include dragging, various sorts of rubber-banding and text field editing (keyboard input). The keyboard input editor also meets our second design objective by freeing the interface designer from specifying his or her own editor, or handling keyboard input event by event.

Note that event/action association is another instance of procedural information in interface descriptions, such as ADO methods and REP procedural elements.

5.3. Observations

Here are several observations about this type of input specification. First, by permitting procedural specification of the actions to be performed when input occurs, the input engine can indeed meet its first objective: Any action realizable on the device can (in theory) be constructed.

Second, in building various user interfaces on workstations, we have found that one of the important but often neglected issues is the perceived response time. People normally think in multiple threads. They should be able to think that way with a multiwindow interface. They should be able to switch contexts and to do something else while the system is performing an operation in the current context. The ability to generate events which are placed at the end of the queue of input events permits the interface designer to break up costly operations into smaller pieces and thereby improve the perceived response time.

Last, although OASIS only provides the interface designers with facilities at the lexical and syntactical levels,[6] it is sufficient for building interfaces for its intended applications.

6. Example Interfaces

This section describes two interfaces, which were developed to test the presentation engine, in order to demonstrate some of the capabilities of OASIS, and how an interface designer uses them. The first is an analog/digital clock, and the second is a graphics interface to an elevator (lift) simulation.

These examples are illustrative rather than typical expert system interfaces. They show how OASIS supports a graphically rich user interface from a minimum application interface, and hint at the power of composition mappings and the procedural elements of REPs. We have also used the clock example to show the design process for an OASIS interface.

6.1. The Clock Example

To build an analog/digital clock, first recognize what information must pass through the interface from the application. In this simple example there is no user input so nothing needs to pass to the application from OASIS. The only information which must pass to OASIS is the actual hours, minutes, and seconds for the current time.

The second step is to examine the representations we want for the interface. There will be analog and digital representations of the same time data. In both cases, all time values (hours, minutes, and seconds) have similar representations. In the analog clock they are all represented by hands. The size of the hands reflects which time value is represented, and the angle of the hands reflect the actual time value. In the digital clock each of the three values is represented as two numerals.

At this point, we could decide that hours, minutes, and seconds should each be different classes of ADOs, perhaps all subclasses of some higher class. However, since there will never be more than one instance of each type of value, and to keep the interface description simple, we will only define one class of time value which we name HAND. Figure 11 shows three instances of the class HAND. The HAND ADO has an instance variable for a time value and another which indicates the type of the time value. In addition to the HAND class, our

---

[6] as defined in Foley and Van Dam (1982).

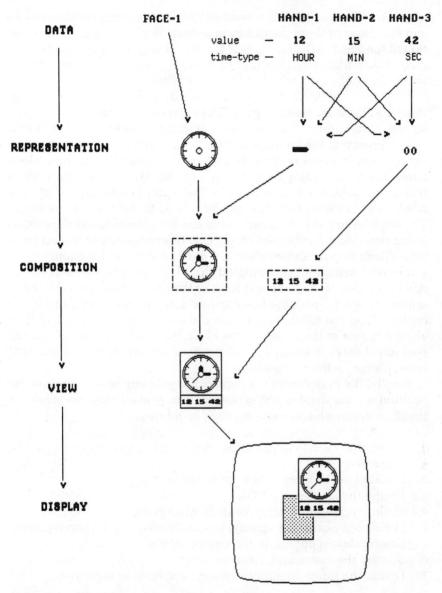

Figure 11.   The Information Levels in a Clock

interface description is simpler if we create a second ADO class named FACE. There will only be one instance of a FACE, and it will be represented by the analog dial and tick marks. However, the side-effects of the FACE are more important than its representation. Our interface description uses the creation of an instance of the FACE class as a trigger for the creation of the hand ADOs, the two compositions spaces and the views of those composition spaces. Similarly, it uses the deletion of the FACE ADO as a trigger for the deletion of these objects. This kind of side-effect provides application and interface designers a mechanism for controlling which ADOs are visible.

Now that the ADO classes are defined, we can build the analog representations for these objects. The representation of the FACE is a simple composite of the available graphics primitives. The HAND ADOs, however, need a more complex representation. We start with a single graphic primitive which defines the general form for a clock hand. Then, depending on the values in the ADO, the representation scales the clock hand as needed for that specific time type. After the clock hand has been scaled, it can be rotated to the appropriate angle. The angle of rotation is based on the current time value and the maximum time value for that time type. One representation serves all three values, and scaling and rotation are done by its reset function.

The representation for the digital clock is much simpler. Each HAND ADO is represented by the text form of the time value. Once the representations are defined, the two composition mappings are built. In the analog clock, the hands always use the same representation and they always appear at the center of the clock face. In the digital clock, the position of the representation is dependent on the time type of the ADO being placed in the composition.

Finally, the mapping of the compositions to adjacent views and the position on the display are specified. The general steps to create an interface description are summarized as follows:

1. Determine what information from the application is to be presented.
2. Decide how to present that information.
3. Define the classes of ADOs.
4. Build a representation(s) for each ADO class.
5. Define composition mappings to specify where and when representations should appear in the compositions.
6. Specify the views and displays.
7. Define the input operations (if any) available in each view.

The resulting OASIS-generated clock is shown in Figure 12. In addition to the ADOs described above there is another for the date string.

Here are some final remarks about this example. The time value (HAND) ADOs have multiple representations which present the same information in different but equally valid ways. The analog clock hand representation is the most complex and the most powerful object in this

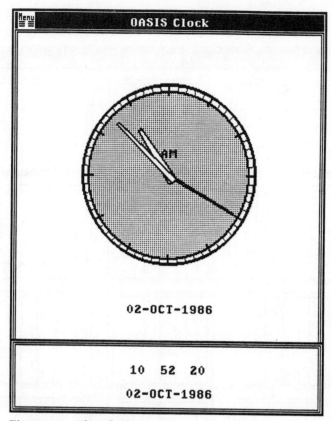

Figure 12.   The Clock

interface. Last, the application interface is extremely limited. The clock
is initialized by creating a FACE ADO and the only other information
passed to OASIS is time values sent at appropriate intervals.

6.2. Lift System Interface

One team in our group has developed a lift (elevator) simulation to test
a protocol engine. We built a user interface for this simulation to test
OASIS. It shows more of the capabilities of OASIS, and it shows a
naturally metaphoric interface for a simple but realistic application.

This interface shows the operation of the elevator simulation in real
time. The elevators move up and down as shown in a floor indicator,
their doors open and close, and floor selection buttons are activated by
clicking on them with a mouse. Elevators are called up or down by
clicking on up/down buttons on each floor.

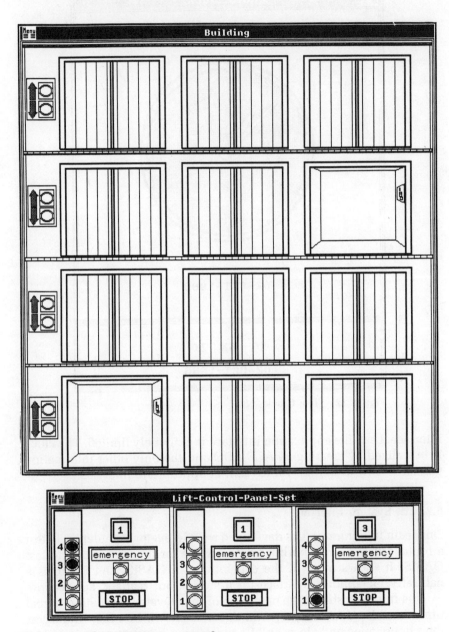

Figure 13.   The LIFT System Interface

The number of elevators and floors is variable and is specified by the application when the simulation starts. With M elevators and N floors, some of the ADO classes representing the interface are:

- START-SIMULATION (1 instance)—models the number of floors and elevators in the simulation. As a side-effect, it defines the necessary views and initializes all the following ADOs for this specific simulation.
- ELEVATOR-DOORS (1 instance which is an M × N array)—models the elevator doors which are either OPEN or CLOSED.
- CALL-BUTTONS (N-element array)—models floor call buttons. Buttons are ON or OFF and represent UP or DOWN requests.
- PANEL (M-element array)—models the control panel and indicators (floor number, STOP/UP/DOWN indicator, etc.).
- FLOOR-BUTTONS (M × N array)—models the floor selection buttons inside each elevator, ON or OFF.

The appearance of the elevator doors is specified in the composition mapping and depends on the ELEVATOR-DOOR condition (OPEN/CLOSE), which chooses between an open and closed representation. Buttons are also represented by two different reps, depending on their condition (ON/OFF). Indicator values are changed directly. Once again, a minimum of information passes through the interface. To initialize, the application creates a START-SIMULATION ADO, giving the number of elevators and floors. This ADO then instantiates all the required ADOs for elevator doors, panels, etc. The composition-mappings for these ADOs compute their locations in the composition based on array indexes of each element.

The only information OASIS sends to the application is a message that button was pressed. In the input mapping defined for the view, a mouse click changes a button's condition slot to ON if it was not already ON.

Similarly, the only information the application sends is:

- Button condition changed to OFF.
- Elevator-door condition changed to OPEN or CLOSE.
- Indicator value change (floor number, UP/DOWN/STOP).

This maps directly internal elements of the lift simulation; no extra information to manage interface behavior is required. All changes in the interface are due to changes in a small number of ADO slots, and those slot values reflect the simulation model rather than the details of the graphics presentation.

7. Conclusions

The primary goal of OASIS is to provide a powerful and appropriate tool for constructing user interfaces for expert systems. The properties and requirements of these systems have been a pervasive influence in its design.

The most important principle in the design of expert systems is the separation of domain knowledge from the problem-solving and inference methods. The distinction between application data and presentation information in OASIS represents a similar separation of domain information from control information. This separation of domain information in expert systems makes it simple and natural to adopt OASIS's data-driven presentation approach for building their user interfaces. Knowledge in an expert system is an abstraction which represents a useful model of a domain and which supports a desired level of reasoning. The mechanisms for representing these abstractions both internally and to users or knowledge engineers are expressive rather than directly representative of physical reality. This quality has led us to a complementary distinction between pictorial and metaphoric interfaces, and to our decision to emphasize and support metaphoric interfaces as the natural type for expert systems.

In developing OASIS we relied on the conceptual model to drive the implementation, rather than using a formal specification or exploratory programming. We have found this approach to have many benefits. First, the model is an excellent vehicle for describing OASIS to users. Second, it provided a principled and coherent guide for implementation design. Finally, considered as a document, it is concise and much easier to maintain than a formal design specification.

We feel several properties of the conceptual model and their implementation in the OASIS prototype will be of particular importance to the tool's success in actual use. These include: the data-driven, multilevel transformation technique which reflects data into a presentation; the narrowness of the application interface and corresponding asynchronous control model; and the open, multilevel architecture to support interface design at different levels of abstraction and programmer skill. We have successfully implemented several interfaces in which the generic presentation system supports an interesting and graphically rich interface driven by a small number of semantically appropriate objects passing through the application interface.

We are currently developing the enhanced functional level of the system, and beginning some exploratory programming of the productivity level. In the near future OASIS will be used to develop some user interfaces for production expert systems. We expect OASIS to become a uniquely powerful and flexible tool for creating both conventional and experimental interfaces for these systems.

Acknowledgments

We are thankful for the editorial assistance and comments of David Buffo and Richard Rubinstein. The LIFT interface example was developed by MIT undergraduate YuChun Lee while he was an intern in our group.

OASIS development has been supported within the Advanced Systems and Tools group of the Intelligent Systems Technologies group, a member of the Artificial Intelligence Center of Digital Equipment Corporation. Ross Faneuf is a Principal Software Engineer, and Steven Kirk is a Senior Software Engineer; they are members of the OASIS project team.

VAX, VMS, and VAXstation are trademarks registered to Digital Equipment Corporation.

References

Baecker, R. (1980). Towards an effective characterization of graphical interaction. In R. Guedj et al. (Ed.), *Methodology of Interaction*. North–Holland, pp. 127–147.

Buxton, W., Sniderman, R. (1980). Iteration in the design of the human-computer interface. In P. Stager (Ed.), Quality of work life and human factors. *Proceedings of the 13th annual meeting of the Human Factors Association of Canada*, pp. 72–81.

Buxton, W. (1983). Lexical and pragmatic considerations of input structures. *Computer Graphics, 17*(3), 31–37.

Buxton, W., Lamb, M. R., Sherman, D., Smith, K. C. (1983). Towards a comprehensive user interface management system. *Computer Graphics, 17*(3), 35–42.

Buxton, W., Myers, B. A. (1986). Creating highly-interactive and graphical user interfaces by demonstration. *Computer Graphics, 20*(3).

Buxton, W. (1986). Chunking and phrasing and the design of human-computer dialogues. *Proceedings IFIP World Computer Congress*.

Coutaz, J. (1985). Abstractions for user interface design. *IEE Computer* (September) 21–34.

Foley, J. D., Van Dam, A. (1982). *Fundamentals of interactive computer graphics*. Reading, MA: Addison–Wesley.

Foley, J. D., Wallace, V. L., Chan, P. (1984). The human factors of computer graphics interaction techniques. *IEEE Computer Graphics and Applications* (November), 13–48.

Hayes, P. J., Szekely, P. A. (1983). Graceful interaction through the COUSIN command interface. *International Journal of Man-Machine Studies, 19,* 285–306.

Hayes, P. J., Lerner, R. A., Szekely, P. A. (1985). Design alternatives for user interface management systems based on experience with COUSIN. *Proceedings CHI'85,* pp. 169–175.

Henderson, D. A., Jr. (1986). The trillium user interface design environment. *Proceedings CHI'86,* pp. 221–227.

Jacob, R. J. K. (1983). Using formal specifications in the design of a human-computer interface. *CACM, 26*(4), 259–264.

Jacob, R. J. K. (1983). Executable specifications for a human-computer interface. *Proceedings CHI'83,* pp. 28–34.

Kaczmarek, T., Mark, W., & Sondheimer, N. (1983). The Consul/CUE interface: An integrated interactive environment. *Proceedings CHI'83,* pp. 98–102.

Olsen, D. R., Jr., Buxton, W., & Ehrich, R. (1984). A context for user interface management. *IEEE Computer Graphics & Applications, 17*(3), 33–42.

Olsen, D. R., Jr., Dempsey, E. P., Rogge, R. (1985). Input/output linkage in a user interface management system. *Proceedings SIGGRAPH'85, 19*(3), 191–197.

Rentsh, T. (1982). Object oriented programming. *SIGPLAN Notices, 17*(9), 51–57.

Schulert, A. J., Rogers, G. T., Hamilton, J. A. (1985). ADM—A Dialog Manager. *Proceedings CHI'85,* 177–183.

Sibert, J. L., Hurley, W. D., Bleser, T. W. (1986). An Object-Oriented User Interface Management System. *Proceedings SIGGRAPH'86,* 259–268.

Stallman, R. M. (1981). EMACS, the extensible, customizable, self-documenting display editor. *MIT AI Lab Memo 519a.*

Tanner, P. P., & Buxton, W. (1985). Some issues in future user interface management system (UIMS) development. In Pfaff, G. (Ed.), *User interface management systems.* Berlin: Springer-Verlag, pp. 67–79.

Stefik, M. J., Bobrow, D. G., Kahn, K. M. (1986). Integrating access-oriented programming into a multiparadigm environment. *IEEE Software, 3*(1), 10–18.

Stefik, M., & Bobrow, D. (1986). Object-oriented programming: Themes and variations. *AI Magazine, 6*(4), 40–62.

Thomas, J. J. et al. (1983). Graphical input interaction technique (GIIT). Workshop Summary, *Computer Graphics, 17*(1), 5–30.

TEN

Explanation: The Role of Control Strategies and Deep Models*

B. Chandrasekaran, Michael C. Tanner, and John R. Josephson

Laboratory for Artificial Intelligence Research, Ohio State University

Abstract

Good explanation can make an expert system's advice more understandable and more believable. But explanation is a large problem, involving issues of presentation, user modeling, and the system's self-understanding. We propose to concentrate on the third, how a system can understand its own problem-solving knowledge and strategy, since we believe this provides the content of any explanation. Unfortunately, most current approaches to expert system construction require expressing knowledge and control at such a low level of abstraction that it is difficult to express explanations at a level appropriate to the problem. In this chapter we propose the generic task methodology as a way of building expert systems so that the basic explanation constructs are available closer to the conceptual level of the user, making them easier to explain at higher levels. In addition we describe a representation for deep models of a domain which can be used to justify problem-solving knowledge by appealing to general domain knowledge.

* Research supported by Defense Advanced Research Projects Agency, RADC Contract F30602–85–C–0010.

1. Introduction

1.1. Need for Explanation in Expert Systems

Explanation is one aspect of user interfaces for expert systems. The ability of a system to explain how it reached a decision is crucial to making it usable. Expert systems will earn their use partly by the range of problems that they can handle and the correctness of their solutions and consultations. But in many applications they will also need, in addition to these qualities, an ability to *justify* and *explain* their advice to the user. This will be necessary for a number of reasons:

1. Because of the rather limited knowledge bases of expert systems, the user may want to know if the system took into account all the knowledge that the user may consider relevant.
2. The user may want to know if the strategies adopted by the system for solving the problem are satisfactory.
3. The user may wish to know if all the relevant data describing the problem state are being considered.

In addition, the ability to explain oneself is generally a reassurance that the expert is more than simply a "rule follower." Thus, it is generally recognized that research on how expert problem-solving systems can generate satisfactory explanations of their behavior is needed.

1.2. What *is* an explanation?

Webster's Dictionary defines the term "explain" from its etymology as, "to make plain; to make something clear." Making something clear is to make the listener "understand." This suggests that there is no general mechanism called an "explainer," but that AI systems will acquire explanatory capabilities in proportion to the distinct kinds of under-standing that the state of AI at a given time is able to represent. Thus a theory of explanation will need to go hand in hand with theories of understanding as they develop.

The main point of the forgoing is the close relationship between structures of understanding and explanation capabilities. This pro-vides the theme of this chapter. In particular, we will describe how explanation is related to understanding problem solving and to deep models of the domain.

1.3. A Decomposition of the Explanation Problem

In this paper we give a decomposition of the problem of explanation generation in knowledge-based systems and propose a mechanism for dealing with a part of that problem. There are three top-level components that can be distinguished:

1. How a problem solver represents its own problem-solving activity and retrieves the relevant portions appropriately in response to user queries. Here the language in which the problem-solving behavior is encoded is very important for making the response perspicuous.
2. How user's goals, state of knowledge, etc., are used to *filter* and *shape* the output of the process in (1) above so that the explanation is responsive to user's needs, is not overly and unnecessarily detailed, is couched in terms which are appropriate to the user's level of understanding, etc. Here *user modeling* is an important issue.
3. How an appropriate human–machine interface displays and presents the information to a user in an effective way. Here the issues include natural language understanding, natural language generation, and principles of effective graphical displays.

No matter how good the theories are for (2) and (3), if a poor representation is adopted for (1) then, at best, inappropriate explanations will be presented packaged in a good interface. That is, the basic *content* of the explanations are generated in stage (1). We need to pay great attention to how a problem solver can *comprehend* its own problem-solving activity. Much of our effort is devoted to developing a good theory of this and testing it by implementation of prototype systems.

The explanation of problem solving itself, i.e., (1) above, has three components:

1. Explaining why certain decisions were made or were not made. This has to do with how the data in a particular case related to the knowledge for making specific decisions or choices.
2. Explaining the elements of the knowledge base itself. For example, if the knowledge base contains plan fragments which are to be instantiated and assembled into longer plans, the problem solver may be called upon to explain the rationale behind the plan fragments. Similarly if, during a particular diagnosis, a troubleshooter uses the knowledge that a low voltage between certain terminals is evidence for a particular malfunction, a user might want to know the reasoning behind the knowledge fragment.
3. Explaining the problem-solving strategy and the control behavior of the problem solver. This would typically be at a higher level of abstraction than in explanations of type 1.

It should be noted that typically types 1 and 3 above involve the *run-time* behavior of a problem solver (and thus cannot in general be precompiled without running into combinatorial problems), while explanation structures for type 2 above can in principle be attached to the knowledge fragments at the time the knowledge base is put together.

In section 3.2 we will propose that our theory of generic types of problem solving (Chandrasekaran, 1984), each with its own architecture, is especially suited to building systems that can explain their control strategy (type 3 above). Systems built using this generic task methodology are composed of knowledge level agents which each perform an epistemically significant task. Thus, they are also capable of producing type 1 explanations, how data match knowledge, based on the memory of each agent for its own problem-solving history. In addition we propose to use the functional representation (Sembugamoorthy & Chandrasekaran, 1986) for deep models of the domain to be used for type 2 explanations, relating the domain knowledge to problem-solving knowledge. We have implemented an expert planning assistant program to test some of our ideas on explanation.

2. State of the Art in Explanation in Expert Systems

The state of the art in explanation can be summarized by three good ideas. The first was due to Davis, Shortliffe, and the others who worked on the original MYCIN system (Davis, 1976; Shortliffe, 1976). The essential idea is that a trace of problem-solving activity at the architecture level can be used to give explanations about what a system is doing. MYCIN had an explanation facility which could answer questions from the user about why certain conclusions were reached: "How a request for data is related to a goal, how one goal leads to another, and how a goal is achieved" (Clancey, 1983). Its explanations were entirely expressed in terms of rules and goals. The question "WHY?" was interpreted as, "Which rule needs this datum, and what is the consequent (goal conclusion) in the rule?" It had explicit representation only of the rules, and not of the *strategies* in problem solving that are implicitly encoded in the rule formalism by the system designer. Thus, it could not answer "WHY?" questions that needed to be interpreted strategically. It also could not justify the rules themselves.

Clancey noted that an expert system typically performs a task at a higher level of abstraction than the goal-subgoal level of a rule base (Clancey, 1983). Further, if its behavior is represented at the task level, the system can produce explanation at the task level. This is the second important idea on explanation. NEOMYCIN (Clancey & Letsinger, 1981) solves the same diagnosis problem as MYCIN but represents the diagnostic task more explicitly. It contains such diagnostic operators as "establish hypothesis space," "explore and refine," and "group and differentiate," which represent the diagnostic strategy and in terms of which it can explain its problem-solving activity (Clancey, 1985). Thus, NEOMYCIN can give strategic explanations which describe its higher-level goals. However, it still cannot justify the rules.

With his XPLAIN system Swartout introduced the third good idea (1983). An expert system has task specific goals and problem-solving knowledge which are *compiled* out of more general domain knowledge. If a trace of the compilation is remembered then rules in the system can be justified in terms of the deeper knowledge. XPLAIN is able to use deep knowledge, called the "domain model," and a representation of problem-solving control strategies, called "domain principles," to compile an expert system. Swartout calls this approach "automatic programming," but from the viewpoint of explanation, what is important is that the control strategy can be explicitly examined for analyzing the system behavior and the deep model can be used to justify the system's rules. This system and the approach are discussed in greater detail in Section 3.1.3.

Our own work fits directly into the spirit of these three ideas, though we differ in some ways. We want our systems to explain themselves at the architecture level in a way that is appropriate to the problem-solving task they are performing and we think it is necessary to have a deep model of the domain which can be accessed by the system for justifying its knowledge. Our differences with the above are subtle, but significant. In this chapter we set up a framework for explanation which we hope will clarify these points of similarity and difference and provide a common ground for discussion of the topic of explanation.

3. Explanation in Expert Systems: A Proposed Framework

3.1. Types of Explanations

In an earlier section, we presented a decomposition of the issues in explanation into three components: the structure of the problem-solving system itself, user modeling, and issues of presentation. In this section, we present the outlines of a new framework that we have developed for research on issues of explanation related to the problem-solving system itself. We identify approaches to explain control strategies and the knowledge structures of expert systems. The issues of explanation related to the problem-solving system itself are broken down into three parts, corresponding to the structures that need to be examined to construct the explanation.

We propose that explanation of problem-solving activity can be categorized into *three distinct types,* viz., Type 1, how the data match the local goals; Type 2, how the knowledge itself can be justified; and Type 3, how the control strategy can be justified. We shall suggest in Section 3.4 that problem-solving knowledge can be justified by tracing how it can be derived from deeper models of the domain. In Section 3.2 we will show that families of control strategies can be identified with our taxonomy of problem-solving types, and how a program can justify the control strategy it used in a certain situation by reference to the type of problem solving it is doing. In the rest of this section, we elaborate further on the three types of explanation.

3.1.1. Type 1: How the Data Match Local Goals

Type 1 Explanation relates the actual problem-solving behavior to problem state or data describing the problem. This involves examining appropriate fragments of the run-time behavior of the system. For example, in a medical diagnosis system, the following question may be asked by a user.

> User: *"Why do you say that the patient has cholestasis?"*
> System: *"Because the patient has high bilirubin in blood, jaundice,and X-rays suggest an obstruction in the biliary duct."*

Or, in an economic-planning consultant,

> User: *"Why do you conclude that a tax cut is appropriate here?"*
> System: *"Because its preconditions are high inflation and trade deficits, and current conditions include these factors."*

These explanations are of how, for this *particular* instance of the problem, problem specific data matched pieces of the knowledge base and certain conclusions were drawn. It is important to note that typically cholestasis may be concludable from a number of different possible combinations of data, or a tax cut may be appropriate for a number of different situations. The user wants to know which data combination was present in this particular problem. This requires keeping a trace of the problem-solving behavior, examining it, and constructing the explanation from the trace.

3.1.2. Type 2: Justification of Knowledge

The user may not be satisfied with this level of explanation. He may ask,

"Why does high bilirubin in blood indicate cholestasis? Does it have to occur in conjunction with jaundice?"

Or,

"Why is a tax cut a good idea for shrinking trade deficits?"

The answer to this does not involve the particular situation at hand. The system is being asked to explain portions of the knowledge base itself. Knowledge of this type can be obtained in at least three ways.

1. By directly being told: The knowledge can only be justified by appeal to authority: "Textbook, p. 85," "Manual, art. 52," etc.
2. By statistical generalization from examples: "89% of all people with liver diseases are known to have jaundice," "68% of the time when a tax cut was tried, the trade deficit went down," etc. Knowledge of this type can be justified by justifying the generalization methodology, but no understanding of the domain is necessarily involved.
3. The third type is the most interesting. This is where a fragment of the knowledge structure is justified by showing how it was *derived* from a *deeper* understanding of the domain. E.g., "Tax cuts generally encourage savings, stimulate investment, and increase production, which decreases prices, makes goods made here attractive, increases exports, and thus reduces trade deficits." Or, "Because cholestasis is a condition in which bile from the liver does not reach the duodenum which normally breaks down the bile, the bile in a cholestatic situation ends up appearing in blood in a relatively unbroken down form, viz., bilirubin. Jaundice is simply an indication of bile fragments being present in blood too, so it gives added confirmation." Notice that this form of reasoning is not *needed* for concluding a tax cut is appropriate, or that the patient has cholestasis, if the knowledge base contains the pieces of knowledge that relate tax cuts to shrinking trade deficits, or that relate bilirubin in blood to cholestasis. But it nevertheless gives confidence to the user that the system's knowledge was derived from a sound understanding of the domain. By the same token it enables the user to decide if the advice should be disregarded on the ground that some aspects of the domain have changed, or that the system is not taking into account some other facts. Here it is important to note that, while the actual derivation of the knowledge from deeper structures need not be done at run-time, it is nevertheless useful to keep the structure of this compilation available so that it can be appropriately used for explanation generation.

We will concentrate in our work in the third category above, viz., reasoning from deep models. We will present in Section 3.4 an approach called *compilation from functional representations*, which shows how such derivations from deeper models can be done for some task domains. In particular, we have developed an approach in which an agent's understanding of how a device works can be used to derive fragments of diagnostic knowledge. Thus a diagnostic expert system can justify a decision by tracing how a piece of diagnostic knowledge, e.g., the one in the example which related high bilirubin in blood to cholestasis, was derived from an understanding of the structure and function of the device involved. This approach can be extended to *plan debugging*, by viewing a plan as a device meant to accomplish certain functions using certain means, and using diagnostic reasoning to analyze failures in a plan.

3.1.3. Type 3: Explanation of Control Strategy

Consider the following questions by a user to an expert system.

    a. "Why didn't you consider portal hypertension in this case?"
    b. "Why aren't you suggesting increased tariffs as a way of decreasing trade deficits?"
    c. "Why are you asking if the patient had jaundice?"

And consider the following answers.

    a'. "Because I had ruled out circulatory diseases, portal hypertension is a special case of circulatory diseases, and *my strategy is not to consider special cases when I have ruled out the general case.*"
    b'. "Because that plan involves political costs. *My strategy is to consider politically easier plans first.*"
    c'. "Because I am trying to *establish* whether or not the patient has cholestasis, *and a way to establish a disease is to see if a special case of the disease can be established.* Jaundice is a case of cholestasis."

In these explanations, it is easy to see that part of what is being explained is the control strategy of the expert system.

This form of explanation can account for "why not?" as well as "why" questions of a certain type. What is needed is an ability to *abstract* the control strategy, and *match* portions of it to the situation. The actual explanation typically involves a combination of explanations of Type 1 and Type 3. E.g., the italicized portions of the explanations above are of Type 3, and the rest are of Type 1.

Swartout (1983) used the idea of explicitly representing control structures for use in explanation in his XPLAIN system. He represented control knowledge, in an explicit form, in a special knowledge base that he called "domain principles." Basically, these consisted of a series of explicit information concerning how to proceed in problem solving for particular goals. For example, it can have a principle such as, "If the goal is to *administer* ⟨drug⟩, then if the knowledge base has knowledge of the form '⟨drug⟩ causes toxicity,' then set up subgoal, *manage toxicity* of ⟨drug⟩." Even though Swartout does not explicitly refer to this as control knowledge, XPLAIN uses it precisely as control information. The expert system will proceed to manage toxicity as a subgoal for administering a drug. An *automatic programmer* translates this explicit control knowledge into an implicit control behavior of the problem-solving system. XPLAIN can then use domain principles to explain parts of the problem-solving process. The explanation system can say, "I am doing x, because x is needed for goal g1," and if asked, "Why goal g1?", it can say, "Because it is a subgoal of g2." And so on. Both in XPLAIN and in a Clancey's work (1983) on explanations in rule-based systems, this goal–subgoal tree is an essential element in the generation of explanations. Later we will propose ways in which the explanatory vocabulary can be enriched and made more illuminating by identifying *generic types* of goal–subgoal structures. Our theory of types of problem solving will be shown in Section 3.2 to provide a framework for identifying some of the elements of the typology of goal-subgoal structures.

3.1.4. Recapitulation

Understanding the problem-solving behavior of an expert system requires inspecting three structures, each corresponding to a type of explanation:

> Type 1: Trace of run-time, data-dependent, problem-solving behavior, viz., which pieces of knowledge were used and how.
> Type 2: Understanding how a piece of knowledge relates to the domain, how it can be justified.
> Type 3: Understanding the control strategy used by the program in a particular situation.

Our work on deep models is a basis for contributions to Type 2, and our framework of problem-solving types (which is, not coincidentally, also a theory of control structure types) is applicable to Type 3. In the next sections we outline these theories and show how they help the explanation problem.

3.2. Types of Problem Solving and Explanation

3.2.1. Problem-solving Types

Let us briefly outline our theory of problem-solving types (these ideas are presented in greater detail in Chandrasekaran, 1984). The central idea is that there are generic tasks in knowledge-based problem solving, and each generic task is characterized by the following:

1. A task specification in the form of generic types of input and output information.
2. Specific organizations of this knowledge particular to the task.
3. A family of control regimes that are appropriate for the task.

A complex knowledge-based problem-solving activity is best decomposed into these generic types. It will in general be necessary to provide for communication between the various structures specializing in these different types of problem solving.

In our work on expert reasoning in medical and mechanical systems, we have identified four generic tasks. There is no claim that these types are exhaustive; in fact, as our research proceeds we expect that we will identify more generic types. Nevertheless the four types that we have identified cover a variety of complex real world tasks and are thus a useful starting point. The tasks can be briefly summarized as follows:
I. *Classification.* Classify a description of a situation as an element, as specifically as possible, in a *classification hierarchy.* The classificatory knowledge is *distributed* among concepts in this hierarchy. Each conceptual *specialist* contains knowledge that helps it determine whether the concept it stands for can be *established* or *rejected.* Problem solving is top-down. Each concept when called tries to establish, that is, it tries to match its description against the situation description. If it succeeds, it calls its successors, which repeat the process. If a specialist fails to establish, it rejects, and all its successors are also automatically rejected. This control strategy is called *Establish-Refine,* and results in a specific classification. (This account is a simplified one. The reader is referred to Chandrasekaran & Mittal, 1983 for details.) Medical diagnosis can often be viewed as a classification problem.
II. *State abstraction.* Given a change in some state of a system, provide an account of the changes that can be expected in the functions of the

system. Knowledge is distributed in conceptual specialists corresponding to systems and subsystems. These conceptual specialists are connected in a way that mirrors the way the system is put together. Control is basically bottom-up, following the architecture of the system/subsystem relationship. The changes in states are followed through, interpreted as changes in function of subsystems, until the changes in the functions at the desired level of abstraction are obtained. This is useful for reasoning about consequences of actions on complex systems.

III. *Knowledge-Directed Information Passing.* Given attributes of some datum, it is desired to obtain attributes of some other conceptually related datum. The concepts are organized as a *frame hierarchy* (Minsky, 1975). Each frame is a specialist in knowledge-directed data inference for a concept. A specialist, when asked for the value of an attribute, first checks to see if the actual value is known, then uses inheritance relationships to determine if the value can be obtained by inference from the values of appropriate attributes of its parent or children, then uses any demons that may be attached to the slot to query other concepts in other parts of the hierarchy for values of their attributes. If none of this succeeds and if it is appropriate, a default value is produced. This is basically a hierarchical information-passing control regime, with demons providing an override of the hierarchy. This is useful for inferring a medical datum from another, when the latter is available but the former is needed for diagnostic reasoning (Mittal, Chandrasekaran, & Sticklen, 1984).

IV. *Design by Plan Selection and Refinement.* Design an object satisfying certain specifications. Specialists corresponding to components are organized in a hierarchy mirroring the object structure. Each specialist has plans which can be used to make commitments for some dimensions of the component. Control is top-down in general. The following is done recursively until a complete plan is worked out: A specialist is called, the specialist chooses a plan based on some specification, and instantiates some parts of the plan which suggests further specialists to call to fill other parts of the plan. Plan failures are passed up the specialist hierarchy until appropriate changes are made by higher-level specialists, so that specialists that failed may succeed on a second try. Useful in some kinds of expert design tasks. This problem-solving type is discussed in more detail in Section 4.4.

3.3. Role of Problem-solving Types in Type 3 Explanation

Now our claim is that such a typology of problem solving, with its associated goal types, is very useful in explaining the control strategy of the problem solver. Let us take some examples:

Classification

Q: Why did you wish to know if the patient had been exposed to anesthetics?

A: Because I was trying to establish hepatitis.

Q: Why?

A: Because I had already established that the patient had liver disease. Now I am trying to subclassify the case, and hepatitis is one of the subcategories. If I can reject hepatitis, I can reject all the following diseases which are its subclasses.

State Abstraction

Let us assume that the user had asked the system, "What will happen if Valve A is closed?"

Q: Why do you wish to know the engine speed?

A: Because I am trying to decide the change in functionality of the cooling system when Valve A is closed, and engine speed is a datum I need for this.

Q: Why are you considering the cooling system?

A: Because, Valve A is a component of the cooling system.

Knowledge-directed Information Passing

Q: Did the patient have exposure to anesthetics?

A: Did he have any surgery?

Q: Why do you ask?

A: I do not have direct record of anesthetic exposure. I could not inherit a value for this attribute from its parent since there is no direct record that no drug had been given. I was also unable to infer no exposure by ruling out all types of anesthetic. Then the anesthetic concept suggested that if there has been surgery, anesthetic can be reasonably inferred.

Design by Plan Selection and Refinement

Q: Why did you choose the standard table top plan?

A: Because I am trying to complete the specification for the table design plan, for refining which I need to design the table top. The table-top design specialist selected the standard table-top plan because all the requirements were normal.

Q: What will you do if the standard table-top plan fails?

A: The table-top design specialist will select the alternate table-top design plan.

Q: What if it fails?

A: *The table design specialist will* redesign *the table design plan, by weakening the constraints on the table top.*

In the forgoing examples, the italicized terms represent the type of goal that is being pursued. We feel that these terms enrich one's understanding of the behavior of the system.

3.3.1. Combining Control Strategy with Problem State Information

The example explanatory pieces in the forgoing, while based on the appropriate fragments of control knowledge, nevertheless combined the control terms with the state of the problem solving. For example, "The table design plan was being *refined,* and the table-top specialist chose the standard table-top plan because the requirements were normal," or "I *established* liver, am now trying to *refine* by considering hepatitis." Thus the actual generation of the explanation requires a mixture of Types 1 and 3 in the list of explanatory types.

3.4. Type 2 Explanation and Deep Models of the Domain

In this section we indicate how certain kinds of Type 2 explanations for expert systems can be obtained from examining a deeper model of the domain. The knowledge-based system uses some knowledge in a problem-solving machinery to arrive at a solution. How the knowledge was used in the context of data was explanation of Type 1, justification in terms of the problem-solving machinery was of Type 3, and justification of the knowledge itself requires explanation of Type 2. Following our problem-solving framework, the knowledge itself has a form that is appropriate for the type of problem solving that the expert system is engaged in. E.g., for a classification problem, the knowledge will be in a form that relates data to evidence for or against classificatory hypotheses. What we will try to outline here is an approach to how this knowledge may be derived from a deeper understanding of the domain.

We will present our ideas in the context of troubleshooting of devices. (The ideas are applicable to domains other than devices; e.g., debugging a plan may be viewed as troubleshooting of an abstract device.) The diagnostic expert system for many devices may be modeled as an MDX-like classificatory system (Chandrasekaran & Mittal, 1983). Thus we will indicate how classificatory knowledge useful for diagnosis can be derived from an understanding of how the device *functions.* The theory is fairly complex and is presented more completely in (Sembugamoorthy & Chandrasekaran, 1986). Here, we content ourselves with an outline of the central idea in a highly simplified form.

The main idea is that an agent's understanding of how a device works is organized in a way that shows how an intended function is accomplished through series of behavioral states of the device, and how each state transition can be understood either as due to a function of a component or in terms of further details of behavior states. This can be repeated for several levels so that ultimately all the functions of a device can be related to its structure and the to function of the components in that structure. For example, the function that we may call "buzz" of an electric buzzer may be represented as:

```
FUNCTION: Buzz:
    TOMAKE buzzing(buzzer)
    IF pressed (switch)
    BY behavior1
```

and the relevant behavior, Behavior1, can be represented as in Figure 1.

Intuitively, the functional specification above says that the purpose of the Buzz function is to put the buzzer in a state called "buzzing," that this will happen if the switch is pressed, and that the details on how pressing the switch changes the device's state is given in the series of behavioral states that is named behavior1. Behavior1, (Figure 1) says that the buzzer, on the switch being pressed, goes to a state where the electrical connections in the clapper alternately close and open, which results in the state where the clapper is repeatedly hit which results in the buzzer being in the state of buzzing. Each transition is further explained either in terms of further details in the state transition or by the functions of the components, e.g., the transition from the clapper being alternately electrically connected and disconnected to its being in the repeated-hit state is explained by relating it to the mechanical function of the clapper.

Let us see how this fragment of functional representation can be used to generate a piece of diagnostic knowledge that may be used by a diagnostic expert system. A *diagnostic compiler* will function as fol-

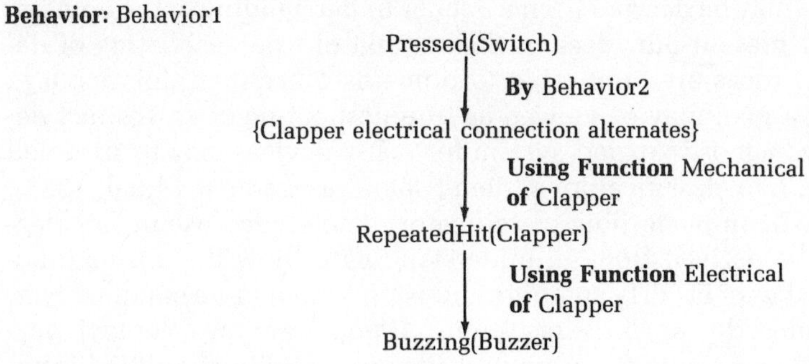

Behavior: Behavior1

Pressed(Switch)

  │   **By** Behavior2
  ↓

{Clapper electrical connection alternates}

  │   **Using Function** Mechanical
  │   **of** Clapper
  ↓

RepeatedHit(Clapper)

  │   **Using Function** Electrical
  │   **of** Clapper
  ↓

Buzzing(Buzzer)

Figure 1. Behavior Specification

lows. Suppose a buzzer does not buzz when its switch is pressed. In order to find out what malfunctions are causing this, the diagnostic compiler will reason thus on the basis of the functional specification and the behavior1 specification. The functional specification tells it that the problem is in behavior1, since the Buzz function is failing. Behavior1, on examination, can result in a series of hypotheses:

R1: If switch is pressed, but the clapper is not alternately electrically connected and disconnected, problem is in behavior2.

R2: If switch is pressed, the clapper's electrical connectivity alternates, but the clapper doesn't hit-repeatedly, the cause of buzzer not buzzing is a mechanical malfunction of the clapper.

Etc.

Each one of the above is a piece of diagnostic knowledge. A diagnostic expert system may either have such diagnostic knowledge directly, or derive it from the functional representation by using a diagnostic compiler. In either case, a system with access to the deep model can retrace the process by which a given rule was compiled from the functional representation, thus providing an explanation of Type 2. For example, suppose someone wants an explanation of how Rule R2 was obtained. The system can say, "Because the buzzing function is accomplished by pressing the switch which causes electrical connection alternation, which in turn causes the clapper to repeatedly hit because of the mechanical function of the clapper, etc., and since the pressing of the switch is resulting in alternate electrical connection of the clapper, but the clapper is not repeated-hitting, we can suspect mechanical malfunction of the clapper."

We need to re-emphasize: (1) Our theory so far has been developed for diagnostic reasoning regarding relatively simple devices, and (2) In this section we have only briefly touched upon the theory, which is elaborated somewhat elsewhere (Sembugamoorthy & Chandrasekaran, 1986). The main point of this section is to indicate that our research can begin to address issues of Type 2 explanation in expert systems.

In the next section we describe our work on a planning system with explanation. This project shows how generic tasks and functional models can be used to construct expert problem solvers which can produce type 2 and type 3 explanations.

4. Implementation of Planning and Explanation

4.1. Introduction

We have chosen "routine planning" as a task for which to build a prototype. In particular, we chose the planning task for Offensive

Counter Air (OCA) missions dealt with by KNOBS (Engelman, Millen, & Scarl, 1983; Scarl et al., 1984) for analysis and implementation. Our goal was to implement a portion of KNOBS, using generic tasks and deep models in order to show how explanation can naturally be derived. A prototype mission planning system with some explanation capabilities has been built, the Mission Planning Assistant (MPA). It ought to be emphasized that the MPA project is not completed, and so what is reported here should be viewed mainly as an interim report. Both the design of the planner and the explanation components are still in the process of further analysis and expansion.

Much of the material in sections 4.2–4.7 is summarized from a report by Chandrasekaran and Josephson (1986). For more details refer to the sections of that report by Herman et al. (1986), Tanner et al. (1986), and Keuneke and Josephson (1986).

4.2. The KNOBS System

The KNOBS system (Engelman, Millen, & Scarl, 1983; Scarl et al., 1984) was built by Mitre Corporation to address the task of planning OCA missions. KNOBS plans by template instantiation, a process of filling in the slots of a frame with acceptable values. The order in which the slots are considered is defined in advance by the plan template, and is determined by the expert's domain-planning knowledge. Slot values are accepted or rejected based upon constraint satisfaction. In order to find values of slots, KNOBS associates a generator with each slot to enumerate potential values. The generator produces a subset of all possible values for the slot.

Given the slot ordering, constraints, and generators, KNOBS plans as follows: The generator of the first slot is asked for its first candidate, the generator for the second slot is asked for its first candidate, and so on. At each slot filling, all applicable constraints are checked. If a value passes all constraints, it is used to fill the slot. But if any constraints are not satisfied, the slot generator is asked for another candidate. If there is another candidate, it is tried, and so on until all slots have accepted values. If a generator runs out of candidates, KNOBS backs up to the most recently filled slot that was involved in the constraint that failed and tries another value there. KNOBS is successful when all slots are filled (and all constraints are satisfied). The basic planning algorithm for KNOBS can thus be described as generate and test with dependency-directed backtracking.

KNOBS was successful in showing the feasibility of AI techniques for certain classes of mission planning. However, the system does not have much problem-solving expertise for planning. Thus the KNOBS mechanism does not allow for two major types of explanation: Neither the planning control strategy, nor knowledge of the domain can be explained. These kinds of explanation for a planner are feasible if the planning and domain knowledge is represented with appropriate structures. It should be added that the designers of KNOBS were also aware of these limitations and are currently building a system called KRS which includes some of the additional functionalities described above.

4.3. Class 3 Design

Our approach to tactical mission planning treats the OCA mission as an abstract device to be designed. The planning of the mission involves a process similar to the process a designer undergoes when faced with a complex device to design. An overview of the design domain will illuminate this analogy. (For a more comprehensive description see (Brown & Chandrasekaran, 1984.)

The general domain of design is vast. It involves creativity, many problem-solving techniques, and many kinds of knowledge. Goals are often poorly specified, and may change during the course of problem solving. However, a spectrum of design classes can be identified, varying from completely open-ended activity to the most routine, depending on what sorts of knowledge is available prior to the start of problem solving.

What we have called "Class 3 Design" characterizes a form of routine design activity. Complete knowledge of both the components and design plans for the device is assumed to be available prior to the problem-solving activity. The problem solving proceeds by using recognition knowledge to select among the previously known sequences of design actions. While the choices at each point may be simple, this does not imply that the design process itself is simple, nor that the components so designed must be simple. It appears that a significant portion of everyday activity of practicing designers falls into this class. In order to explore this class of design problems, the Design Structures and Plans Language (DSPL) was developed.

4.4. Design Structures and Plans Language

We consider the routine design task to be a hierarchical planning task, where typically each level makes some design commitments, and the design is further refined by the lower-level planners. A design problem solver in DSPL consists of a hierarchy of cooperating, conceptual specialists, with each specialist responsible for a particular portion of the design. Specialists higher in the hierarchy deal with the more general aspects of the device being designed, while lower specialists design more specific subportions of the device, or address other design subtasks. The organization of the specialists and the specific content of each is intended to precisely capture the designer's expertise in the problem domain.

Each specialist in the design hierarchy contains locally, within itself, the design knowledge necessary to accomplish that portion of the design for which it is responsible. There are several types of knowledge represented in each specialist, but for simplicity only three are described here. (For full details on DSPL see (Brown & Chandrasekaran, 1984, 1985.) First, explicit *design plans* in each specialist encode sequences of possible actions to complete the specialist's task successfully. Different design plans within a specialist may encode alternative action sequences, but plans within a particular specialist are always aimed at achieving the specific design goals of that specialist. A second type of knowledge encoded within specialists is encoded in *design plan sponsors*. Each design plan has an associated sponsor to determine the appropriateness of the plan in the run-time context. The third type of planning knowledge in a specialist is encoded in *design plan selectors*. The function of the selector knowledge is to examine the run-time judgments of the design plan sponsors and determine which of the design plans within the specialist is most appropriate to the current problem context.

Control in a DSPL system proceeds from the top-most specialist in the design hierarchy to the lowest. Beginning with the top-most specialist, each specialist selects a design plan appropriate to the requirements of the problem and the current state of the solution. The selected plan is executed by performing the design actions specified by the plan. This may include computing and assigning specific values to attributes of the device, running constraints to check the progress of the design, or invoking subspecialists to complete another portion of the design. Thus design plans which refer to a subspecialist are refined by passing control to that subspecialist. (In the language of Section 3.2 this process is called "design by plan selection and refinement.")

Our discussion of the control strategies in a DSPL system only includes successful plan execution. However, DSPL does include facilities for handling various types of plan failures, and for controlling redesign suggested by such failures. (The details of these features of the language can be found in Brown & Chandrasekaran, 1984.)

4.5. Mission Planning as Class 3 Design

Our view of tactical mission planning is that it is essentially a class 3 design task. The problem can be decomposed into the design of subcomponents of the mission plan. In the device design domain, the design of a device is decomposed into the design of subassemblies and their components, etc., where each subassembly or component can be designed in a fairly independent fashion. In the tactical mission planning domain, the OCA is decomposed into various parts of missions where each part can be planned relatively independently of the others. In both domains, of course, each of the solutions to the subproblems must be appropriately combined into a solution for the overall problem. Due to the well-known limitations of human problem-solving capacities, it is apparent that a human problem solver can be successful in a planning situation only to the extent that he or she can also decompose the problem into a manageable number of somewhat independent subproblems which can be solved separately and combined into a final solution. Using DSPL as a natural mechanism for representing the necessary knowledge, the MPA system closely mirrors these ideas.

The additional context of the DSPL control structure provides the framework for a more comprehensive explanation facility. In addition to the necessary ability to examine particular attributes of a mission plan, the control structure provides the ability to examine the problem-solving strategies of the planning system. This kind of explanation is not easily extracted from a system which uses template instantiation and constraint satisfaction as its primary mechanisms for problem solving, since problem-solving strategies are absent or at best implicitly represented.

4.6. Explanation in the Mission Planning Assistant

We have implemented a Mission Planning Assistant as a class 3 designer which solves the OCA mission-planning problem. Our implementation of explanation in MPA is based on the organizing principle that the agent which makes a decision is responsible for justifying it. MPA is built in DSPL so the agents which contribute to the final plan include: Specialists, Design Plans, and Design Plan Sponsors. In the present implementation there are some 200 of these agents, though not all of them contribute to any particular plan. All of these agents perform knowledge-level tasks (i.e., epistemically significant) so explanation of any one agent's problem-solving decisions can be given in terms of the goals of the agent which uses it, and the function of the agents it uses.

The final answer produced by the MPA is essentially a list of attribute-value pairs as in KNOBS. That is, a list of the form:

```
Target = Berlin
Aircraft Type = F-111
Number of Aircraft = 6
    .   .   .
```

We have decided to concentrate on questions of the form, "How was it decided?" which can be asked of the value of any attribute. For example, selecting F-111 in the above list would initiate a dialogue on the question of how MPA decided to use F-111 as the value of **Aircraft Type.** Questions of this form directly ask about the problem solving which led to final decisions. While the answers do not exhaust the kinds of things a problem solver can say about its actions, we feel that it is a reasonable place to start working on explaining problem solving.

To support "How was it decided?" explanations, and in keeping with our organizing principle given above, we determined three basic questions which all agents must be able to answer:

1. "What did you do?" This question is answered with a summary of the result of the agent's action.
2. "What is your purpose?" This question is posed by subagents who want to have knowledge of the context they are operating in, and is answered by a short description.
3. "How did you do it?" This question would be answered by giving a complete explanation of the context of the agent's activation followed by a functional description of its action. The agent may have to ask its subagents Q1 and its superagent Q2.

Then, in general, the explanation for "How was it decided?" is the answer to question 3 above. The answer to q3 is a combination of the answer to q2 for the calling agent and q1 for all subagents. So an explanation contains:

```
In the context of ⟨answer to Q2 for calling agent⟩
     we did the following:
        ⟨answer to Q1 from subagent1⟩
        ⟨answer to Q1 from subagent2⟩
        ⟨answer to Q1 from subagent3⟩
                  . . .
```

Which can produce explanations such as:

```
In the context of selecting the aircraft type for the
     mission
     we did the following:
        chose the F-111 plan
        filled in parts of the OCA as appropriate for
        F-111 aircraft
```

In the next section we give a detailed example of a single-agent type, namely, Sponsors, and the explanations it can produce. Explanations from agents of the other types are produced in a similar fashion.

```
(SPONSOR A-10
   (SETQ target (KB-FETCH TARGET))
   (SETQ timeOverTarget (KB-FETCH TIMEOVERTARGET))
   (SETQ threat
      (TABLE (airborne) (AAA) (SAM)
         (IF     T        ?        ?      THEN UNSUITABLE)
         (IF     ?        T        ?      THEN UNSUITABLE)
         (IF     ?        ?        T      THEN UNSUITABLE)
         (IF     ?        ?        ?      THEN PERFECT)))
   (SETQ conditions
      (TABLE (night) (weather)
         (IF     F       FULL     THEN UNSUITABLE)
         (IF     F     PARTIAL    THEN SUITABLE)
         (IF     F      GOOD      THEN PERFECT)))
   REPLY
      (TABLE    conditions        threat
         (IF UNSUITABLE       ?           THEN RULE-OUT)
         (IF     ?        UNSUITABLE THEN RULE-OUT)
         (IF  SUITABLE        ?           THEN SUITABLE)
         (IF     ?            ?           THEN PERFECT)))
```

Figure 2.   DSPL code for a Design Plan Sponsor

4.6.1. Explanation of Plan Sponsors

Rather than give examples of explanation from all of the types of agent
in MPA we will concentrate here on a particular type—the sponsors.
Sponsors operate in the context of a DSPL design specialist. A specialist's job is to design a component of the device. To do this a specialist has available several alternative courses of action, called plans.
Each plan is appropriate, or perhaps most likely to succeed, under
some conditions and not others. So associated with each plan is a
sponsor which matches characteristics of the plan to information about
the problem at hand and produces a measure of how useful the plan
will be on a scale of: Ruled-Out, Unsuitable, Suitable, and Perfect. The
specialist then chooses a plan based on what the sponsors return. The
code for a sponsor is given in Figure 2. This is a sponsor for a plan
which uses A-10s (an aircraft type) on the mission. It first sets some
local variables by looking them up in the data base (using *KB-FETCH*, a
data-base access function which simply returns the value of an attribute). The *TABLE* construct is essentially a group of rules which all
depend on predicates of the same values. For example, the table setting
the variable *conditions* contains three rules which depend on the values returned by the functions *night* and *weather*. The first rule requires
night to return F and *weather* to return *FULL*. If the predicates are true,
then *conditions* will be *UNSUITABLE*. The symbol '?' in the tables
represents a predicate which is always true. The table is finished when

The context of *selecting an aircraft to consider for the mission* determined that:

• target is **BrandenburgSAM**

• timeOverTarget is **1300**

• threat is **UNSUITABLE** because:
  o SAM is TRUE

• conditions are **PERFECT** because:
  o weather is GOOD

I determined the value of plan A-10 to be **RULE-OUT** because:

• threat is UNSUITABLE.

Figure 3.   Explanation for a Design Plan Sponsor

one rules matches. REPLY tells DSPL that what follows is the main function of the sponsor, i.e., rating the suitability of a plan.

The explanation for this sponsor is given in Figure 3. This explanation can be produced by inspection of the sponsor code because sponsors are problem-solving agents of known type and which follow a known form in their implementation. Values for the local variables are given, those fetched from the data base are not justified while those determined by tables are given justification. The final REPLY is used to determine the actual decision made by the sponsor. This explanation describes how the data matched problem-solving knowledge at run-time (type 1 explanation). MPA does not have an explicit representation of its control strategy; however, some explanation of control is possible. The italicized phrase at the beginning of the explanation comes from the agent, a specialist, which uses the sponsor to do its job. The user of MPA can follow up by getting an explanation from that specialist which would spell out the sponsor's context in more detail by giving the problem-solving strategy MPA was pursuing at the point where the sponsor was invoked. Thus, the explanation for the calling agent gives a problem specific explanation of the control strategy in service of which the agent was called (type 3 explanation).

4.7. Understanding an OCA Mission Plan

The planning task accomplished by the MPA system involves specifying a set of pre-established components. That is, the planner knows the mission needs a certain type of component—its job is to make a concrete commitment as to which specific component of that type would be best. The planner requires only a limited knowledge of these components in order to make such decisions. Its understanding of the resultant mission plan is thus restricted.

For example, suppose a user of the mission planner asks the question, "Why was an F-111 used?" The question could be answered in various ways. For a *particular* mission, the question might be addressed directly by the mission planner. Here, the inquiry is interpreted as, "Why did you use an F-111 *instead of* any other aircraft for this mission?" Explanation would indicate what makes the F-111 appropriate (speed, weather-compatible, etc., as seen in Section 4.6.1). Since this is the specific information the system used in making its decision, the planner can explain it.

In the above, interpretation of the question was, "Why choose an F-111?." An alternate interpretation could be, "Why is the F-111 used in the mission plan?." A good response here might be, "The F-111 is an aircraft. Aircraft are used in OCAs because they have the ability to fly and to deliver the ordnance. These functions are used to get to the target location and to destroy the target—the primary goal of an OCA mission." This explanation requires a deeper understanding of the domain than the planner has readily available within its compiled planning knowledge. Here we need a structure to represent distinctly *how the plan works*.

To represent this understanding, we use the *functional representation of devices* as given by Sembugamoorthy and Chandrasekaran (1986). A device is any structure (concrete or abstract) that serves a purpose. Thus, a plan can be viewed as an abstract device in that it has components which act together in order to achieve a desired goal. A functional representation for a plan can serve as a knowledge structure from which a more complete understanding of the specific planning domain can be derived.

4.7.1. The Functional Representation of a Mission Plan

In the course of describing the functional representation of OCA missions we will also give a brief recap of the basic idea of functional representations. An agent's understanding of how a device works is organized to show how an intended function is accomplished as a series of behavioral states of the device. The device itself is represented at various levels. The topmost level describes the function of the device in terms of the roles of its components. The next level describes the function of these components using the roles of their subcomponents, and so on.

A part of the *functional specification* of the abstract device OCAMission describes the main function of an OCA—to destroy a target, as shown below.

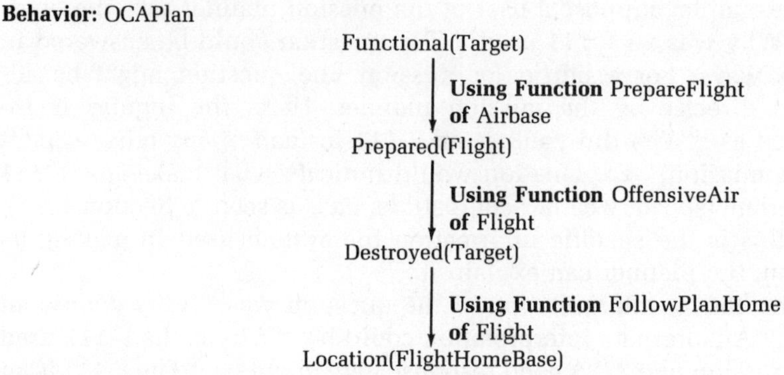

Behavior: OCAPlan

Functional(Target)

> **Using Function** PrepareFlight
> **of** Airbase

Prepared(Flight)

> **Using Function** OffensiveAir
> **of** Flight

Destroyed(Target)

> **Using Function** FollowPlanHome
> **of** Flight

Location(FlightHomeBase)

Figure 4.   Behavior Specification in MPA

```
FUNCTION: DestroyTarget:
        TOMAKE Destroyed(Target)
        IF Functional(Target)
        PROVIDED Functional(Flight)
        BY OCAplan
```

This description indicates that the plan, OCAMission, has a *function* called DestroyTarget. This function is used *if* a target is operational (functional). When this function is used, the target will be destroyed *by* a behavior called OCAplan. This behavior should succeed in accomplishing the goal of target destruction *provided* the flight is operational throughout the behavior.

The *behavioral specification* of a device describes the manner in which a function is accomplished by using the functions of components, generic knowledge, and subbehaviors. The behavior for an OCA plan is described by a chain of events caused by the specified actions given in Figure 4. This structure is meant to represent the temporal sequence (from top to bottom) of states which occur as a result of actions taken. The diagram thus indicates that the OCAPlan's behavior begins when a Target is in a Functional state. Here an OCA plan will use the function PrepareFlight of the component AirBase to make the Flight Prepared. Upon achieving this state, the plan uses the component Flight since it has the function (OffensiveAir) to Destroy the Target, and so on.

The important characteristics which make this representation useful for the design and repair of devices and plans include:

1.   A component is specified independent of the representation of the device which contains it. That is, the specification of a component

does not refer to its role in the composite. If replacements are necessary, this property makes it possible to determine permissible substitutes by simply comparing functional capabilities of current components with those of alternatives.

2. Only the names of the component functions are carried over to a higher level, not their behavior specifications. This property is important if an agent needs to replace a malfunctioning component by a functionally equivalent but behaviorally different one. That is, it is not *how* the function is achieved that is important, but *what* is achieved.

Since much of planning involves adaptations of already established plans, these traits which allow for such adaptations of components and behaviors are valuable.

4.7.2. Enhancements to the Representation

In the course of using the functional representation for MPA we are learning about enhancements needed both to further the capabilities for adaptation and for richer understanding and explanation capabilities. For example, we are learning that it is sometimes necessary to distinguish between a device's *primary* functions and its *secondary* functions. These secondary functions are present in order to *support* the primary functions. Specification of such functions is needed for proper explanation and for information when considering replacement of components.

4.7.3. Explanation of Plans

Understanding of an OCA plan can now be demonstrated through the explanation capabilities inherent in its functional representation. The representation is capable of answering questions about its devices, functions, and behaviors. Examples of answers to questions will be given in the context of a top-level device of OCAMission. Explanation responses are built using access to the functional primitives.

I. *Devices*

QUESTION: "Why is this device needed?"

ANSWER: Device d is used because it has the functional capabilities to *fun1, fun2,* and *fun3*.

EXAMPLE: "The device Flight is used because it has the functional capabilities to achieve offensive counter air missions, to reach the target, to return to the home base after a mission."

II. *Functions*

QUESTION: "Why is this function needed?"

ANSWER: This function is needed to ensure that *goal*. (Here, secondary functions specify that they are needed to support the conditions for functions *fun1* and *fun2*.)

EXAMPLE: "The function Protection of ECM is needed to protect the aircraft and crew, to ensure that the Aircraft is not threatened, and to support conditions for the function DestroyTarget."

QUESTION: "What does this function do?"

ANSWER: The function *fun* is accomplished by behavior *b* to ensure that *goal*. The behavior can be used if *condition*.

EXAMPLE: "The function Offensive Air is accomplished by behavior OffensiveAirTactics to ensure that the target is destroyed. The behavior can be used if the target is functional, the flight is loaded, and the constraint FuelSufficientForPlan is satisfied by FlightPlan."

QUESTION: "Where is this function used?"

ANSWER: The function *fun1* is used in behavior *b* of function *fun2*.

EXAMPLE: "The function Fly is used in the behavior GetThere of function FollowPlanToTarget and in the behavior GetBack of function FollowPlanHome."

III. *Behaviors*

QUESTION: "Why is this action performed?"

ANSWER: The function *fun* is used in *behavior* because it achieves *goal*.

EXAMPLE: "The function LoadOrdnance is used in OffensiveAirTactics because it ensures that the flight is loaded which is needed for the primary goal to destroy the target."

5. Overview of the Work of Explanation

Our work so far has contributed to each of the three types of explanation. Our theoretical position is that in order to generate explanation of type 1 and type 3 *at the appropriate level of abstraction*, the problem-solving process needs to be represented at what we have called the *generic task level*. The essence of the argument is that most of the current approaches to expert system construction use knowledge representation languages and control primitives at too low a level of abstraction (the rule/frame/logical formulae level). This makes both system design and explanation difficult, since the system designer has to transform the problem into a low-level implementation language and explanation requires translating back to the problem level. We have identified a set of higher-level building blocks in terms of which systems can be conceptualized, designed, and implemented. The basic explanation constructs are then available closer to the conceptual level of the user than they would be if they had to be extracted from the implementation language level. This point of view has led us to propose a new approach to the design of knowledge-based systems, namely, *generic tasks*. In order to facilitate expert system construction at the generic task level, we have devoted a considerable amount of energy to the design and implementation of a set of higher-level tools for the construction of expert systems of various types. One such tool is DSPL (Brown & Chandrasekaran, 1984, 1985), a language for building design systems described in section 4.4. Several others are in various stages of design and implementation, including CSRL (Bylander, Mittal, & Chandrase-karan, 1983; Bylander & Smith, 1983; Tanner & Bylander, 1985), a language for building classification systems. Together these tools will constitute a high-level tool set for the construction of knowledge-based systems capable of explanation.

The theory itself is being put to the test at this stage for what can be called *routine planning* or *routine design* tasks. We have identified the OCA mission problem as a problem of this type, used one of our generic task languages (DSPL) for both knowledge acquisition and system implementation, and by using the constructs in DSPL effectively, have been able to show how explanation at higher and more appropriate levels of abstraction can be automatically generated from the problem solver.

Explanation of Type 2, viz., explanation of knowledge fragments in the knowledge base, has been approached by us in the context of the OCA mission as explanation of *plans*, i.e., the plans themselves, not the planning process. We propose that plans can be viewed as *devices*, and as such an earlier representation developed in our laboratory for representing device functions can be used effectively for explaining plans.

6. Conclusions and Future Work

In section 2 we characterized previous work on explanation as producing three good ideas. These are:

1. Meaningful explanation can be given at the architecture level.
2. Justification of knowledge requires access to deep models.
3. Some kinds of explanation require explicit representations of problem-solving strategies.

These correspond to our type 1, type 2, and type 3 explanations, respectively. The generic task methodology provides a higher level architecture for problem solving and a representation of control strategies, both of which can be used for explanation. Our functionally represented deep models can be used both to compile problem solving and to justify problem solving knowledge.

The MPA prototype system has demonstrated the viability of the generic task approach to explanation in expert systems. However, it is limited both in the scope of its problem-solving knowledge and in the completeness of its explanations. We are in the process of finding domain experts who will help us extend MPA's problem-solving knowledge beyond that available in the original KNOBS system. We are also working on extending the explanatory capabilities beyond "How was it decided?" questions to include such things as "Why not?" questions and interactive questions which allow the user to query the system during its problem-solving activity. In spite of its present limitations, we believe MPA has fulfilled our original goal of showing how explanation can naturally be derived from deep models and an understanding of the problem-solving task.

Acknowledgments

We gratefully acknowledge the assistance of Mitre Corporation for providing the KNOBS source code and taking the time to help us understand KNOBS.

References

Brown, D. C., Chandrasekaran, B. (1984). *Expert systems for a class of mechanical design activity.* Paper for IFIP WG5.2 working conference.

Brown, D. C., Chandrasekaran, B. (1985). *Plan selection in design problem solving.* Ohio State University, Department of Computer and Information Science, LAIR.

Bylander, T., Mittal, S., Chandrasekaran, B. (1983). CSRL: A language for expert systems for diagnosis. *IJCAI-83.* Karlsruhe, West Germany, pp. 218–221.

Bylander, T., Smith, J. W., M.D. (1983). Using CSRL for medical diagnosis. *Proceeding of MEDCOMP'83.* Athens, OH.

Chandrasekaran, B. (1984). Expert systems: Matching techniques to tasks. In W. Reitman (Ed.), *Artificial Intelligence in Business.* Norwood, NJ: Ablex ch. 4, pp. 41–64.

Chandrasekaran, B., & Josephson, J. (1986). Explanation, problem solving, and new generation tools: A progress report. *Expert Systems Workshop Proceedings,* DARPA, Pacific Grove, CA, April 16–18, pp. 101–126.

Chandrasekaran, B. & Mittal, S. (1983). Conceptual representation of medical knowledge for diagnosis by computer: MDX and related systems. In M.

Yovits (Ed.), *Advances in Computers.* London: Academic Press, pp. 217–293.

Clancey, W. J. (1983). The epistemology of a rule-based expert system—A framework for explanation. *Artificial Intelligence, 20*(3), 215–251.

Clancey, W. J. (1985). *Representing control knowledge as abstract tasks and metarules.* Working Paper KSL 85–16, Stanford Knowledge Systems Laboratory, Palo Alto, CA, April. Draft. To appear in M. Coombs & L. Bolc (Eds.), *Computer Expert Systems,* Springer-Verlag, Berlin, Germany.

Clancey, W. J. & Letsinger, R. (1981). NEOMYCIN: Reconfiguring a rule-based expert system for application to teaching. *Proceedings of the 7th IJCAI,* Vancouver, BC, August 24–28, pp. 829–836.

Davis, R. (1976). *Applications of meta-level knowledge to the construction, maintenance and Use of Large Knowledge Data Bases* (Tech. Rep. STAN–CS–76–552). Stanford University, Stanford, CA.

Engelman, C., Millen, J. K., Scarl, E. A. (1983). *KNOBS: An integrated AI interactive planning architecture.* DSR 83–162, Mitre Corp., Bedford, MA.

Herman, D., Keuneke, A., Tanner, M. C., Hartung, R., Josephson, J. (1986). Design and construction of the Mission Planning Assistant. *Expert Systems Workshop Proceedings,* DARPA, Pacific Grove, CA, April 16–18, pp. 103–106. Also, in Chandrasekaran & Josephson, 1986.

Keuneke, A., Josephson, J. (1986). Understanding an OCA mission plan. *Expert Systems Workshop Proceedings,* DARPA, Pacific Grove, CA, April 16–18, pp. 112–116. Also in Chanrasekaran & Josephson, 1986.

Minsky, M. (1975). A framework for representing knowledge. In P. H. Winton (Ed.), *The psychology for computer vision.* New York: McGraw–Hill.

Mittal, S., Chandrasekaran, B. & Sticklen, J. (1984). PATREC: A knowledge-directed data base for a diagnostic expert system. *IEEE Computer Special Issue* (September), pp. 51–58.

Scarl, E. A., Engelman, C., Pazzani, M. J., Millen, J. (1984). *The KNOBS system.* Mitre Corp. , Boston, MA.

Sembugamoorthy, V. & Chandrasekaran, B. (1986) Functional representation of devices and compilation of diagnostic problem solving systems. In J. L. Kolodner & C. K. Riesbeck (Eds.), *Experience, memory and reasoning.* Hillsdale, NJ: Erlbaum, ch. 4, pp. 47–73.

Shortliffe, E. H. (1976). *Computer-based medical consultations: MYCIN.* Amsterdam: Elsevier/North-Holland.

Swartout, W. R. (1983). XPLAIN: A system for creating and explaining expert consulting programs. *Artificial Intelligence, 21*(3) 285–325.

Tanner, M. C., Allemang, D., Josephson, J., DeJongh, M. (1986). Explanation in the Mission Planning Assistant. *Expert Systems Workshop Proceedings,* DARPA, Pacific Grove, CA, April 16–18, pp. 106–112. Also in Chandrasekaran & Josephson, 1986.

Tanner, M. C., Bylander, T. (1985). Application of the CSRL language to the design of expert diagnosis systems: The Auto-Mech experience. In J. J. Richardson (Ed.), *Artificial intelligence in maintenance.* Park Ridge, NJ: Noyes, pp. 149–169.

ELEVEN

Facilitating Change in Rule-based Systems

Robert J. K. Jacob,
Judith N. Froscher

Naval Research Laboratory,
Washington, DC

Abstract

Current expert systems are typically difficult to change once they are built. This chapter describes a design method intended to make a knowledge-based system easier to change, particularly by people other than its original developer. The solution proposed is to divide the information in a knowledge base and reduce the amount that each knowledge engineer must understand to change the knowledge base. The method divides the domain knowledge in an expert system into groups and then attempts to limit carefully and specify formally the flow of information between these groups, in order to localize the effects of typical changes within the groups.

1. Introduction

If expert systems are to come into wide use in practical applications, the problem of continuing maintenance and modification of the knowledge base must be addressed in the development stage. Most current expert systems began as research tools, often developed in universities and maintained by their originators and their students. Now many observers believe that this technology shows promise of solving practical problems in industry and government, but knowledge-based systems continue to be ad hoc, one of a kind, and difficult to maintain.

Changing a knowledge base typically requires a knowledge engineer who is well grounded in the design of the system and the structure of the knowledge base. Most often, it requires the same knowledge engineer who originally wrote the system.

This study develops a design and programming methodology for builders and maintainers of knowledge-based systems. The user in this case is the programmer or knowledge engineer who develops or modifies a knowledge base, rather than the end user who obtains information or advice from the expert system. The design technique, similar to those used in software engineering (Parnas, 1972, 1984), will make a knowledge-based production system easier to change, particularly by people other than its original developer. It will provide an interface to the developer and maintainer that allows them to organize and more easily modify the information in the system. It could also be used as the basis of the user interface for a knowledge-base browser (Baroff, 1987). We have chosen to concentrate on production systems because they are the most widely used type of knowledge representation in expert systems, particularly among those existing systems large enough and mature enough to have experienced the types of maintenance problems we hope to alleviate. In the future, we will attempt to extend the approach to suit other, newer knowledge representations.

2. Background

While few knowledge-based systems are currently being used in commercial or military environments, one of the most successful exceptions is R1/XCON, developed by McDermott at Carnegie–Mellon University (McDermott, 1981). R1 configures the many components that make up a DEC VAX 11/780 computer and is implemented as a production system in OPS5. The development of R1 illustrates the problems encountered when an expert system is used in a practical setting. Since the VAX computer line was constantly being changed and expanded, it was continually necessary to add more knowledge and greater capability to R1. Before long, the system became complex enough that it was necessary to reimplement it entirely. To support R1, DEC established a special software support group, which had to invest considerable effort in understanding R1 before they could make any changes to it.

As commercial promise for expert system technology grows, more researchers have become concerned with the practical problems of building these systems for end users, who have a limited background in artificial intelligence. They have proposed several methods for partitioning these systems to make the knowledge bases more understandable, maintainable, efficient, or suitable for parallel processing. One simple approach is to build a system made up of several knowledge bases; examples of this approach are seen in ACE (Wright, 1984) and PROSPECTOR (Duda et al., 1978). The developers of LOOPS (Bobrow & Stefik, 1981) use the notion of a rule set, which is called like a subroutine. Each rule set returns a single value, which can then be used elsewhere in the knowledge base. Clancey has abstracted the inference goals in a knowledge base in order to separate the control strategy, encoded as meta-rules, from the specific domain knowledge (Clancey, 1983). Rules that contribute to a particular goal in a knowledge base can then be grouped together; in fact, R1/XCON is partitioned into several subtasks in this fashion (Stefik et al., 1983). Because expert systems generally use large amounts of computer resources, researchers are studying how both the knowledge base and working memory can be separated so that each independent group can be processed on a parallel processor (Gupta & Forgy, 1983). Such a separation can also make the system easier to change, although this was not the original purpose of the study.

3. Approach

The basic approach we have taken for building maintainability into an expert system is to divide the information in the knowledge base and attempt to reduce the amount of information that each single knowledge engineer must understand before he or she can make a change to the knowledge base. We thus divide the domain knowledge in an expert system into groups and then attempt to limit carefully and specify formally the flow of information between these groups, in order to localize the effects of typical changes within the groups.

Production systems comprise a knowledge base, expressed as if-then rules, and a relatively simple inference mechanism or rule interpreter. The interpreter tests the values of the facts on the left-hand side of a rule; if the test succeeds, new values for facts are set according to the right-hand side of the rule.

In the present approach, we divide these rules into separate groups. The general principle for grouping two rules together is: *If a change were made to one rule, to what extent would the other rule be affected?* In this study, a *fact* refers to some isolable portion of the data representation that, if changed by one rule, would affect another rule in some way. In a simple production system where the data are attribute-value pairs, a fact corresponds to one attribute. The knowledge engineer building the system would group together rules that use or produce values for the same sets of facts. With this arrangement, a fact in the knowledge base can be characterized either as being generated and used by rules entirely within a single rule group or else as spanning two or more groups. The latter will prove critical to future changes to the knowledge base, since they are the "glue" that holds the groups together. Baroff and colleagues (Baroff et al., 1987) propose a complementary approach, in which they divide the facts into groups and then characterize the rules according to which groups of facts they operate on.

Whenever rules in one group use facts generated by rules in other groups, such facts will be flagged, so that the knowledge engineer will know that their values may have been set outside this group. More importantly, those facts produced by one group and used by rules in other groups must be flagged too. For each such fact, the programmer of the group that produces the fact makes an assertion, comprising a brief summary of the information represented by that fact. This assertion is the only information about that fact that should be relied upon by the programmers of other groups that use the fact. It is not a formal specification of the information represented by the fact, but rather an informal summary of what the fact should "mean" to other programmers.

Given this structure, programmers who want to change the system must understand thoroughly and preserve the correct workings of a single group of rules (but not the entire body of rules, as with conventional systems). They could change rules in the group provided that they preserve the validity of the assertions associated with facts produced by this group and used by other groups. Similarly, whenever a programmer used a fact produced by another group, he or she would rely on the assertion provided for it by the programmer of the other group, but not on any specific information about the fact that might be obtainable from examining the inner workings of the other group.

4. Programming Methodology

To apply the proposed method, the developer of a rule-based system first divides the rules into groups. This can be done manually or automatically, as described below. One approach is to apply the automatic grouping algorithm to a prototype of the expert system and use the resulting grouping to guide the organization and development of the production version.

Next, a software tool characterizes each fact as being produced and used entirely within one group (a local or intragroup fact) or being produced or used by two or more groups (an intergroup fact); the latter are flagged. The developer of each rule group that produces intergroup facts then provides an assertion describing each such fact. The assertion describes what the programmer of the fact-producing group asserts will be true of that fact—upon which the programmers of the groups using that fact can rely. It summarizes the workings of the group that produces it. It is generally inappropriate for this assertion to provide a formal specification of the conditions for producing the fact, because that would essentially repeat the entire group of rules as they are presently. Rather, what is desired is an informal statement of the aspects of the output that will not change and may be considered externally visible. For example: *Fact X estimates whether the patient has heart disease;* rather than: *X will be true if input A <0.6 and B ≥ 2.1.* This assertion is the only information about the fact that should be used in the development of other groups containing rules that use the value of the fact; information about the internal workings of the rules in the group should not be used, because such details are not guaranteed to remain unchanged.

Facts simultaneously produced by a large number of groups are not handled in precisely this way, since they constitute the "global" data for the system. Their assertions are part of the overall system design, rather than the design of the individual groups. Logically, the assertion for such a fact could be the "or" of the assertions generated by all groups that produce the fact, but such would not be very useful. Instead, the overall system designer will identify these facts in the early design and provide more abstract assertions, which indicate how he or she expects the global data to be used by all the groups together. A well-designed system will minimize the number of facts of this kind.

Thus, the set of rules will be divided into groups, the intergroup facts used and produced by each group will be identified, and assertions will be entered for those produced by each group. The example below illustrates the language used to provide this information, using a simple example knowledge base (Winston, 1980).

```
(GROUP isamammal
    (PRODUCES
        (mammal "is it a mammal, by conventional
        English usage"))
    (RULES
        (r1 (IF hair) (THEN mammal))
        (r2 (IF milk) (THEN mammal)))))

(GROUP isabird
    (PRODUCES
```

```
                    (bird "is it a bird, by English usage"))
            (RULES
                    (r3 (IF feather) (THEN bird))
                    (r4 (IF flies ovip) (THEN bird))

                    (rx (IF a) (THEN c))
                    (ry (IF b) (THEN c))
                    (rz (IF c) (THEN bird)))))

    (GROUP isacarn
        (PRODUCES
                (carn "is it a carnivorous creature"))
        (RULES
                (r5 (IF meat) (THEN carn))
                (r6 (IF pointed claws fwdeyes) (THEN
                    carn))))

    GROUP isungulate
        (PRODUCES
                (ungulate "is it an ungulate"))
        (USES
                (mammal))
        (RULES
                (r7 (IF mammal hoofs) (THEN ungulate))))

    (GROUP kind-of-carn
        (USES
                (mammal)
                (carn))
        (RULES
                (r8 (IF mammal carn tawny darksp)
                    (THEN cheetah))
                (r9 (IF mammal carn tawny blackst)
                    (THEN tiger))))

    GROUP kind-of-ungulate
        (USES
                (ungulate))
        (RULES
                (r10 (IF ungulate longn longl darksp)
                    (THEN giraffe))
                (r11 (IF ungulate blackst) (THEN zebra))))

    (GROUP kind-of-bird
        (USES
```

```
    (bird))
(RULES
    (r12 (IF bird notfly longn longl blackwh)
    (THEN ostrich))
    (r13 (IF bird notfly swims blackwh)
    (THEN penguin))
    (r14 (IF bird flyswell) (THEN albatross)))))
```

The rules above are given in an abstract notation that lists their input and output facts, but no further details. This is the same representation used as input for the analyses described subsequently.

Note that three extra rules have been added for illustration to group isabird above. They indicate that the animal is considered a bird if c is true, which in turn depends on a and b. These rules appear to produce fact c, but c is not shown in the PRODUCES list for group isabird and does not have an assertion. This is because c is not used by rules in any other group—it is thus an intragroup fact, analogous to a local variable with no bearing on the connectivity of the modules of the system. Also, group kind-of-carn appears to produce facts cheetah and tiger, but they, too, are not listed. The reason is that those facts are not used by rules in any other groups and, again, have no effect on the connections between groups. In fact, they are top-level outputs of this expert system.

Some of the steps required to produce a knowledge base like the above are manual, and some can be automated. To prepare this example, the rules were divided into groups by hand, although this could have been done automatically, as described below. Then, a software tool was used to analyze the groups and automatically list the intergroup facts produced and used by each group. The programmer then manually wrote the (here, trivial) assertions for all intergroup facts produced by each group. That last step is not automatic and is critical to the success of the method. The methodology and tools find and highlight the intergroup facts and then require the programmer to give them special attention and provide special declarations for them. In this example, all information except for the rules themselves—i.e., the groupings, PRODUCES and USES lists, and assertions—are essentially comments. They need have no effect on the actual execution (or efficiency) of the expert system.

After a knowledge base is developed in this fashion, the knowledge engineer who wants to modify a group must understand the internal operations of that group, but not of the rest of the knowledge base. If he or she preserves the correct functioning of the rules within the group and does not change the validity of the assertions about its intergroup facts, the knowledge engineer can be confident that the change that has been made will not adversely affect the rest of the system. Conversely, if he or she wants to use additional intergroup facts from other groups, he or she should rely only on the assertions provided for them, not on the internal workings of the rules in the other group. (Of course, changes that pervade several groups would still have to be handled as they always have been, but the grouping is intended to minimize these.)

An interesting aspect of this approach is that it draws distinctions between the facts contained in working memory of a production system. Certain facts are flagged as being important to the overall software structure of the system, while others are "internal" to particulate modules and thus less important. Programmers can be advised to pay special attention to rules that involve the "important" facts. This is in contrast to the homogeneous way in which the facts of a rule-based system are usually viewed, where they must all command equal attention or inattention from the programmer.

5. Algorithms for Partitioning a Knowledge Base

It is possible to develop an algorithm that will take a set of rules and divide them into groups suitable for use with this method. Such an algorithm can help in developing a rule-based system and also in evaluating the wider applicability of the proposed method by grouping the rules of existing systems, as described subsequently. It is somewhat easier to develop a grouping algorithm for rule-based systems than for code written in conventional programming languages because both the syntax and semantics of production languages are quite simple and regular. (Some refinements needed to handle OPS5, a relatively complex production language, are discussed below.)

The basic problem is to partition a set of rules into groups that will aid in their maintenance. Rules that affect each other and are likely to be changed at the same time should be grouped together. Several approaches to the grouping problem have been explored (Jacob & Froscher, 1985, 1986), and the best results were obtained from an algorithm based on cluster analysis. A clustering algorithm takes a collection of objects and partitions them into groups of like objects.

Measure of Similarity or Distance Between Rules. In order to use a clustering algorithm, a measure of distance or "relatedness" between the objects to be clustered (the rules) must be defined. Since our ultimate concern is for a programmer making changes to the knowledge base, this similarity between two rules should measure the likelihood

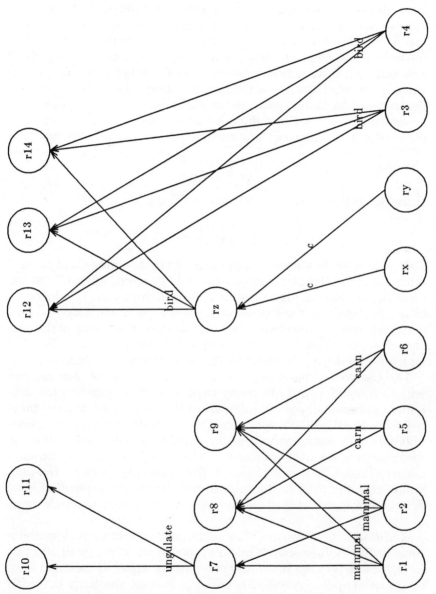

Figure 1.   Plot of individual rules of a very simple expert system. Rules are shown as circles and facts, as lines connecting them.

that a change made to one rule would require a change in the other rule. The rules in a production system are related through the facts whose values they use or modify. These relationships can be depicted in a graph, showing the inference hierarchy for the system. Figure 1 depicts the animal system given above. In it, each node, or circle, represents a rule and each link, or line, between two rules represents a fact whose value is set by one rule and used by the other. The "relatedness" between two rules is thus measured by the number of facts that are mentioned in both rules. Since there are several ways in which two rules could refer to the same fact, a weighting factor is applied. The two rules

```
if A then B
if B then C
```

share fact B in common; so do the two rules

```
if A then B
if C then B.
```

The rules of the former pair have a greater programming effect on each other than the latter pair, and hence should be more "related." The top three illustrations in Figure 2 summarize the three ways in which two rules can share a fact and the weight given to each. The total "relatedness" measure between two rules is, then, a weighted count of the facts shared by both rules. Each fact is weighted by the score that indicates in which of the three possible ways the two rules use the fact.

The Clustering Algorithm. Given such a measure, we can proceed with a straightforward clustering algorithm. First, measure the similarities between all pairs of rules, select the closest pair, and put those two rules together into one cluster. Then, repeat the procedure, grouping rules with each other or possibly with already-formed clusters. In the latter case, we must measure the "relatedness" between a rule and a cluster of rules. This is the mean of the similarities between the individual rule and each of the rules in the cluster, corresponding to an average-linkage clustering procedure. The algorithm proceeds iteratively.

Additional Refinements. The algorithm presently used contains some further refinements. While they have a relatively small effect on its operation, they are significant at iterations where the best and next-best possible pairings would be close in average similarity but differ substantially on other criteria. First, other values of the weights for the cases shown in Figure 2 were tested, and the clusterings obtained were generally insensitive to any choice of plausible weights. Then, an additional case was added to cover facts *not* shared by two rules. Without it, the pair of rules

Score = 1.0

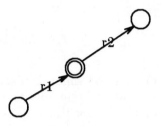

Score = 0.75

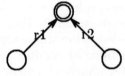

Score = 0.5

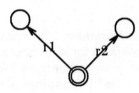

Score = -0.25

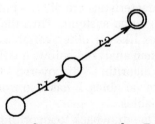

Figure 2. Components of "relatedness" measure between two rules. Rules are shown as lines, facts are shown as circles, and the fact whose score is given is shown as a double circle.

```
if A then B
if B then C
```

and the pair

```
if A then B
if B then C and D and E and F
```

would have the same similarity; but, in determining a grouping, the former pair is preferable to the latter. Hence a negative weight, as shown in the last illustration of Figure 2, is added to the similarity between two rules for facts that appear in one of the rules but not the other. In addition, the square root of each between-rule similarity is taken before combining them into the between-group similarity measure. These two changes reduce the tendency of the algorithm to use a few pivotal rules to form a long, "spindly" group that gradually annexes its neighbors in all directions. The other refinement is an additional term added to the similarity between two groups, which slightly favors combinations of smaller groups over larger ones. This takes into account the practical consideration that the groupings are ultimately going to be used as the basis for assignment of programming responsibilities to individuals, hence very small or very large groups would likely be manually overridden in the end. The quantity *2/(size of the combined group)* is added to the similarity between two groups for this purpose.

State Variables. The clustering algorithm described makes no special provision for state or goal variables in the rule set. They are treated exactly as any other facts. While one could use the state variables as a key to identify groupings of rules, such a method will only divide the rules temporally, that is, according to *when* they operate. That is not always the appropriate grouping for modifying the program. For modification, we are concerned with how two rules affect each other in the long run, not whether they affect each other in sequence. The two characteristics are often—but not guaranteed to be—the same in well-structured systems. Thus the clustering algorithm treats the state variables like all other variables in identifying groups. In the particular system analyzed below, it will be seen that, by following this approach, the algorithm "discovered" the same grouping as that implied by the state variables. It has also worked well for systems that do not use state variables.

One drawback to algorithms of this type is that on each iteration the algorithm makes the best possible agglomeration of two groups, but it never backtracks, in case there might be a better grouping for the system considered as a whole. Also, like most clustering algorithms, if it runs for enough iterations it will eventually group all the rules into one large group. One stopping rule that has worked in several cases is to stop when the similarity between the next two groups to be combined is no longer positive (since there is a term with a negative weight in the similarity between rules). Another approach is to use the distribution of the sizes of the groups as a guide.

6. An Example

A somewhat larger rule-based system appears in Appendix A. It has 34 rules and 21 facts. This system will illustrate the programming method, but it should be remembered that it is used for exposition; the proposed method will seem excessive for a system of this size and relative simplicity. The system is written in the OPS5 language (Brownston et al., 1985; Forgy, 1981) by Ralph Fink et al. of the Naval Air Development Center and describes the interactions between two opposing military battle groups. The original system, in OPS5, is shown in Appendix A. Some details in the bodies of the rules, such as `write` statements and some literal values, have been deleted or replaced with ellipses to save space. This is an unusually well-structured rule-based system, and it makes heavy use of state variables (the `status` attributes of goal–rules, plan–rules, etc.) These variables are used to enable or disable groups of rules. The system thus already contains an implicit structure; for example, all rules that depend on the left-hand side

(goal–rules ˆstatus active)

will be enabled or disabled together and constitute a logical grouping to the original system developer as well as a temporal grouping.

Using the new method, this set of rules would appear as shown in Appendix B, with the rules divided into groups and the intergroup facts declared. "Facts" in OPS5 are not always simple static variables; the next section will explain how they have been interpreted in this framework. The division into groups shown was obtained from the clustering algorithm. Note that the groupings are similar to those implied by the state variables; that is, the clustering algorithm "discovered" the structure already implicit in this rather well-structured set of rules. Examination of the PRODUCES and USES lists gives an indication of the structure of the system. It becomes clear that four of the attributes of class `target` are the only real nonlocal data in the system (the remaining 17 facts are all either local variables or state variables). The method helps to identify and focus attention on these four key variables. In addition to using and producing these four tar–

get variables, each group is seen to use those state variables that enable
its own rules and produce state variables that enable exactly one other
group, which indicates a particularly straightforward pattern of activation among these rule groups.

7. "Facts" in Working Memory Elements

Several production system languages, in particular OPS5, add some
wrinkles to the straightforward conception of static facts examined and
modified by rules. A rule in OPS5 can test and set values of one or more
attributes of one or more "working memory elements" and can create
or remove such elements. The "facts" of interest are thus dynamic—
they cannot be statically enumerated in advance. Each working memory element is identified as belonging to some *class*, and rules generally
identify the class of each element they examine or change.

For example, the following OPS5 rule

```
(p goal-rule-1
   {(goal-rules ^status active) (goal-rules)}
   {(target ^present-position 123
     ^relative-behavior 456) (target)}
   - ->
   (modify (target) ^goal attack)
   (remove (goal-rules))
   (make plan-rules ^status active))
```

examines the status attribute of a working memory element of class
goal-rules and the present-position and relative-behavior
attributes of one of class target. It changes the goal attribute of the
target element, removes the goal-rules element, and creates a new
element of class plan-rules and sets its status attribute. For the
purposes of the software engineering method, each of the possible
classes of elements in a system could be treated as a separate "fact,"
with a multifaceted value consisting of all the attribute values of elements of that class. The above rule would then be considered to use
facts goal-rules and target and produce facts target, goal-
rules, and plan-rules. In the notation we use for abstract description of rules, it would be written:

```
(RULE goal-rule-1
   (IF goal-rules target)
   (THEN target goal-rules plan-rules))
```

The problem with this interpretation is that it is a rather coarse-
grained abstraction of the working of the rules. For example, nearly

every rule in the system shown in the appendices tests some attribute of target. A finer-grained abstraction of the information used and produced by each rule is needed. The basic goal of this abstraction is to identify which items in the right-hand sides of rules could affect the firing or not firing of which items in the left-hand sides. Observe that the right-hand side item

(modify ⟨target⟩ ˆgoal attack)

in the above would not affect any rule with a left-hand side containing

(target ˆpresent-position 789).

It would affect only those rules that test the goal attribute of working memory elements of class target. Thus each attribute of each class is treated as a separate "fact," e.g., target-goal and target-present-position are separate facts.

Since working memory elements are created and destroyed dynamically, there is not really a single static variable target-goal in the system; it is considered to occur whenever a working memory element of class target uses an attribute named goal. The fact target-goal is an abstraction of all possible uses of the goal attribute of *all* working memory elements of class target.

We observe, similarly, that a right-hand side

(make plan-rules ˆstatus active)

can only affect rules whose left-hand sides test the status attribute of class plan-rules, since no other attributes of plan-rules were set. Hence it is considered to set "fact" plan-rules-status only. However, the right-hand side

(remove ⟨goal-rules⟩),

which deletes an entire working memory element of class goal-rules, potentially affects any rule that examines any portion of a goal-rules element. It is considered to set a new "fact," goal-rules, which may be thought of as an abbreviation for *the effect of removing an element of class* goal-rules. All left-hand sides that examine any part of a goal-rules working memory element are then considered to use the fact goal-rules in addition to the facts for any individual attributes of goal-rules they use.

The OPS5 rule above thus finally becomes, in our representation:

```
(RULE goal-rule-1
    (IF goal-rules goal-rules-status
        target target-present-position
        target-relative-behavior)
    (THEN target-goal goal-rules plan-rules-status))
```

As noted, these facts are not individual static variables but abstractions of the manipulations of working memory data by which two rules can affect each other.

8. Support Software

We have developed software tools to support this programming methodology and to analyze the connections between the rules of a production system. The input is a set of rules expressed in the abstract form shown above. We have built software that translates from OPS5 into this representation, including the separation of OPS5 working memory elements into their component "facts." For expert systems written in other languages, we have performed the translation manually or semi-automatically with text-processing programs.

The developer of a rule-based system can define the grouping of rules and input the knowledge base in the form shown in the previous examples, or he or she can use the clustering algorithm discussed to produce the grouping. Given such a grouping, the software then identifies the intragroup and intergroup facts. It flags all intergroup facts produced by a group, so the programmer can provide assertions for them; and it flags all intergroup facts used by a group and retrieves their assertions, so the programmer can rely on them when using such facts.

Other software tools can trace all effects of changing a given rule and can find any unused rules or groups. Statistics about the characterization of the facts in the system are also produced. For example, the following data describe the system discussed in Section 6:

34	Rules
4	Groups
21	Facts
3	bottom
1	top
9	x–x
4	x–y
0	x–xy
0	xy–x
0	xy–xy
1	x–any
2	any–x
1	any–any

Of the 21 facts found, 3 of them were characterized as bottom, meaning input data, not produced by any rules, and 1 was top, meaning an output, not used by any rules. The x–x category denotes intragroup facts. The remaining categories describe subspecies of intergroup facts: x–y denotes facts produced by just one group and used by just one other group; x–xy are those produced by one group and used by that group and one other group; xy–x are produced by two groups and used only by one of those two; xy–xy are produced by two groups and used by the same two; x–any are produced by one group and used by two or more groups; any–x are produced by two or more groups and used by one group; and any–any covers the remaining more complex cases. Finally, software tools are available to compute the measures of coupling and cohesion discussed below.

9. Evaluating the Methodology

To decide whether partitioning a knowledge base is a feasible approach, we are analyzing existing expert systems to determine how the rules in the system are related to each other. We are using the software tools to determine whether the rules are indeed thoroughly intertwined or sufficiently separated that they could be divided into the groups required by the methodology. The approach is to use the clustering algorithm to divide the rules of the existing system into groups. By examining the resulting groupings, we hope to determine how well the structure implied by the new programming method can fit the structures observed in actual rule bases, that is, whether the existing systems could have been cast in the mold required by the method or whether it would have imposed excessive restrictions and unnatural structure on the developers. To date, we have analyzed several knowledge bases and found that there is considerable separability and latent structure to the relationships between the rules in these systems, which permits the present approach to be imposed. However, such structure has not been exploited to improve maintainability.

For example, Figure 3 shows a graph for a larger expert system. It was developed by James Reggia of the University of Maryland, using the KES language and is used to diagnose stroke and related diseases (Reggia et al., 1984). It contains 373 rules and 116 distinct variables. Unlike OPS5, the KES language uses static variables, in which all instantiations are declared in advance. However, 21 of the variables in this system can be assigned more than one value simultaneously. The presence of each possible value for each multivalued variable is treated as a separate fact in our framework, so that the system has 244 facts. In Figure 3, like Figure 1, each node represents a rule and each link between two rules represents a fact whose value is set by one rule and used by the other. To reduce clutter, labels like those in Figure 1 have

Figure 3.   Plot of rules of a more complex expert system. Rules are shown as dots and facts, as lines.

266

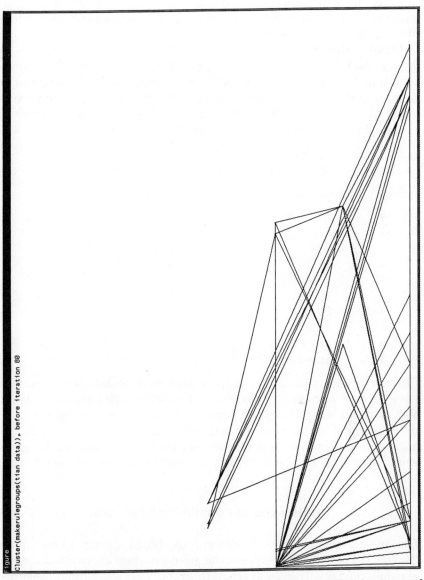

Figure Cluster(makerulegroups(tian data)), before iteration 80

Figure 4.   Rules of Figure 3, clustered. Rule groups are shown as dots and intergroup facts, as lines.

been suppressed, and rules, which were represented by circles in Figure 1, are now shown as points. A graph of this type can be used to give a general indication of the structure of the rule set and the interdependencies between rules.

Figure 4 shows the same system as Figure 3, after clustering into 30 groups. Each node now represents a group of rules, and each link represents a fact that is produced by rules in one group and used by those in another group. Facts that are produced and used entirely within a single group do not appear in the graph, and the resulting structure is clearly simpler. Statistics for this grouping are as follows:

```
373      Rules
 30      Groups

244      Facts

 94      bottom
 30      top
 66      x-x
 12      x-y
  6      x-xy
  7      xy-x
  0      xy-xy
 21      x-any
  5      any-x
  3      any-any
```

Observe that 66 of the 120 nontop- or bottom-level facts in this system have become intragroup facts or local variables. The groupings were also found to be substantially similar to the arrangement suggested by the rule author's naming of the original rules and his comments in the code; approximately 90% of all pairs of rules were handled in the same way (either both separated or both joined) by the two arrangements.

10. Measures of Coupling and Cohesion

The division of a set of rules into groups should attempt to minimize the amount of coupling between the groups and maximize the amount of cohesiveness within each group (Stevens, 1974). Defining measures for these notions will provide data to help compare alternative groupings of a given set of rules. Once a set of rules is divided into groups, each fact in the system is characterized as intergroup or intragroup. One simple measure of coupling is the proportion of intergroup facts, while cohesion is represented by the proportion of intragroup facts. For the battle-planning system shown previously, this measure gives 8/17 for coupling and 9/17 for cohesion (top- and bottom-level facts are excluded from this count).

Another approach to these measures is also being investigated. For coupling, it uses the average "relatedness" between all pairs of rules, where members of the pairs lie in different groups. For overall cohesion, it uses the average relatedness of every pair of rules that lie in the same group. For the battle system, these quantities are -0.2443 average coupling and $+4.1631$ average cohesion, suggesting, at the least, a far better than random organization.

11. Conclusions

By studying the connectivity of rules and facts in rule-based expert systems, we found that they indeed have a latent structure, which can be used to support a new programming methodology. We have developed a method based on dividing the rules into groups and concentrating on those facts that carry information between rules in any two different groups. We have developed an algorithm for grouping the rules of a knowledge base automatically and a simple notation and set of software tools to support the new method.

The resulting programming method requires the knowledge engineer who develops a rule-based system to declare groups of rules, flag all between-group facts, and provide descriptions of those facts to any rule groups that use such facts. The knowledge engineer who wants to modify such a system then gives special attention to the between-group facts and preserves or relies on their descriptions when making changes. In contrast to the homogeneous way in which the facts of a rule-based system are usually viewed, this method distinguishes certain facts as more important than others and directs the programmer's attention to them.

A future step in this research will be to attempt to measure the extent to which the new method helps or hinders maintenance of an expert system. We will attempt to make changes both to a conventional expert system and to one divided into groups following the proposed method and compare the results. A second future direction will be to apply these basic ideas to newer knowledge representations, such as frames and semantic nets, as large systems begin to be written using them. The basic approach will likely remain the same: divide the information in the knowledge base into groups, then specify and limit the flow of information between the groups. The specifics of the programming method will, of course, differ.

Acknowledgments

We are most grateful to several AI researchers who have made knowledge bases they developed available to us: Ralph Fink of the Naval Air Development Center and James Reggia of the University of Maryland developed the systems discussed in this chapter. Anne Werkheiser of the Army Engineer Topographic Laboratory and Mark Lerner of Columbia University also contributed their systems to this work. We also thank David Parnas for his comments on an earlier version of this chapter.

References

Baroff, J., Simon, R., Gilman, F., & Shneiderman, B. (1987). Direct manipulation user interfaces for expert systems. In J. A. Hendler (Ed.), *Expert systems: The user interface*. Norwood, NJ: Ablex.

Bobrow, D. G., & Stefik, M. (1981). *The LOOPS manual* (Tech. Rep. KB–VLSI–81–13), Knowledge Systems Area, Xerox Research Center. Palo Alto: CA.

Brownston, L., Farrell, R., Kant, E., & Martin, N. (1985). *Programming expert systems in OPS5: An introduction to rule-based programming*. Reading, MA: Addison–Wesley.

Clancey, W. J. (1983). The advantages of abstract control knowledge in expert system design. *Proceedings National Conference on Artificial Intelligence*, pp. 74–78.

Duda, R. O., Hart, P. E., Nilsson, N. J., & Sutherland, G. L. (1978). Semantic network representations in rule-based inference systems. In D. A. Waterman & F. Hayes–Roth (Eds.), *Pattern-directed inference systems*, pp. 203–221. New York: Academic Press.

Forgy, C. L. (1981). *OPS5 User's Manual* (Tech. Rep. CMU–CS–81–135), Computer Science Department, Carnegie–Mellon University, Pittsburgh.

Gupta, A., & Forgy, C. L. (1983). *Measurements on production systems*, CMU–CS–83–167. Computer Science Department, Carnegie–Mellon University, Pittsburgh.

Jacob, R. J. K., & Froscher, J. N. (1985). Developing a software engineering methodology for rule-based systems. *Proceedings 1985 Conference on Intelligent Systems and Machines*, pp. 179–183, Oakland University, Rochester, Michigan.

Jacob, R. J. K., & Froscher, J. N. (1986). Software engineering for rule-based systems, *Proceedings Fall Joint Computer Conference*, Dallas, pp. 185–189.

McDermott, J. (1981). R1: The formative years. *AI Magazine*, 21–29.

Parnas, D. L. (1972). On the criteria to be used in decomposing systems into modules. *Communications of the ACM, 15*, 1053–1058.

Parnas, D. L. (1984). Software engineering principles. *INFOR Canadian Journal of Operations Research and Information Processing*.

Reggia, J. A., Tabb, R., Price, T. R., Banko, M., & Hebel, R. (1984). Computer-aided assessment of transient ischemic attacks: A clinical evaluation. *Archives of Neurology, 41,* 1248–1254.

Stefik, M., Aikins, J., Balzer, R., Benoit, J., Birnbaum, L., Hayes–Roth, F., & Sacerdoti, E. (1983). The architecture of expert systems. In F. Hayes–Roth, E. A. Waterman, & D. B. Lenat (Eds.), *Building expert systems.* Reading, MA: Addison–Wesley, pp. 89–126.

Stevens, W. P., Meyers, G. J., & Constantine, L. L. (1974). Structured design. *IBM Systems Journal, 13,* 115–139.

Winston, P. H., & Horn, B. K. P. (1980). LISP. Reading, MA: Addison–Wesley.

Wright, J. B., Miller, F. D., Otto, G. V. E., Siegfried, E. M., Vesonder, G. T., & Zielinski, J. E. (1984). ACE: Going from prototype to product with an expert system. *Proceedings 1984 ACM Annual Conference on the 5th Generation Challenge,* pp. 24–28.

Appendix A

The example system discussed in Section 6, original OPS5 rules. Note: some details in the bodies of the rules, such as `write` statements and some literal values have been deleted or replaced with ellipses to save space.

```
(p goal-rule-1
    {(goal-rules ^status active) <goal-rules>}
    {(target ^present-position . . . ^relative-behavior
        . . . ) <target>}
    - ->
    (modify <target> ^goal attack)
    (remove <goal-rules>)
    (make plan-rules ^status active))

(p goal-rule-2
    {(goal-rules ^status active) <goal-rules>}
    {(target ^present-position . . . ^relative-
        behavior . . . ) <target>}
    - ->
    (modify <target> ^goal attack)
    (remove <goal-rules>)
    (make revision-rules ^status active))

(p goal-rule-3
    {(goal-rules ^status active) <goal-rules>}
    {(target ^present-position . . . ^relative-
        behavior . . . ) <target>}
    - ->
    (modify <target> ^goal attack)
    (remove <goal-rules>)
    (make revision-rules ^status active))
```

```
(p goal-rule-4
    {(goal-rules ^status active) <goal-rules>}
    {(target ^present-position . . . ^relative-
       behavior . . . ) <target>}
    - ->
    (modify <target> ^goal attack)
    (remove <goal-rules>)
    (make revision-rules ^status active))

(p goal-rule-5
    {(goal-rules ^status active) <goal-rules>}
    {(target ^present-position . . . ^relative-
       behavior . . . ) <target>}
    - ->
    (modify <target> ^goal advance)
    (remove <goal-rules>)
    (make plan-rules ^status active))

(p goal-rule-6
    {(goal-rules ^status active) <goal-rules>}
    {(target ^present-position . . . ^relative-behavior
       . . . ) <target>}
    - ->
    (modify <target> ^goal no-attack)
    (remove <goal-rules>)
    (make plan-rules ^status active))

(p goal-rule-7
    {(goal-rules ^status active) <goal-rules>}
    {(target ^present-position . . . ^relative-
       behavior . . . ) <target>}
    - ->
    (modify <target> ^goal retreat)
    (remove <goal-rules>)
    (make revision-rules ^status active))

(p goal-rule-8
    {(goal-rules ^status active) <goal-rules>}
    {(target ^present-position arrived-at) <target>}
    - ->
    (make battle-group ^status dead)
    (modify <target> ^goal achieved)
    (remove <goal-rules>)
    (make plan-rules ^status active))

(p goal-rule-9
    {(goal-rules ^status active) <goal-rules>}
    {(target ^relative-behavior inconsistent) <target>}
    - ->
    (modify <target> ^goal dont-know)
    (remove <goal-rules>)
    (make plan-rules  status active))
```

```
(p plan-rule-1
    {(plan-rules ^status active) ⟨plan-rules⟩}
    {(target ^goal attack) ⟨target⟩}
    - -⟩
    (modify ⟨target⟩ ^plan-of-action course-to)
    (remove ⟨plan-rules⟩)
    (make expectation-rules ^status active))
(p plan-rule-2
    {(plan-rules ^status active) ⟨plan-rules⟩}
    {(target ^goal no-attack) ⟨target⟩}
    - -⟩
    (modify ⟨target⟩ ^plan-of-action no-course-to)
    (remove ⟨plan-rules⟩)
    (make expectation-rules ^status active))
(p plan-rule-3
    {(plan-rules ^status active) ⟨plan-rules⟩}
    {(target ^goal dont-know) ⟨target⟩}
    - -⟩
    (modify ⟨target⟩ ^plan-of-action wait-and-see)
    (remove ⟨plan-rules⟩)
    (make expectation-rules ^status active))
(p plan-rule-4
    {(plan-rules ^status active) ⟨plan-rules⟩}
    {(target ^goal achieved) ⟨target⟩}
    - -⟩
    (modify ⟨target⟩ ^plan-of-action succeeded)
    (remove ⟨plan-rules⟩)
    (make expectation-rules ^status active))
(p plan-rule-5
    {(plan-rules ^status active) ⟨plan-rules⟩}
    {(target ^goal advance) ⟨target⟩}
    - -⟩
    (modify ⟨target⟩ ^plan-of-action course-to)
    (remove ⟨plan-rules⟩)
    (make expectation-rules ^status active))
(p revision-rule-1
    {(revision-rules ^status active) ⟨revision-rules⟩}
    {(target ^relative-behavior . . . ^present-
      position . . . ^goal . . . ) ⟨target⟩}
    - -⟩
    (modify ⟨target⟩ ^plan-of-action feint)
    (remove ⟨revision-rules⟩)
    (make expectation-rules ^status active))
(p revision-rule-2
    {(revision-rules ^status active) ⟨revision-rules⟩}
    {(target ^relative-behavior . . . ^goal retreat)
      ⟨target⟩}
```

```
        --)
      (modify <target> ^plan-of-action no-course-to)
      (remove <revision-rules>)
      (make expectation-rules ^status active))

(p revision-rule-3
    {(revision-rules ^status active) <revision-rules>}
    {(target ^relative-behavior . . . ^present-
      position . . . ^goal . . . ) <target>}
    --)
    (modify <target> ^plan-of-action feint)
    (remove <revision-rules>)
    (make expectation-rules ^status active))

(p revision-rule-4
    {(revision-rules ^status active) <revision-rules>}
    {(target ^relative-behavior . . . ^present-
      position . . . ^goal . . . ) <target>}
    --)
    (modify <target> ^plan-of-action wait-and-see)
    (remove <revision-rules>)
    (make expectation-rules ^status active))

(p expectation-rule-1
    {(expectation-
      rules ^status active) <expectation-rules>}
    {(target ^plan-of-action course-to) <target>}
    --)
    (make computational-rules ^status active)
    (remove <expectation-rules>)
    ;; Note: update-attributes is an external function,
    ;; which sets the transition and present-position
    ;; attributes of target
    (modify <target> (update-attributes)))

(p expectation-rule-2
    {(expectation-rules ^status active) <expectation-
      rules>}
    {(target ^plan-of-action no-course-to) <target>}
    ---)
    (make computational-rules ^status active)
    (remove <expectation-rules>)
    (modify <target> (update-attributes)))

(p expectation-rule-3
    {(expectation-rules ^status active) <expectation-
      rules>}
    {(target ^plan-of-action feint)
      <target>}
    --)
    (make computational-rules ^status active)
    (remove <expectation-rules>)
    (modify <target> (update-attributes)))
```

```
(p expectation-rule-4
    {(expectation-rules ^status active) (expectation-
      rules)}
  * {(target ^plan-of-action wait-and-see) (target)}
    - ->
    (make computational-rules ^status active)
    (remove (expectation-rules))
    (modify (target) (update-attributes)))
(p expectation-rule-5
    {(expectation-rules ^status active) (expectation-
      rules)}
    {(target ^plan-of-action succeeded) (target)}
    - ->
    (halt))

(p computation-rule-1
    {(computational-rules ^status active) (computational-
      rules)}
    {(target ^relative-behavior . . . ^transition recede)
      (target)}
    - ->
    (modify (target) ^relative-behavior 1-move-away)
    (remove (computational-rules))
    (make goal-rules ^status active))
(p computation-rule-2
    {(computational-rules ^status active) (computational-
      rules)}
    {(target ^relative-behavior . . . ^transition
      approach) (target)}
    - ->
    (modify (target) ^relative-behavior moved-towards)
    (remove (computational-rules))
    (make goal-rules ^status active))
(p computation-rule-3
    {(computational-rules ^status active) (computational-
      rules)}
    {(target ^relative-behavior . . . ^transition recede)
      (target)}
    - ->
    (modify (target) ^relative-behavior 2-moves-away)
    (remove (computational-rules))
    (make goal-rules ^status active))
(p computation-rule-4
    {(computational-rules status active) (computational-
      rules)}
    {(target ^relative-behavior . . . ^transition recede)
      (target)}
    - ->
    (modify (target) ^relative-behavior 3-moves-away)
    (remove (computational-rules))
    (make goal-rules ^status active))
```

```
(p computation-rule-5
   {(computational-rules ^status active) ⟨computational-
    rules⟩}
   {(target ^relative-behavior . . . ^transition recede)
    ⟨target⟩}
   - -⟩
   (modify ⟨target⟩ ^relative-behavior 4-moves-away)
   (remove ⟨computational-rules⟩)
   (make goal-rules ^status active))

(p computation-rule-6
   {(computational-rules ^status active) ⟨computational-
    rules⟩}
   {(target ^relative behavior . . . ^transition
    approach) ⟨target⟩}
   - -⟩
   (modify ⟨target⟩ ^relative-behavior reapproach)
   (remove ⟨computational-rules⟩)
   (make goal-rules ^status active))

(p computation-rule-7
   {(computational-rules ^status active) ⟨computational-
    rules⟩}
   {(target ^relative-behavior reapproach ^transition
    recede)
    ⟨target⟩}
   - -⟩
   (modify ⟨target⟩ ^relative-behavior inconsistent)
   (remove ⟨computational-rules⟩)
   (make goal-rules ^status active))

(p computation-rule-8
   {(computational-rules ^status active) ⟨computational-
    rules⟩}
   {(target ^transition none) ⟨target⟩}
   - -⟩
   (remove ⟨computational-rules⟩)
   (make goal-rules ^status active))

(p computation-rule-9
   {(computational-rules ^status active) ⟨computational-
    rules⟩}
   - -⟩
   (remove ⟨computational-rules⟩)
   (make goal-rules ^status active))

(p starter-rule-1
   {(first-starter-rule ^status active) ⟨first-starter-
    rule⟩}
   {(target ^present-position none) ⟨target⟩}
   - -⟩
   (remove ⟨first-starter-rule⟩)
   ;; Note: initial-position sets the present-position
   ;; attribute of target
   (modify ⟨target⟩ (initial-position)))
```

```
(p starter-rule-2
    {(other-starter-rules ^status active) <other-starter-
      rules>}
    {(target ^present-position . . . ) <target>)
    --)
    (remove <other-starter-rules>}
    (modify <target> (update-attributes))
    (make computational-rules ^status active))
```

Appendix B

The system discussed in Section 6, after grouping the rules and applying the new method.

```
(GROUP computation-rules
    (PRODUCES
        (target-relative-behavior
            "Describes direction of target with respect to
            current position and how many moves it would
            take to reach the target.
            Possible values are: arrived-at, moved-
            towards, 1-move-away, 2- moves-away, 3-moves-
            away, 4-moves-away, reapproach, and
            inconsistent.")
        (goal-rules-status
            "State variable, enables firing of goal
            rules"))
    (USES
        (target-relative-behavior)
        (target-transition)
        (computational-rules-status))
    (RULES
        (computation-rule-1
            {(computational-rules ^status active)
              <computational-rules>}
            {(target ^relative-behavior . . .
              ^transition recede) <target>}
            --)
            (modify <target> ^relative-behavior 1-move-
            away)
            (remove <computational-rules>)
            (make goal-rules ^status active))
        (computation-rule-2
            {(computational-rules ^status active)
              <computational-rules>}
            {(target ^relative-behavior . . .
```

```
            ^transition approach) ⟨target⟩}
        - -⟩
        (modify ⟨target⟩ ^relative-behavior moved-
          towards)
        (remove ⟨computational-rules⟩)
        (make goal-rules ^status active))
(computation-rule-3
    {(computational-rules ^status active)
        ⟨computational-rules⟩}
    {(target ^relative-behavior . . .
        ^transition recede) ⟨target⟩}
        - -⟩
        (modify ⟨target⟩ ^relative-behavior 2-moves-
          away)
        (remove ⟨computational-rules⟩)
        (make goal-rules ^status active))
(computation-rule-4
    {(computational-rules ^status active)
        ⟨computational-rules⟩}
    {(target ^relative behavior . . .
        ^transition recede) ⟨target⟩}
        - -⟩
        (modify ⟨target⟩ ^relative-behavior 3-moves-
          away)
        (remove ⟨computational-rules⟩)
        (make goal-rules ^status active))
(computation-rule-5
    {(computational-rules ^status active)
        ⟨computational-rules⟩}
    {(target ^relative-behavior . . .
        ^transition recede) ⟨target⟩}
        - -⟩
        (modify ⟨target⟩ ^relative-behavior 4-moves-
          away)
        (remove ⟨computational-rules⟩)
        (make goal-rules ^status active))
(computation-rule-6
    {(computational-rules ^status active)
        ⟨computational-rules⟩}
    {(target ^relative-behavior . . .
        ^transition approach) ⟨target⟩}
        - -⟩
        (modify ⟨target⟩ ^relative-behavior
          reapproach)
        (remove ⟨computational-rules⟩)
        (make goal-rules ^status active))
(computation-rule-7
    {(computational-rules ^status active)
        ⟨computational-rules⟩}
```

```
        {(target ^relative-behavior reapproach
           ^transition recede) (target)}
        - -)
        (modify (target) ^relative-behavior
          inconsistent)
        (remove (computational-rules))
        (make goal-rules ^status active))

    (computation-rule-8
        {(computational-rules ^status active)
          (computational-rules)}
        {(target ^transition none) (target)}
        - -)
        (remove (computational-rules))
        (make goal-rules ^status active))

    (computation-rule-9
        {(computational-rules ^status active)
          (computational-rules)}
        - -)
        (remove (computational-rules))
        (make goal-rules ^status active))))
```

```
(GROUP expectation-plan-revision
    (PRODUCES
        (target-transition
            "Tells whether target is currently receding or
            approaching")

        (target-present-position
            "Tells which of 3 possible sectors the target
            currently occupies")

        (computational-rules-status
            "State variable, enables firing of
            computational-rules"))

    (USES
        (target-goal)
        (target-present-position)
        (target-relative-behavior)
        (plan-rules-status)
        (revision-rules-status))

    (RULES
        (expectation-rule-1
            {(expectation-rules ^status active)
              (expectation-rules)}
            {(target ^plan-of-action course-to)
              (target)}
            - -)
            (make computational-rules ^status active)
            (remove (expectation-rules))
            (modify (target) (update-attributes)))
```

```
(expectation-rule-2
    {(expectation-rules ^status active)
     ⟨expectation-rules⟩}
    {(target ^plan-of-action no-course-to)
     ⟨target⟩}
    --⟩
    (make computational-rules ^status active)
    (remove ⟨expectation-rules⟩)
    (modify ⟨target⟩ (update-attributes)))
(expectation-rule-3
    {(expectation-rules ^status active)
     ⟨expectation-rules⟩}
    {(target ^plan-of-action feint) ⟨target⟩}
    --⟩
    (make computational-rules ^status active)
    (remove ⟨expectation-rules⟩)
    (modify ⟨target⟩ (update-attributes)))
(expectation-rule-4
    {(expectation-rules ^status active)
     ⟨expectation-rules⟩}
    {(target ^plan-of-action wait-and-see)
     ⟨target⟩}
    --⟩
    (make computational-rules ^status active)
    (remove ⟨expectation-rules⟩)
    (modify ⟨target⟩ (update-attributes)))
(expectation-rule-5
    {(expectation-rules ^status active)
     ⟨expectation-rules⟩}
    {(target ^plan-of-action succeeded)
     ⟨target⟩}
    --⟩
    (halt))
(plan-rule-1
    {(plan-rules ^status active) ⟨plan-rules⟩}
    {(target ^goal attack) ⟨target⟩}
    --⟩
    (modify ⟨target⟩ ^plan-of-action course-to)
    (remove ⟨plan-rules⟩)
    (make expectation-rules ^status active))
(plan-rule-2
    {(plan-rules ^status active) ⟨plan-rules⟩}
    {(target ^goal no-attack) ⟨target⟩}
    --⟩
    (modify ⟨target⟩ ^plan-of-action no-course-
     to)
    (remove ⟨plan-rules⟩)
    (make expectation-rules ^status active))
```

```
(plan-rule-3
    {(plan-rules ^status active) ⟨plan-rules⟩}
    {(target ^goal dont-know) ⟨target⟩}
    - -⟩
    (modify ⟨target⟩ ^plan-of-action wait-and-
      see)
    (remove ⟨plan-rules⟩)
    (make expectation-rules ^status active))
(plan-rule-4
    {(plan-rules ^status active) ⟨plan-rules⟩}
    {(target ^goal achieved) ⟨target⟩}
    - -⟩
    (modify ⟨target⟩ ^plan-of-action succeeded)
    (remove ⟨plan-rules⟩)
    (make expectation-rules ^status active))
(plan-rule-5
    {(plan-rules ^status active) ⟨plan-rules⟩}
    {(target ^goal advance) ⟨target⟩}
    - -⟩
    (modify ⟨target⟩ ^plan-of-action course-to)
    (remove ⟨plan-rules⟩)
    (make expectation-rules ^status active))
(revision-rule-1
    {(revision-rules ^status active) ⟨revision-
      rules⟩}
    {(target ^relative-behavior . . . ^present-
      position . . .^goal . . . ) ⟨target⟩}
    - -⟩
    (modify ⟨target⟩ ^plan-of-action feint)
    (remove ⟨revision-rules⟩)
    (make expectation-rules ^status active))
(revision-rule-2
    {(revision-rules ^status active) ⟨revision-
      rules⟩}
    {(target ^relative-behavior . . . ^goal
      retreat) ⟨target⟩}
    - -⟩
    (modify ⟨target⟩ ^plan-of-action no-course-
      to)
    (remove ⟨revision-rules⟩)
    (make expectation-rules ^status active))
(revision-rule-3
    {(revision-rules ^status active) ⟨revision-
      rules⟩}
    {(target ^relative-behavior . . . ^present-
      position . . .^goal . . . ) ⟨target⟩}
    - -⟩
    (modify ⟨target⟩ ^plan-of-action feint)
```

```
                    (remove ⟨revision-rules⟩)
                    (make expectation-rules ˆstatus active))

            (revision-rule-4
                {(revision-rules ˆstatus active) ⟨revision-
                    rules⟩}
                {(target ˆrelative-behavior . . . ˆpresent-
                    position . . .ˆgoal . . . ) ⟨target⟩}
                - -⟩
                (modify ⟨target⟩ ˆplan-of-action wait-and-
                    see)
                (remove ⟨revision-rules⟩)
                (make expectation-rules ˆstatus active))))

    (GROUP goal-rules

        (PRODUCES
            (target-goal
                "Gives objective currently being sought with
                respect to target, i.e., attack, no-attack,
                retreat, advance, achieved, or dont-know")

            (revision-rules-status
                "State variable, enables firing of revision-
                rules")

            (plan-rules-status
                "State variable, enables firing of plan-
                rules"))

        (USES
            (target-present-position)
            (target-relative-behavior)
            (goal-rules-status))

        (RULES
            (goal-rule-1
                {(goal-rules ˆstatus active) ⟨goal-rules⟩}
                {(target ˆpresent-position . . . ˆrelative-
                    behavior . . . ) ⟨target⟩}
                - -⟩
                (modify ⟨target⟩ ˆgoal attack)
                (remove ⟨goal-rules⟩)
                (make plan-rules ˆstatus active))

            (goal-rule-2
                {(goal-rules ˆstatus active) ⟨goal-rules⟩}
                {(target ˆpresent-position . . . ˆrelative-
                    behavior . . . ) ⟨target⟩}
                - -⟩
                (modify ⟨target⟩ ˆgoal attack)
                (remove ⟨goal-rules⟩)
                (make revision-rules ˆstatus active))
```

```
(goal-rule-3
    {(goal-rules ^status active) 〈goal-rules〉}
    {(target ^present-position . . . ^relative-
     behavior . . . ) 〈target〉}
    - -〉
    (modify 〈target〉 ^goal attack)
    (remove 〈goal-rules〉)
    (make revision-rules ^status active))
(goal-rule-4
    {(goal-rules ^status active) 〈goal-rules〉}
    {(target ^present-position . . . ^relative-
     behavior . . . ) 〈target〉}
    - -〉
    (modify 〈target〉 ^goal attack)
    (remove 〈goal-rules〉)
    (make revision-rules ^status active))
(goal-rule-5
    {(goal-rules ^status active) 〈goal-rules〉}
    {(target 〈present-position . . . ^relative-
     behavior . . . ) 〈target〉}
    - -〉
    (modify 〈target〉 ^goal advance)
    (remove 〈goal-rules〉)
    (make plan-rules ^status active))
(goal-rule-6
    {(goal-rules ^status active) 〈goal-rules〉}
    {(target ^present-position . . . ^relative-
     behavior . . . ) 〈target〉}
    - -〉
    (modify 〈target〉 ^goal no-attack)
    (remove 〈goal-rules〉)
    (make plan-rules ^status active))
(goal-rule-7
    {(goal-rules ^status active) 〈goal-rules〉}
    {(target ^present-position . . . ^relative-
     behavior . . . ) 〈target〉}
    - -〉
    (modify 〈target〉 ^goal retreat)
    (remove 〈goal-rules〉)
    (make revision-rules ^status active))
(goal-rule-8
    {(goal-rules ^status active) 〈goal-rules〉}
    {(target ^present-position arrived-at)
     〈target〉}
    - -〉
    (make battle-group ^status dead)
    (modify 〈target〉 ^goal achieved)
    (remove 〈goal-rules〉)
    (make plan-rules ^status active))
```

```
              (goal-rule-9
                  {(goal-rules ^status active) (goal-rules)}
                  {(target ^relative-behavior inconsistent)
                   (target)}
                  - -)
                  (modify (target) ^goal dont-know)
                  (remove (goal-rules))
                  (make plan-rules ^status active))))
    (GROUP starter-rules

        (PRODUCES
            (target-transition
                "Tells whether target is currently receding or
                approaching")

            (target-present-position
                "Tells which of 3 possible sectors the target
                currently occupies")

            (computational-rules-status
                "State variable, enables firing of
                computational-rules"))

        (USES
            (target-present-position))

        (RULES
            (starter-rule-1
                {(first-starter-rule ^status active) (first-
                starter-rule)}
                {(target ^present-position none) (target)}
                - -)
                (remove (first-starter-rule))
                (modify (target) (initial-position)))

            (starter-rule-2
                {(other-starter-rules ^status active)
                 (other-starter-rules)}
                {(target ^present-position . . . ) (target)}
                - -)
                (remove (other-starter rules))
                (modify (target) (update-attributes))
                (make computational-rules ^status active))))
```

TWELVE

The Evolution of Interface Requirements for Expert Systems

Marilyn Stelzner,
Michael D. Williams

IntelliCorp
Mountain View, CA

Abstract

The user interface requirements for expert systems have evolved considerably since the days when a consultation system first conducted a dialogue with the user. These changes are due in part to the transition from expert systems to expert advisory systems, the increasing use of deep models of knowledge, and the increasing size and complexity of the systems. Because the user is actively involved in the decision-making process, there is increased necessity for the user interface to support the user's cognitive task. This requirement encourages use of the interface as model world metaphor, a metaphor that is directly supported by a deep model of knowledge. At the same time, increasing size and complexity of the expert systems implies an increasing amount of resources required to implement user interfaces, motivating the development of general tools that accelerate interface development and facilitate experimentation with user interface design.

1. Introduction

The user interface requirements for expert systems have evolved considerably since the days when a consultation system first conducted a dialogue with the user. These changes are due in part to the transition from expert systems to expert *advisory* systems, the increasing use of deep models of knowledge, and the increasing size and complexity of the systems. The more experience we gain at IntelliCorp building commercial expert systems, the more we are convinced of the importance of user interfaces to the overall acceptance and success of such systems. At the same time, we see no indications that the requirements for user interfaces to expert systems are yet stabilizing since expert systems themselves continue to evolve.

The major difference between the classical expert systems, such as MYCIN, R-1, or Prospector, and the expert advisory systems we frequently see today is that the human remains very much in the decision-making loop. Early examples of expert systems asked the user many questions and then returned an answer. In an expert advisory system, the user typically makes decisions based on help and information provided by the advisory system; that is, the user and the system share the reasoning and decision-making tasks. Because the user guides and participates in the reasoning tasks, there is an increased necessity to support the user's cognitive task. Both the quantity and quality of communication between the system and user must be increased. While consultation systems may be adequately supported by the metaphor of *interface as conversation*, expert advisory systems make the metaphor of *interface as model world* (Hutchins, Hollan, & Norman, 1985) much more appropriate since such interfaces have demonstrated that they can increase the user's problem-solving capabilities (Hollan et al., 1986).

Early lists of requirements for expert systems stated that a limited scope, or a fairly narrow problem, was desirable. Today we are seeing growth in these systems along two different dimensions:

1. The increasing scope of these systems is reflected in the size of the knowledge bases involved, independent of the underlying representation; i.e., the number of rules, the number of objects, or the amount of procedural knowledge, is increasing.
2. The number of uses of the same knowledge is expanding. The knowledge encoded in knowledge bases is a valuable asset, and system developers and users frequently want to do more than one thing with it.

Sharing reasoning tasks with the user, multiple uses of the same knowledge, and larger and more complex domains, all encourage representing underlying knowledge in the form of a "deep" model, rather than a heuristic, or "shallow" model. (The term "model" is used here to mean a systematic description of the objects and the relationships among objects in a domain.) Model-based reasoning is demonstrating significant architectural advantages in the implementation of expert systems by separating knowledge about the domain from knowledge about problem-solving processes. At the same time, model-based reasoning can provide explicit representational support for user interfaces designed using the interface as model world metaphor.

Larger-scale expert systems have also increased requirements for the user interface to help in managing complexity. The ability to browse quickly through large amounts of knowledge and to obtain multiple views of the same knowledge becomes critical to both system development and use. When the same model is used for more than one task, multiple interfaces accessing the same knowledge are required. A model of a factory, for example, might be used for capacity planning, financial analysis, scheduling, and alarms management, each of which would probably require separate interfaces.

Larger scale also implies that the development of user interfaces consumes an increasing amount of development resources. This provides motivation for the development of general tools that speed up interface development and facilitate experimentation with user interface design. Not surprisingly, realization of the evolving requirements for expert system interfaces has been reflected in the tools we produce, as they evolve from release to release. Each release has included new tools for constructing end user interfaces as well as additional interface support for system developers.

The next section of this chapter discusses the interface requirements that we see resulting from these changes. Section 3 describes each of our interface tools and some of the reasons for their evolution. Finally, we discuss our general approaches to the development of interface tools and what we consider to be some of the hard problems in the area.

2. The Requirements for User Interfaces to Expert Systems

Requirements for interfaces to expert systems should be categorized into those supporting system developers and those supporting end users, although the distinction between developer and end user is frequently blurred. This is because expert advisory systems tend to be constantly evolving. In many cases, tasks considered knowledge acquisition in the past, such as the definition of a model of the system to be analyzed, are now tasks performed by the end user. At the same time, as the heuristics employed by expert users of an expert advisory system become better understood, knowledge in the system may be expanded so that additional tasks are performed automatically.

The interface requirements for these two classes of users are obviously not the same, although they may overlap. Specifically, end user interfaces can be very useful for developers, though not necessarily the other way around. Interfaces originally designed for an expert system developer are frequently inappropriate for an end user. (Richer & Clancey, 1985). Major differences in these requirements stem from the different focus of the two classes of users:

- The major focus of the developers is on the *representation of the domain* and the reasoning processes.
- The major focus of the end users is on the *domain itself.*

Developers' interface tools, therefore, will enable the developer to look at the underlying representation of the domain and allow tracing of the various reasoning processes. The end users' interface, on the other hand, should make their mental models of the domain explicit.

Given the desirability of the interface as model world metaphor and the need to assist both users and developers in managing complexity, we have identified five major requirements for user interfaces to expert systems:

1. The interface should represent the domain in the user's natural idiom.
2. The interface should provide immediate feedback to the user on the effects of changes to system state by explicitly maintaining and displaying complex constraints and interrelationships.
3. The user must be able to recover easily from trying different alternatives.
4. The user interface must support the user at different granularities, or levels of abstraction.
5. User interfaces must be implemented in such a way that it is possible to have multiple interfaces to the same knowledge.

2.1. The Natural Idiom

Mental models are systematic descriptions of objects and relationships between objects (Genter & Stevens, 1983), and computational models are logical extensions when problems are too large or complex to be dealt with using a mental model. The interface needs to map directly onto this perception, reflecting how the knowledge in the program maps onto the mental model. Hutchins, Hollan, and Norman contrast such interfaces to more conventional interfaces:

> Historically, most interfaces have been built on the conversational metaphor. There is power in the abstractions that language provides . . . but

the implicit role of interfaces as an intermediary to a hidden world denies the user direct engagement with the objects of interest. Instead, the user is in direct contact with linguistic structures, structures that can be interpreted as referring to the objects of interest, but that are not those objects themselves. We argue that the central metaphor of the interface should be that of the model world: Instead of describing the actions of interest, the user should be doing them. In the conventional interface, the system describes the results of the actions: In the model world the system would present directly the actions taken upon the objects.

More specifically, this implies a need to provide interactive displays of the user's model *in the natural idiom* (Kunz, personal communication), an idiom that is frequently graphic. Spreadsheets are an early example of using the natural idiom in a decision support environment, while Steamer (Hollan, Hutchins, & Weitzman, 1984) is the canonical example in the AI community. The ONCOCIN project has attempted to provide this type of interface by graphically representing medical documents for doctors to enter patient information. Additional examples of this type of interface are found in many of the applications built using Impulse (Smith, Dinitz, & Barth, 1986), Paragon (Siemens, Golden, & Ferguson, 1986), KEE™9, and other environments providing knowledge-based interface tools.

A NASA Life Support System application has an interface using a schematic based on an engineering diagram, as shown in Figure 1. Genetic engineers using the Strain Management System to study the effects of gene splicing operate directly on a graphic representation of a gene, as shown in Figure 2. A set of knowledge-based tools for the nuclear power industry is centered around interactive plant models that allow nuclear engineers to construct models of plant subsystems graphically, as shown in Figure 3.

2.2. Immediate Feedback

As well as displaying the domain in the natural graphic idiom, the displays must allow the user to act directly upon them, and then provide immediate feedback on the effects of the user's actions. A project management and scheduling application uses an interactive Gantt chart, shown in Figure 4, for indicating scheduled activities and the constraints between activities. When the user changes the duration of an activity with the mouse, the starting and end dates of all dependent operations are immediately modified.

The advantages of rapid feedback have been well documented:

> Rapid feedback in terms of changes in the behavior of objects not only allows for the modification of actions even as they are being executed, but

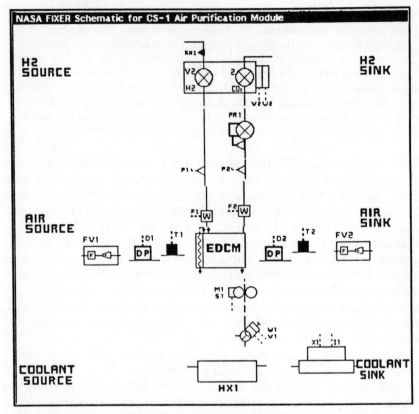

Figure 1.   The NASA Life Support System Interface.

also supports the feeling of acting directly on the objects themselves. It removes the perception of the computer as an intermediary by providing continual representation of system state. In addition, rapidity of feedback and continuous representation of state allows one to make use of perceptual faculties in evaluating the outcome of actions. (Hutchins, Hollan, & Norman, 1985).

Immediate feedback on system state frequently requires that the graphics reflect the running of the model, through some sort of animation. Animation aids the *envisionment* process (described by de Kleer as "an inference process which, given the device's structure, determines its function") (de Kleer & Brown, 1983) and the user's understanding of system behavior. Steamer provides an interactive graphical interface to a steam propulsion plant simulation that is used to train plant operators (Hollan, Hutchins, & McCandless, 1986). A knowledge-based simulation of a factory (Faught, 1986) has a detailed layout of the factory

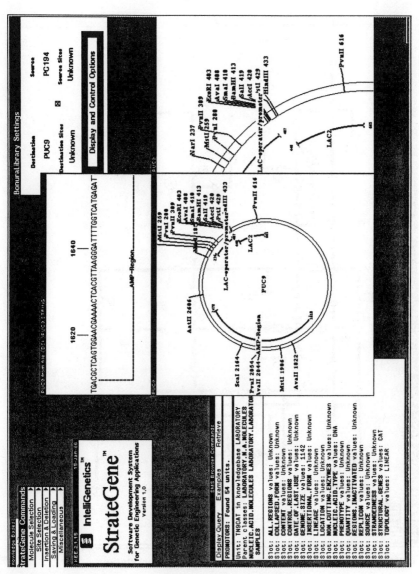

Figure 2. The Strain Management System Interface.

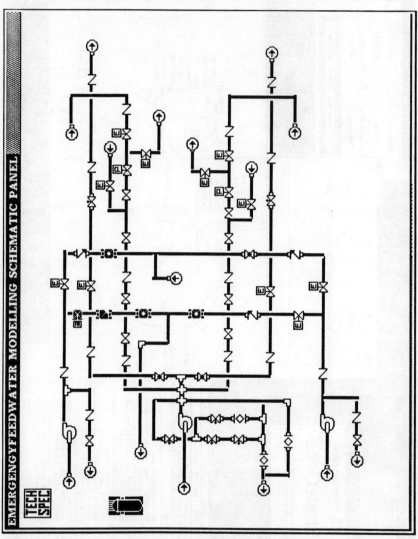

Figure 3.   Interface for the Nuclear Engineers Workstation.

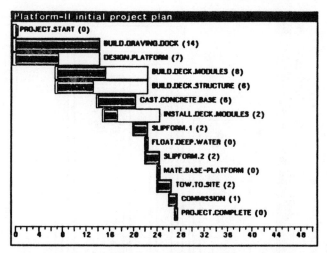

Figure 4.   Gantt Chart Interface for Project Management.

floor, shown in Figure 5, to assist manufacturing engineers in evaluating the performance of different operating strategies. Animation of basket movement through the factory allows the engineer to identify quickly bottlenecks and underutilized resources.

2.3. Recoverability

The end users of expert systems tend to be highly skilled knowledge workers, who may or may not be experts in the precise area addressed by the system. Aside from the fact that such users tend to be less patient with "unfriendly" systems, the success of the system is directly related to the users' ability to try out various decisions on the system and then change their minds. They must be able to recover easily from situations they don't want to be in and to experiment with different responses without much penalty.

Recoverability implies more than standard undo facilities and may impose computational requirements on the underlying system for maintenance of history lists, checkpointing capabilities, or even truth maintenance. The ability to guess at an answer to a question with little or no penalty, and to see the implications of the guess quickly, makes the system easier to learn to use.

2.4. The Appropriate Granularity

As applications become larger and more complex, an overall requirement of the interface is to assist both developers and end users in

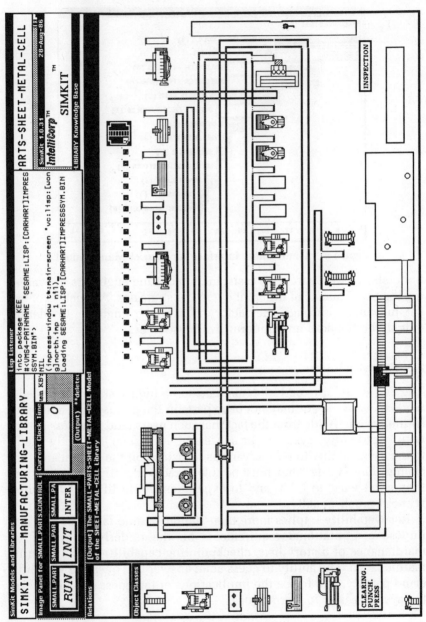

Figure 5. Interface to the Factory Floor Simulation.

dealing with complexity. This implies that interface design issues become more important, the larger the application is. To assist in dealing with complexity, the interface must, first, assist the developer in decomposing the problem, and, secondly, help the end user to understand the relationships between the component parts of the problem and between various levels of abstraction. To support these two requirements, the interface must allow both types of users to work at the appropriate *granularity* (Hobbs, 1985), a granularity that changes frequently during a user session.

In particular, the interface should support both end users and developers at the following levels:

- The object description level;
- The intraobject level, reflecting user-specified relationships between individual objects;
- Object hierarchies indicating both class/subclass or class/member relationships, as well as composite/component (or part-of) relationships;
- Collections of object classes (libraries) and collections of objects (models).

Changing the level of abstraction viewed by the user serves to simplify the interaction by filtering out information that is not relevant at a given level.

2.5. Multiple Interfaces to the Same Knowledge

Multiple, overlapping problems using the same knowledge implies different interfaces for different types of problems, but integrated into the same system. The same knowledge, therefore, will be reflected in more than one interface or view. (Richer & Clancey, 1985). The requirement for multiple views of the same knowledge has implications about the implementation of interfaces. An approach similar to Smalltalk's Model-View-Controller (Goldberg, 1984). separates interface from the underlying representation of the domain. A distinct separation of the programmatic interface and the interactive interface to knowledge are also features of OASIS (Faneuf), and ActiveImages™ (Stelzner & Williams, 1986).

3. Building Tools to Support User Interfaces

IntelliCorp markets knowledge-based programming tools appropriate for building a wide range of expert systems applications. Our general

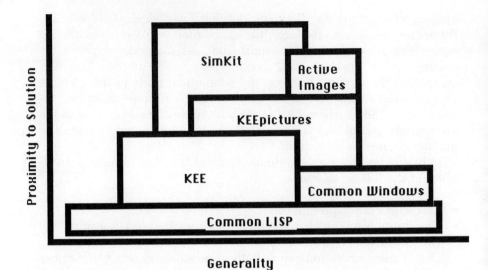

Figure 6.   The Layered Architecture of IntelliCorp's Tools.

approach to supporting the design and development of user interfaces to expert systems has been to develop a layered set of tools that facilitate design and implementation of highly interactive, graphic interfaces. Our goal is to free system developers from many of the details of building graphic interfaces so that they can focus their attention on matching the interface to the users' cognitive task. Since interface design is still very much an art, it is important that these tools facilitate experimentation and incremental tuning.

Early versions IntelliCorp products primarily had developer interfaces, but recent versions have included significant new tools for building end-user interfaces. In release 3.0, approximately 55–60% of the code is interface-related. The goal of our interface tools is to provide reusable chunks of code that can be easily tailored by developers who are not necessarily experienced graphics programmers. These tools vary in the degree of generality, as shown in Figure 6. That is, we have put effort into tools that support some types of interfaces more than others. For example, we have developed more extensive tools for constructing graphic interfaces than textual interfaces. Each of IntelliCorp's major interface tools is described below.

3.1. The KEE™ Interface

The Knowledge Engineering Environment™ (KEE) software development system is an integrated package of tools that allows programmers

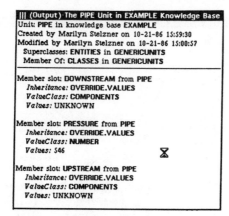

Figure 7.   Display of a KEE Unit.

to develop knowledge-based systems without extensive training in artificial intelligence technologies. The first release, KEE 1, had early versions of the KEE interface featuring the unit display, shown in Figure 7, and the knowledge-base graph, shown in Figure 8. These displays help the developer to examine knowledge-base structures at both the object level and the object hierarchy level. Both displays serve as active browsers, since all boldface names are mouseable and can be used to access the named object. The user is acting upon an object, but in this case, the object is a knowledge structure. One command that can be selected by mousing on an object is "display," which allows the user to trace relationships from one object to another by successively displaying objects referred to in the display of another object.

By the time that KEE 1.2 was released, an "active rule graph" had been added. This graph animates the firing of rules, assisting the developer in debugging rules, and the end user in understanding the reasoning strategies the system is taking.

3.2. The ActiveImages™ Package

Early KEE users soon asked for more help in building end user interfaces, which was provided in KEE 2 in the ActiveImages system. ActiveImages is a package that provides facilities for building control panel interfaces to knowledge structures in knowledge-based applications (Stelzner & Williams, 1986), heavily influenced by Steamer (Hollan, Hutchins, & Weitzman, 1984) and LOOPS (Stefik et al., 1983). The user interfaces built with ActiveImages explicitly mimic operator panels for many control systems. The ActiveImages package provides a set of predefined graphic objects, such as gauges, thermometers, bargraphs,

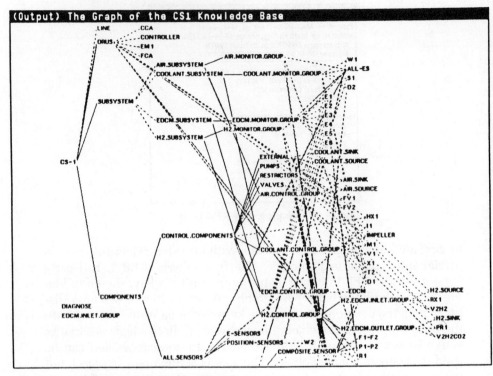

Figure 8.   A KEE Knowledge Base Graph.

and histograms, which can be used to display and control the state of a knowledge-based system.

Interfaces built with ActiveImages are primarily focused at the object description level since most of the images attach to object attributes, or *slots*. To attach an image to an object's attribute, the user mouses on the name of the attribute and selects the command "Attach Image." The user then chooses a particular image from a menu of images appropriate for the data type of the attribute. After shaping and positioning the image on the screen, the image is ready to use. The thermoactuator shown in Figure 9 is an example of the kind of image that can be constructed in this manner.

ActiveImages are immediately updated when the value of an attribute is modified, providing feedback to the user on changes in system state. Many of the images are *actuators*, images that add the ability to control the state of a knowledge base with a direct-manipulation style interaction. For example, the user mouses on top of a graphic

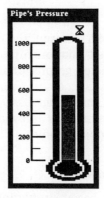

Figure 9.   Display of a Thermoactuator, a Class of ActiveImages.

image, such as the thermometer shown in Figure 10, and changes the value stored in the attached slot by "pulling" the height of the bar reflecting the value up or down.

Because ActiveImages can be created quickly and easily, system developers frequently build control panels to help them debug their applications. This is a case where an end user interface is also valuable for system developers.

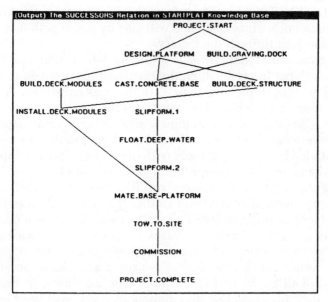

Figure 10.   Slotgraph Showing the Successors Relation Between Activity Objects.

3.3. Slotgraph

By the time that KEE 2.1 was released, the need for a general interface tool reflecting user-specified relationships between objects had been determined. *Slotgraph* creates graphs of user-specified relations, as shown in the graph of the "successors" relation between activity objects in Figure 10. Like the knowledge-base graph, objects in Slotgraph displays are active, and commands relevant to the object can be obtained by mousing on the object name.

3.4. SimKit® Interface Tools

SimKit, a set of knowledge-based simulation and modeling tools built on top of KEE 2.1, includes our first general tool on the "interface as model world" metaphor. The SimKit Model Editor, provides a direct manipulation interface for building complex system models, such as the factory floor layout model shown in Figure 5. The user mouses on the desired object class, such as PUNCHPRESSES, in the Object Classes Viewport on the left, creating a new member of the PUNCHPRESSES class. The new punchpress is then placed on the design canvas in the center, and an icon appears as its graphic representation. To connect the new punchpress into the network, the user mouses first on the punchpress and then on the conveyor section below it. That action will define a DOWNSTREAM relation from the punchpress to the conveyor, and a number of such connections will specify a new path that baskets of parts can take through the factory.

Supporting the Model Editor is a Library Editor, which assists the system developer in establishing the relationships between model objects and relationships, and their graphic representations. A simple dialogue is used to define new object classes and new types of relationships. The Library Editor automatically creates default graphic representations, icons, for the new classes, and they can then immediately be instantiated by pointing at them with the mouse. The developer then edits the icons to be pictures of the real world object.

SimKit also supports the graphic specification of part/whole or composite/component relationships, a facility that assists the user in viewing a problem at multiple levels of abstraction. To define a composite object "by example," the user mouses on an example of each component of the composite. To define a composite object that represents a computer processor, for example, the user might mouse on an input queue, a PROCESSOR, and an output queue, as shown in Figure 11. The user then indicates that all component parts have been selected, and names the new composite class. A new class icon appears, and the

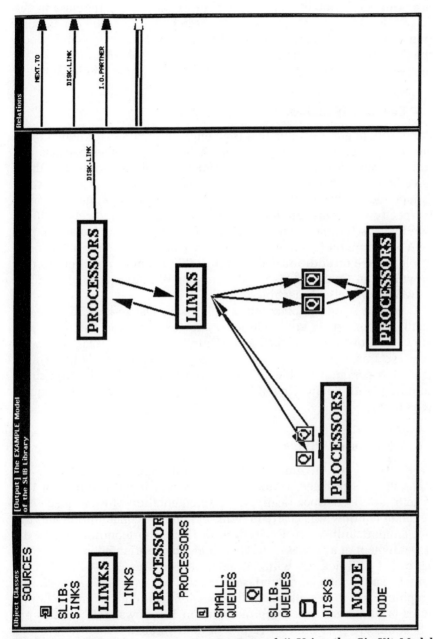

Figure 11. Defining a Composite "By Example" Using the SimKit Model Editor.

301

user can immediately create a member of the composite class in the same way that any other member is created. To show the decomposition of a composite object graphically, the user mouses on it and selects the "Show parts" option. To go up a level of abstraction, the user mouses on a component object and select the "Show whole" option.

3.5. Common Windows℠

Portability of graphic interfaces is an engineering issue for which there are no easy answers. We have had to face these issues because our software runs on a variety of different kinds of hardware, and there have been no satisfactory tools in the past for developing hardware-independent graphic interfaces. Our approach to this problem has been to specify Common Windows (Drascher, Sharpe, & Tidwell, 1986), a window system that is an extension to Common Lisp. We have implemented Common Windows on a number of systems and it has been implemented on additional systems by other vendors. An interface that is written in Common Lisp and Common Windows is then portable between a variety of machines.

Common Windows places the emphasis on system-building tools by featuring constructs and techniques that have proven useful in previous window systems, such as the Interlisp-D℠ and ZetaLisp℠ window systems. Many high-level facilities have been provided to handle the most common problems which interface builders face, such as scrolling and *hotspotting* (making a region of a window mouse-sensitive).

3.6. KEEpictures℠ Toolkit

Early prototypes of SimKit's Model Editor were built on top of the ActiveImages package, which lacked several desired features for that type of interface. Specifically, the implementation of each image as a separate window was costly in terms of memory consumption and did not support animation. Realization of these shortcomings led to the development of a new, and more general, object-oriented graphics toolkit called KEEpictures, which enables users of the KEE system to construct a variety of iconic interfaces. Its intended uses range from simple graphic displays to sophisticated animation techniques. Since KEEpictures is implemented on top of Common Windows, KEEpictures applications are portable to a variety of hardware.

The KEEpictures environment provides a set of primitive standard picture classes, such as circles, axes, lines, and strings. Each of these primitives can be shaped, enlarged, shrunk, and altered in a variety of ways. Pictures can be combined together to form larger, composite pictures. As well as using the standard building blocks provided by KEEpictures, users can also draw their own pictures using bitmaps. These bitmaps can then be added together, or to other types of pictures, to form the final picture.

KEEpictures was released in KEE 3, and ActiveImages has now been reimplemented to be built using KEEpictures primitives.

4. A General Approach to Implementing Interface Tools

KEEpictures, ActiveImages, and SimKit all implement their various interface primitives through object-oriented programming, using inheritance over object hierarchies of class/subclass and class/member relationships in KEE. Behavior of the graphic objects is implemented by sending the object a message to, for example, create a member of itself, delete itself, move itself, or reshape itself. Specialization of class definitions provides modularity when defining object behaviors.

The second major requirement for these interface tools is to establish a one-to-one correspondence between graphic objects and model objects. Changes made directly to the representation of the model must be reflected in the graphics, as well as reflecting changes made on the graphic representation back on the model. The correspondence from model to graphics is typically implemented using active values, a demon-like mechanism that invokes specified procedures whenever a slot is accessed or modified. The correspondence between the graphics and the model object is maintained by message sending from the graphic object to the model object.

These tools have a combination of interaction styles, ranging from direct manipulation (Schneiderman, 1982) to mouse-and-menu to conversational. The choice among these styles depends on a number of factors, but a brief summary follows:

- A mouse-and-menu style is used when the user must make a number of choices, and the choices can be constrained to a limited set of options.
- A conversational style is used when the choices to be made by the user cannot be constrained, as is typically the case when the user is naming objects or object attributes.
- A direct manipulation style is used in selected situations when user options can be preconceived and sufficiently limited.

The approach taken to make these systems easy to use has been to implement multiple levels of editors. Interactive interfaces, in either a direct manipulation or mouse-and-menu style, provide easy access to the most frequently used functions with minimal user input. Contextual information is used to assume reasonable defaults whenever possible in an attempt to reduce the number of user inputs, since minimizing the number of user inputs seems to make an interface easier to use. Given the number of different options that must be available to users of the class of expert systems we are building, however, this is not a straightforward task. Our approach has been to try to assume reasonable defaults, whenever possible taking advantage of contextual information.

The problem then becomes one of determining what is a reasonable default? A number of criteria seem to be evolving:

- The user frequently does not need to change the assumed value.
- If the user will need to change the value, they are happy to defer changing it. An example is generation of a default bitmap for new object classes created through the SimKit Library Editor. The user is typically satisfied to work with a default graphic display when getting started, but later wants the ability to go in and create a domain specific bitmap such as the work station and conveyor bitmaps shown in Figure 5.
- If the user will need to change the value, it can be made easy to change later.

The problems are in determining what can be assumed as a reasonable defaults. There is a need to take advantage of as much contextual information as possible, which is easier in a knowledge-based environment. Finding reasonable defaults involves trial and error, or the "muddling through" and experimental approach to interface design advocated by Norman (1986).

Flexibility is critical to the success of these tools also because of the evolving nature of interface requirements and special-purpose requirements for specific domains. To relax the standard tradeoff between ease of use and flexibility, we have adopted an approach to interface design called *specification by reformulation* (Stelzner & Williams, 1986). This approach involves making the results of a partial specification quickly visible, and then allowing the user to refine the specification incrementally and view the results. This approach requires a particular relationship between knowledge representation and interface design. The interface design features two distinct, but integrated, interfaces:

- An intelligent, interactive interface that enables the user to create quickly approximate specifications, or prototypes. While the interactive interface provides access to the major functionality of the

tool, it is limited to the subset of the tool's total functionality necessary to optimize usability and flexibility.
- A programmatic interface that enables the user to modify and refor-
mulate the products of the interactive interface. The programmatic
interface, while harder to use than the interactive interface, is op-
timized for expressiveness and completeness.

Reformulation is dependent on a declarative representation of the
graphic images for communication between the two interfaces. The
declarative representation, which in this case is a KEE unit, must be
used consistently as the central reference point for attributes of the
graphic representation. Both the interactive and programmatic interfaces must retrieve values from the graphic object's unit and note any
changes back on the unit.

5. Conclusions

The evolution of expert systems is making interface design a more
critical factor in the overall development of the system. This is due in
part to the increasing size and complexity of the systems, the transition
from expert systems to expert advisory systems, and the increasing
focus on model-based reasoning. At the same time, since expert systems are continuing to evolve, the requirements for user interfaces have
not yet stabilized.

The difficulties in designing user interfaces to expert systems do not
seem to be in the area of building commercial-grade, interface tools
such as the ones just described. There are myriad details involved in
getting complete functionality, but no serious technical difficulties.
Instead, the difficult part of interface design is matching the interface to
the user's cognitive task. This makes the work being done in the field of
cognitive science on interface design and on how people solve problems extremely relevant. The combination of new understandings arising from cognitive science research and the representational power of
AI languages is contributing to the rapid progress being made in interface design for expert systems, even as the interface requirements of
expert systems change rapidly.[1]

---

[1]KEE, Knowledge Engineering Environment, ActiveImages, SimKit, KEEpictures, and
Common Windows are trademarks of IntelliCorp. Interlisp-D is a trademark of Xerox.
ZetaLisp is a trademark of Symbolics.

References

de Kleer, J. & Brown, J. S., (1983). Assumptions and ambiguities in mechanistic mental models. In D. Genter & A. L. Stevens (Eds.), *Mental Models*. Hillsdale, NJ: Erlbaum.

Drascher, E., Sharpe, D., Tidwell, K., (1986). *Common Windows Manual.* (Mountain View, CA:) IntelliCorp.

Faneuf, R. et al., (unpublished, 1986). OASIS: Object–oriented adaptable sapient interface system.

Faught, W. S., (1986). Applications of AI in engineering. *IEEE Computer*, July.

Genter, D., & Stevens, A. L., (Eds.) (1983). *Mental models*. Hillsdale, NJ: Erlbaum.

Goldberg, A., (1984). *SMALLTALK–80: The interactive programming environment.* Menlo Park, CA: Addison-Wesley.

Hobbs, J. R., (1985). Granularity. *Proceedings of the International Joint Conference on Artificial Intelligence*, Los Angeles, August.

Hollan, J. D., Hutchins, E. L., McCandless, T. P., Rosenstein, M., & Weitzman, L., (1986). *Graphical interfaces for simulation* (Tech. Rep. 8603) Institute for Cognitive Science, San Diego, CA.

Hollan, J. D., Hutchins, E. L. & Weitzman, L., (1984). STEAMER: An interactive inspectable simulation–based training system. *AI Magazine*.

Hutchins, E. L., Hollan, J. D., & Norman, D. A., (1985). *Direct manipulation interfaces*, (Tech Rep. 8503), Institute for Cognitive Science, San Diego, CA.

Kunz, J. Personal communication.

Norman, D. A., (1986). *CHI '86 debate*. Resolved: Interface design doesn't matter.

Richer, M. H., & Clancey, W. J., (1985). Guidon–watch: A graphic interface for viewing a knowledge–based system. *IEEE Computer Graphics and Applications*, 5, (November), 51–64.

Schneiderman, B., (1982). The future of interactive systems and the emergence of direct manipulation. *Behavior & Information Technology*, 1, 237–256.

Siemens, R. W., Golden, M., & Ferguson, J. C., (1986). StarPlan II: Evolution of an expert system. *Proceedings: AAAI-86, Fifth National Conference on Artificial Intelligence*, Philadelphia.

Smith, R. G., Dinitz, R., & Barth, P., (1986). Impulse-86: A substrate for object-oriented interface design. *OOPSLA '86: Conference Proceedings*, Portland, OR.

Stefik, M., Bobrow, D. G., Mittal, S., & Conway, L., (1983). Knowledge Programming in LOOPS. *AI Magazine*, (Fall).

Stelzner, M., & Williams, M. D., (unpublished, 1986). Specification by reformulation: An approach to knowledge-based interface design.

THIRTEEN

Cognitive Impacts of the User Interface

Paul E. Lehner

George Mason University

Mary M. Kralj

Human Resources Research Organization

Acknowledgement

The research reported herein was supported under Contract N0014-83-C-0537 from the Office of Naval Research. Preparation of this manuscript was supported by Office of Naval Research, Contract No. N00014-84-C-0526. Both contracts were to PAR Technology Corporation.

1. Introduction

Interactive computer systems are becoming increasingly complex. As systems become more complex, the human engineering of these systems will become increasingly dominated by cognitive rather than perceptual factors. While factors such as display size, perceptual resolution of characters, contrasting colors, etc., are important, it is generally cognitive factors that will determine whether or not a user can effectively use a complex system. In the case of decision-aiding systems, such as expert systems, these cognitive factors include the consistency between the user's and expert system's problem-solving procedures, knowledge structures and knowledge elements, as well as a user's cognitive model of the "reasoning" processes within the system.

In this chapter we will explore two issues related to the cognitive factors affecting user/expert system interaction. First, we will present an overview of our work demonstrating that a dominant factor in the quality of user/expert system interaction is the extent to which the user has an accurate *cognitive model* of the expert system's reasoning process. Second, we present a theory of user interface design that heavily emphasizes the cognitive impacts of a user interface. We will explore the impact of alternative user interface features on a user's cognitive model of an expert system's processes. The main premise is that since research has demonstrated a user's cognitive model to be a dominant factor in the quality of user/complex system interaction, then the extent to which a user interface promotes an accurate cognitive model should be a primary determinant of whether or not that interface can be classified as a good or "user friendly" interface.

2. Cognitive Models and User/Expert System Interaction

Conventional wisdom within expert system technology suggests that in order for an expert system to be accepted by its users, it must utilize the same problem-solving procedures, knowledge structures and elements as the system's users. That is, there must be significant *cognitive consistency* between the user's and the expert system's cognitive structures. Unfortunately, as is explained below, in many applications of expert system technology, cognitive consistency between the user's and expert system's knowledge-base and problem-solving processes is a criterion that can not, in principle, be satisfied.

Historically, most expert systems have been developed to operate in time-relaxed consultation environments where the system requests from the user a substantial amount of information about the problem at hand. Systems such as MYCIN and PROSPECTOR are prototypical of this. Recently, however, expert-system technology has focused on the use of the expert system as *intelligent interfaces* between a user and larger complex information-processing system. These *expert interface systems* (sometimes referred to as expert advisory systems) use the same program architectures found in consultation systems, but automatically acquire data from an external source rather than requiring data information from the user. The primary function of the expert interface system is to enhance a user's ability to utilize an external data source, often a large system that operates independently of the *expert interface system* (See Lehner, in press for examples).

From a human-engineering perspective, there are some key aspects of expert interface systems that make them very different from expert consultation systems. Expert interface systems are often designed to address problems for which practiced human experts do not exist (e.g., rapidly correlate and interpret large volumes of data). The human expertise that does exist is usually dispersed over several types of experts. Some people will be knowledgeable about the problem domain while others will be experts on the characteristics of baseline data base or information-processing system for which the expert system provides an interface. As a result, the knowledge base of an expert interface system is not likely to reflect a single source of human expertise. This is compounded by the fact that expert interface systems have a much broader variety of potential users than consultation systems. In a consultation system, the user must be sufficiently knowledgeable about the problem domain to answer the questions the system asks the user. Expert interface systems automatically obtain their data from an external source and are basically turnkey systems that even a user who is totally inexperienced in the problem domain can use.

For these reasons, it is not likely that user's of an expert interface system will utilize the same problem-solving procedures, knowledge structures and elements as the expert system. Cognitive consistency cannot be assumed.

An important issue then is that of identifying the conditions required for user/expert system interaction to be effective in the context of cognitive inconsistency. In a research program initially presented in Lehner and Zirk (1987) we hypothesized that a good *cognitive model* of expert system processing would satisfy this requirement. Indeed our hypothesis went considerably further such that in cases where both the user and machine were expert problem solvers, and the user possessed an accurate cognitive model of machine processing, significant *inconsistency is often better than consistency* between the two cognitive structures. Whenever two experts collaborate, the opportunity for a significantly better solution to emerge from this collaboration is greater when the two experts do not reflect redundant expertise.

Several experiments were performed to test this theory. These experiments are discussed in detail in Lehner and Zirk (1987) and Hall (1985). The results are summarized herein. Experiments 1 through 3 used a simple stock market game as the problem domain. In Experiment 1 we set up a condition in which both the subject and expert system had isomorphic decision rules (i.e., they would come up with the same answers), but there was inconsistency in their respective data sets. The expert system had access to data the subjects did not initially have, while the data the subjects had were somewhat more accurate than the expert system's (i.e., subject's data were more recent). Under this condition, subjects needed to interact with the expert system to get all relevant data, but the expert system did not necessarily generate the correct answers. A 2×2 factorial design was used to create the experimental conditions. The two independent variables were: (1) cognitive consistency, and (2) cognitive model. The two levels of cognitive consistency were created by the nature of the problem-solving style used by the subject. In each problem, the expert system operated in a goal-driven, backward-chaining manner through the rule base to evaluate goals. High cognitive consistency was defined when the user was taught to problem solve in a similar goal-driven, backward-chaining manner. Low cognitive consistency occurred when the user problem solved in an almost opposite, data-driven, forward-chaining process. The application of both procedures resulted in identical final solutions for all data possibilities.

The two levels of the second independent variable, cognitive model, were (1) accurate cognitive model, and (2) no cognitive model. Subjects in the accurate cognitive model condition received as part of their instructions a written description of an inference network. This section described the structure of a general inference network, explained how the expert system identified goals, intermediate hypothesis, and data items, and chained up and down the network to obtain degree of certainty values for each goal. Included in this section were a pictorial display of an inference net and a simple example of its operation. By working through this (2½) page section, the user developed a cognitive model of how the expert system solved problems. The primary results for this experiment are shown in Figure 1. When the subjects and the expert system used similar decision processes, the quality of the user's cognitive model had little impact. When the subjects and expert system employed different decision processes, the impact of the quality of the user's cognitive model was dramatic.

We hypothesized that the dramatic impact of cognitive model in Experiment 1 was due to the fact that subjects with a good cognitive model were able effectively to use the expert systems logic trace capabilities to extract missing data, while poor cognitive model subjects were not effective in using this capability. In Experiment 2 we replicated the cognitive inconsistent good and poor mental models conditions of Experiment 1 with one exception. The cognitive inconsistent, poor cognitive model subjects were given an additional command that resulted in the display of all problem-relevant data. If our hypothesis was correct, then the 54% difference between these two conditions would disappear. In fact, in this experiment there was only a 9% nonsignificant difference between these two groups.

In Experiment 3, we examined the extent to which a good cognitive model affected a user's ability to isolate "errors" in an expert systems rule set. Experiment 3 replicated the four-cell design of Experiment 1 (quality of cognitive model x cognitive consistency) with three differences: (1) both subject and machine had identical data sets, (2) one or more of the expert system's production rules differed from the problem-solving procedures taught to the subjects, and (3) the subject's task

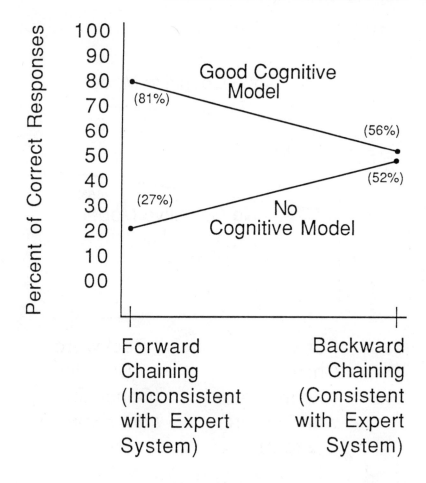

Figure 1.   Performance in Experiment 1 as Percentage of Optimal Responses

was to isolate the rules (parameter values) that resulted in the expert system generating a different conclusion from the subject. Figure 2 shows the percentage of problems in which subjects were able to properly find "errors" in the expert systems rule set under the same four conditions as Experiment 1. Once again, cognitive model had a dramatic impact.

Finally, in a following study, we performed a preliminary confirmation of some of our findings with a "real world" expert system. We used MYCIN and medical students as subjects. Subjects with a good cognitive model significantly outperformed poor cognitive model sub-

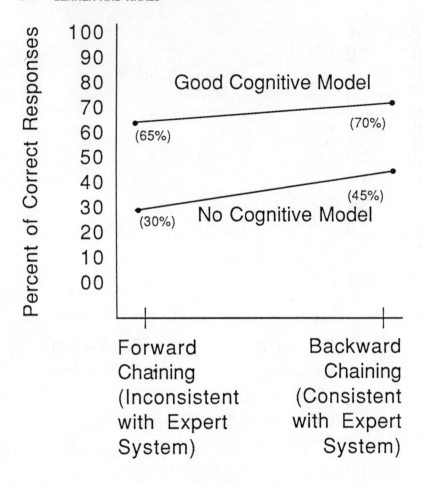

Subject Problem Solving Procedure

Figure 2. Performance in Experiment 3 as Percentage of Inconsistent Rules Identified

jects in their ability to identify why MYCIN generated a particular recommendation. Unfortunately, we were limited to only three subjects per cell, with a result that significance was only at the 0.1 level.

Overall, these experiments provided strong support for the theory that "Cognitive Model" is a dominant factor in the quality of user/expert system interaction. It is also probable that this finding will generalize to other complex system where the system is performing significant amounts of automated analytical reasoning, such as is typical of most decision aids.

3. Cognitive Impacts of the User Interface

If a user's cognitive model is a dominant factor in the quality of user/expert system interactions, then the determinants of a user's cognitive model become, by definition, significant factors in the effectiveness of user/expert system interaction. It is our contention that the user interface of an expert system is a primary determinant of the user's perception of expert system processing. Furthermore, the extent to which a user interface promotes an accurate cognitive model should be a primary determinant of whether or not that interface can be classified as a good or "user friendly" interface.

3.1 Impacts of the User Interface on a User's Cognitive Model: A Theoretical Framework

There is considerable evidence to suggest that people evaluate decision aids, including expert systems, on the basis of the frame of reference they bring into the user/machine setting. For instance, research by Adelman, Rook, and Lehner (1985) suggests that substantive experts evaluate expert systems on the basis of the perceived match of the system to their organizational and problem-solving environment, while technologists evaluate expert systems on the basis of technical characteristics, such as perceptual features of the human interface. We propose taking this argument one step further. Namely, that when confronted with an expert system, people quickly match what they are seeing with something analogous in their own frame of reference, and that this analogy forms the basis of their initial cognitive model. Computer experts compare the new system with other systems with which they are familiar. Domain experts assume that the expert system solves a substantive problem using procedures similar to their own. In other words, people construct a cognitive model of expert system processing through a process of anchoring and adjustment (Tversky & Kahanemann, 1974). They initially create an "anchor model" based on their own frame of reference, and then they adjust this anchor model on the basis of interactive experiences that are not consistent with their model.

Beyond the assertion that users adjust their model on the basis of interactive experiences, the key issue is precisely how this adjustment takes place. Our theory for this is based on Einhorn and Hogarth's work on causal inferencing in humans. As they described it:

> Causal inference is an essential cognitive activity that combines judgments of causation with judgments-under-uncertainty. Thus, causal inference involves judgments of probable cause. A framework for under-

standing how judgments of probable cause are made is presented that consists of three major elements: (1) a causal background [against which] the causal strength of a variable depends on it being a deviation of difference in a background (2) various cues-to-causality such as covariation, temporal order, contiguity in time and space, and similarity of cause and effect, and (3) discounting of an explanation of specific alternatives. (1984)

In our view, a cognitive model of expert system processing is essentially a complex model of causations. Machines, in most people's minds, are well-defined entities that are both predictable and understandable. Consequently, people try to understand a machine (intelligent or not) by building an internal representation of how that machine works. Expert systems are machines that are designed to solve problems in the same domain in which the user is an experienced problem solver. Consequently, users should have little difficulty making inferences about how the machine makes inferences. This is similar to making inferences about how other people are making inferences ("I can see how you came to that conclusion, . . ."), except that machines are perceived as more predictable.

Given this perspective, a cognitive model can be thought of as a collection of causal inferences about how a machine makes inferences (many of which are themselves causal inference), or more simply a "causal model." Consistent with the perspective of Einhorn and Hogarth, a user's initial causal model will be based on the frame of reference the user brings to the user/expert system setting. Furthermore, in our conception, "cues to causality" translate into characteristics of the user interface that provide cues to the user as to how the expert system works. This leads to a number of interesting thoughts as to how the user interface will impact a user's causal model.

Our main contention is that in complex systems humans process a user interface as a source of *cues to internal causality* about how that complex system works. This leads to some interesting corollaries. First, if an expert system interface is designed so as to provide little or no rationale for its recommendations, (e.g., it only gives results) then interacting with that system will generally not change a user's initial causal model. This is because there are few cues to internal causality.

Another more interesting corollary is that in addition to cues that come from the content of output displays, there are likely to be many *spurious* cues to internal causality arising from the output displays. Potential types of spurious cues include the following:

Covariance—If the value of two output parameters appear to covary, or if these outputs are consistently displayed together, the user might infer from this covariance that these outputs are causally connected. That is, the value of one output cannot change independent of the value of the second output.

Contiguity—If the preconditions leading to a conclusion are not displayed contiguously (i.e., in close temporal and physical proximity) with the conclusion, users will not naturally infer which preconditions and conclusions are related. Similarly, preconditions presented or queries made will naturally be associated with the next conclusion that is displayed.

Temporal Order—Precondition values should be displayed/requested prior to displaying output conclusions. Without the proper temporal order, users may fail to perceived proper causality.

Similarity—Similar looking commands or instructions often lead users to infer that these commands are somehow causally related.

Consider the example of a user/expert system interaction in Figure 3. This is an example of a user interaction with an illustrative expert system for diagnosing engine difficulties in a car. User inputs are on a 5 (definitely yes) to a −5 (definitely no) scale (Lehner & Barth, 1985).

Based on the interaction shown in Figure 3, a user could infer several conclusions about how the system determines whether the carburetor fuel mix is too weak. First, if asked which factors lead to the conclusion that the weak mix was unlikely, the likely response would be gray plug deposits and engine overheating. These were the only two factors the system asked about just before (temporal order and contiguity) it reported that weak mix was unlikely. Second, since (a) the user had no information on grey plugs (0 = don't know), and (b) there was no change in degree for weak-mix (lack of covariance) the user might infer that grey plugs are the only real indicator of a weak mix.

The knowledge base that actually generated the above interaction is depicted in Figure 4. Note that a lack of power is one of the determinants of a weak mix. The cues to causality embedded in the interaction depicted in Figure 3 gave little if any indication that this was the case.

4. Summary

As is evidenced by the demand for this book, there is an increasing interest in the impact of cognitive factors in user/complex system interaction. In this chapter, we have presented a theoretical framework which suggests that (1) a user's cognitive model of system processing is a dominant factor in user/expert system interaction, and (2) that the user interface is a primary source of cues to causality of expert system processing and therefore an important determinant of a user's cognitive model.

The current goal is whether or not the carburetor fuel mix is too rich (rich-mix). Current degree is -5.0.

How certain are you that the exhaust is smoky?
>5

How certain are you that the car is backfiring?
>-5

How certain are you that there is a lack of power?
>3

After considering all significant questions, the degree that the carburetor fuel mix is too rich (rich-mix) initially was -5.0. It is now 11.0.

There are no more significant questions for the current goal.

Investigated goals with degree of belief > = 2.0 are:

The carburetor fuel mix is too rich (rich-mix). Prior degree was -5.0. Current degree is 11.0.

Other goals with degree > = 2.0 are:

None.

The current goal is whether or not the carburetor fuel mix is too weak (weak-mix). Current degree is 1.0.

How certain are you that there is a grey deposit on the sparkplugs?
>0

How certain are you that the engine overheats?
>-5

After considering all significant questions, the degree that teh carburetor fuel mix is too weak (weak-mix) initially was -5.0. Current degree is -5.0.

There are no other significant questions for the current goal.

Investigated goals with degree of belief > = 2.0 are:

The carburetor fuel mix is too rich (rich-mix). Prior degree was -5.0. Current degree is 11.0.

Other goals with degree > = 2.0 are :

None.

At this point, AL/X would begin to consider yet unanswered evidence for any other goals.)

Figure 3.   Example of User/Expert System Interaction

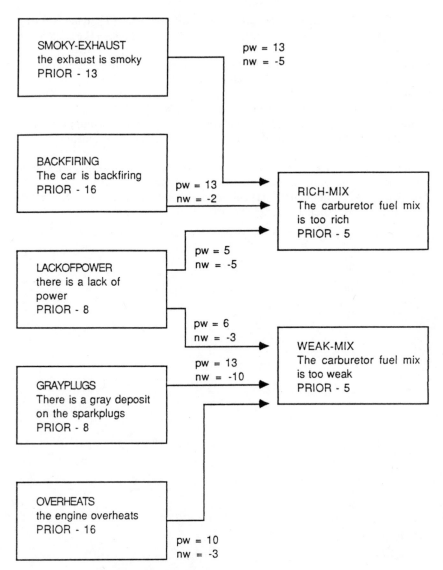

Figure 4.   Actual Inference Network

References

Adelman, L., Rook, F., & Lehner, P. E. (1985). User and R&D specialist evaluation of decision aids: A questionnaire and some empirical results. *IEEE Transactions and Systems, Man and Cybernetics* (May/June).

Einhorn, H. J., & Hogarth, R. M. (1985). *Probable cause: A decision making framework.* University of Chicago, Center for Decision Research.

Hall, R. (1985). *Mental models and problem solving with a knowledge Based Expert System* (PAR Report No. 85–108), PAR Technology Corpo. Reston, VA.

Lehner, P. E. (in press). On the role of artificial intelligence in C². *IEEE Transactions on Systems, Man and Cybernetics.*

Lehner, P. E. (in press). *Artificial intelligence and national defense: Opportunity and challenge.* Princeton, NJ: Petrocelli Books.

Lehner, P. E., & Barth, S. W. (1985). Expert Systems and Microcomputers. In S. Andriole (Ed.), *Applications in artificial intelligence,* Princeton, NJ: Petrocelli Books.

Lehner, P. E., & Zirk, D. (in press). Cognitive factors in user/expert system interactions. *Human Factors.*

Tversky, A., & Kahnemann, D. (1974). Judgment under uncertainty: Heuristics and biases. *Science 185,* 1124–1131.

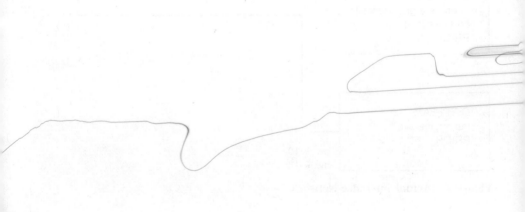

Author Index

Subject Index

A

Abstraction
  control, 27
  procedural, 28
ABSTRIPS, 93
Acceptance, 3, 9, 11, 54
ACE, 251
ActiveImages, 295, 296–300, 303
Ada, 146
AGE, 38
Anaphora
  natural language, 166–168
  pointing, 169–174
AP5, 147
ART, 103, 115

B

Bayes Theorem, 48, 50

C

Caseframe, *see also* Natural language, 156, 164
CENTAUR, 94
Cognitive model, 2, 9, 174–177, 289, 307–318
Cognitive Science, 305
Command languages, 163
CommonLoops, 201
CommonWindows, 302
Conflict resolution, 11, 133, 143
CRL, 160
CSRL, 245

D

DARN, 12, 57–59
DART, 58
Data-driven systems, 115
Debugging (of expert systems), 99, 116

Direct manipulation, 23, 29, 31, 99–125, 154, 159, 185, 303
  benefits
    expert systems, 113
    general, 101
  definition, 100
  inappropriate when, 163
DRACO, 147
DSPL, 235–240, 245, 246

E

EMACS, 208
EMYCIN, 129
Envisionment, 290
Error tracing, 99
Evaluation, 4, 49–51, 53, 121
EXPERT, 147
Expert advisory system, 285–287, 308
Expert interface system, *see* expert advisory system
Explanation, 10, 144, 219–247

F

Fault identification, 70
Form filling, 115
Fortran, 54, 146
Frame-based systems, 82, 229

G

Generic task methodology, 222, 228–229
Gist, 146
Granularity, 295

H

HEARSAY III, 127, 145
Help facilities, 2
Hierarchical knowledge, 43, 59, 81–98, 228, 229, 303
Hierarchical browsing, 124